Legacy of the Chicago School
A Collection of Essays in Honour of the Chicago School of Sociology During the First Half of the 20th Century

Other books by Christopher Hart

Englishness: Diversity, Differences & Identity
Literature Reviewing: Releasing the Social Science Imagination
Doing A Literature Search: A Comprehensive Guide for the Social Sciences
Doing Your Masters Dissertation
Talcott Parsons: Theories, Developments & Applications
Englishness: Heroes, Heroines, Symbolism and Narratives
1984 Commercial for MacIntosh

Legacy of the Chicago School

A Collection of Essays in Honour of the Chicago School of Sociology During the First Half of the 20th Century

Edited by CHRISTOPHER HART

Midrash Publications

Editorial arrangements and Introduction ©2010 *Chris Hart*

Chapter 1   *Ian Shaw*, ©2010
Chapter 2   *Roger A. Salerno*, ©2010
Chapter 3   *Brian Roberts*, ©2010
Chapter 4   *Dennis W. MacDonald*, ©2010
Chapter 5   *Julie L. Kirby*, ©2010
Chapter 6   *Martyn Hammersley*, ©2010
Chapter 7   *Matthias Gross*, ©2010
Chapter 8   *Howard S. Becker*, ©2010
Chapter 9   *Shane Blackman*, ©2010
Chapter 10 *Filipa Subtil and José Luís Garcia*, ©2010

First published in 2010.

All rights reserved. No part of this publication may be reproduced.

Midrash Publications
100 Towers Road
Poynton
Cheshire, England
SK12 1DF
Email: midrash@mac.com
Available from: http://www.lulu.com/9238347

British Library Cataloguing in Publication Data
A catalogue record for this publication is available from the British Library.

ISBN 9 781905 984145

Dedication

This volume is dedicated to all those who have got the seats of their pants dirty.

Legacy of the Chicago School

A Collection of Essays in Honour of the Chicago School of Sociology During the First Half of the 20th Century

Contents

edited by *Christopher Hart*

	Dedication	
	Preface	
	Introduction	1
Chapter 1	An Unresolved Legacy of the Chicago School *Ian Shaw*	44
Chapter 2	Ernest Burgess: Exploring Urban Marginality *Roger A. Salerno*	65
Chapter 3	'Ahead of its Time?': The Legacy and Relevance of W.I. Thomas and F. Znaniecki (1918-20) The Polish Peasant in Europe and America *Brian Roberts*	74
Chapter 4	Human Ecology and the Emergence of Global Society: The Theoretical Insights of Roderick D. McKenzie *Dennis W. MacDonald*	105
Chapter 5	Mind, Self and Society: The Overlooked Potential of G.H. Mead's Legacy *Julie L. Arthur Kirby*	126
Chapter 6	Blumer's Dilemma Revisited: Is Social Science Possible? *Martyn Hammersley*	153

Chapter 7	'All Life is Experimentation': The Chicago School and the Experimenting Society *Matthias Gross*	174
Chapter 8	The Art of Comparison: Lessons from the Master, Everett C. Hughes *Howard S. Becker*	185
Chapter 9	'The Ethnographic Mosaic' of the Chicago School: Critically Locating Vivien Palmer, Clifford Shaw and Frederic Thrasher's Research Methods in Contemporary Reflexive Sociological Interpretation *Shane Blackman*	195
Chapter 10	Communication: An Inheritance of the Chicago School of Social Thought *Filipa Subtil and José Luís Garcia*	216

Preface

The chapters in this volume have their origins in the conference *The Legacy of the Chicago School*, held from the 13th to the 14th September, 2007 at the magnificent Britannia Hotel Manchester, England. The conference organizers were, Dr Dave Francis, Manchester Metropolitan University, England, Dr Chris Hart, University of Chester, England and Dr Pete Martin, University of Manchester, England. The papers presented at the conference were: *The Chicago School and the Emergence of Global Society: The Insights of Roderick D. McKenzie*, Dennis W. MacDonald, (Chair) Department of Sociology, Saint Anselm College, Manchester, USA; *'Ahead of its Time?': The Legacy and Relevance of W.I. Thomas and F. Znaniecki (1918-20) The Polish Peasant in Europe and America*, Brian Roberts, University of Glamorgan, Pontypridd, Wales; *Playing Chicago Against Chicago: The Natural History of Public Problems*, Cédric Terzi, Daniel Cefaï and Louis Quéré, Faculté des sciences économiques, et sociales de l'Université de Fribourg (Suisse), Paris; *Preschooling – Recovering the Early Sociological Tradition at the University of Chicago (1892–1918)*, Rainer Egloff, Wissenschaftlicher Mitarbeiter Collegium Helveticum, in gemeinsamer Trägerschaft von Universität, Zürich, Switzerland; *Sociology and Social Work: an Unresolved Legacy of the First Chicago School*; Ian F. Shaw, University of York, England; *The Theoretical Metaphors of Human Ecology*, Svetlana Bankovskaya, The Moscow State Institute of International Relations (University), Moscow; *Blumer's Dilemma Revisited: Causality and Analytic Induction*; Martyn Hammersley, The Open University, England; *"All Life is Experimentation": The Chicago School and the Experimenting Society*; Matthias Gross, Department of Urban and Environmental Sociology, Helmholtz Centre for Environmental Research – UFZ, Permoserstr. Leipzig, Germany; *James Carey and the Legacy of Chicago School of Sociology on Communication and Media Studies*, Filipa Brito Subtil, Instituto de Ciências Sociais da Universidade de Lisboa, Portugal; *The Ethnographic Mosaic': Critically Locating Clifford Shaw's Research Method of the Young Person's 'own story' in Contemporary Reflexive Sociological Interpretation*, Shane Blackman, Canterbury Christ Church University, England; *Mind, Self and Society: Have we Utilised the Full Radical Potential of G.H. Mead's Thought?* Julie Kirby, Faculty of Health, Edge Hill University, Lancashire, England; *The Use of Cartography in the Chicago School of Sociology*, A. Javier Treviño, (Chair) Department of Sociology, Wheaton College, Norton, MA, USA; The LA School of Urban Studies: Students of Legacy or Claimants of Inheritance of the Chicago School, Nikita A. Kharlamov, Moscow Higher School of Economics; *Ernest Burgess: Exploring Urban Marginality*, Roger Salerno, (Chair, Sociology/Anthropology) Pace University, New York City, USA; *The Chicago School as the First "school" of Empirical Sociology: a Standard Bearer?* Martin Bulmer, University of Surrey, England; and *Everett Hughes and the Art of Comparison: A Chicago Method*, Howard S. Becker, San Francisco, USA. Not all of the papers presented have been published here and nor were all the papers submitted for consideration presented to the conference. Published in this volume is a selection of papers which represent and span several nationalities, generations and subject disciplines. In particular and in keeping with the general ethos of the conference several younger social scientists have been included in this volume.

Regrettably we could not accommodate all those who wished to present a paper. This was because we decided from the start this would be a conference that would not have streams with quick 20 minute papers but be one where all presenting would have nearly one hour and would present to all delegates. One of the notable and striking features of this conference was the collegial community that quickly developed among the participants. All papers were presented to all delegates in the tranquil and beautiful environment of the historic Britannia Hotel in Manchester. The conference was an exemplar of trans-disciplinarity, a genuine sharing of different research subjects and approaches to analysis from different scholarly traditions. The chapters in this modest volume represent the diversity of scholarship on, and which is still developing new studies, sociological knowledge generated by members of the Department of Sociology.

Finally, my I say thank you to all contributors for their patience given the time it has taken to produce this book.

Chris Hart
University of Chester, 2010.

Introduction

Crescat Scientia, Vita Excolatur
'Let knowledge grow from more to more; and so be human life enriched'

"The question before us is how to become one in spirit, not necessarily in opinion."
William Rainey Harper,
First President of the University of Chicago

The 'Chicago School' of sociology is famous. So famous it has become a generic term for a range of perspectives, approaches and methods that are rarely cited. Who now cites Robert Ezra Park (1864-1944), Albion W. Small (1864-1944), George E. Vincent (1864-1941)[1], Charles Horton Cooley (1864-1929), Walter C. Reckless (1898-1988), Ruth Shonle Cavan (1896-), Edward Franklin Frazier (1894-1962), Everett Cherrington Hughes (1897-1983), Roderick D. McKenzie (1885-1940), Elsworth Faris (1874-1953), William Ogburn (1886-1959), Frederick M. Thrasher (1892-1970), Ernest Burgess (1886-1966), Homer Hoyt (1895-1984), Clifford Shaw (1895-1957), Herbert Blumer (1900-1986), Vivien M. Palmer[2] or Louis Wirth? One occasionally sees W.I. Thomas (1863-1947) and Florian Znaniecki (1882-1958) cited but not Dorothy Swaine Thomas (1899-1977). George Herbert Mead (1863-1931) is still a major source of theory and concepts, that is, in a very general sense. But what of the detailed empirical work of Edwin H. Sutherland (1883-1950), Charles Edward Merriam (1874-1953), Paul G. Cressey[3] (1901-1955), Harvey Warren Zorbaugh (1896-1965), Samuel C. Kincheloe (1890-1981), Harold Foote Gosnell (1897-1997) and Nels Anderson (1889–1986)?

---

[1] Vincent was co-author with Albion W. Small of *An Introduction to the Study of Society* (1895) and during this initial period was President of the American Sociological Association (1915–1916).

[2] Despite repeated searches and enquiries we have not been successful in locating much biographical information about Vivian Palmer even though her work is widely cited from the 1930s onwards, especially her (1928) *Field Studies in Sociology: A Student's Manual*. Chicago: University of Chicago Press and (1929) "Social backgrounds of Chicago's local communities." Chicago: Local Community Research Committee. Papers of Ernest W. Burgess, Special Collections. Regenstein Library, University of Chicago.

[3] Paul G. Cressey (1901-1955) is now mostly known for his *Taxi Dance Hall* study but what of the monumental work he and others did on the effects of motion pictures in America? See, 'The Motion Picture Experience as Modified by Social Background and Personality.' *Journal of Educational Sociology* 7 (1934):504-515.

The theoretical and empirical works of the 'first' Chicago School have become largely forgotten sources of so much taken-for-granted by contemporary sociologists, psychologists, criminologists, policy makers, and practitioners in education and the social work professions. The methods of ethnographic fieldwork, participant observation, life histories, personal documents (letters, diaries), population statistics, maps, real estate pricing, and interviewing – among other methods - were all developed and widely used by members and students of the Department. The list of topics they investigated and established is long and includes, urban sociology, community studies, immigration, racism, inequality, identity and adaptation, political participation, leisure and commercialized entertainment, African American politics, exclusion, community radicalism, religion, white peoples' perceptions of black communities, social problems, traditions, sub-cultures, urban planning, institutionalization, social reform, social mobility… and many more. Few departments of sociology have made such an impact for so long on so many disciplines and fields of practice.

Introduction: The Beginnings

The University of Chicago, founded by American Baptist Education Society and financed initially by John D. Rockefeller, opened in 1892. Crescat Scientia, Vita Excolatur - 'Let knowledge grow from more to more; and so be human life enriched' – became it's motto. Designed to look like the best British universities, principally Oxford and Cambridge, architect Henry Ives Cobb fashioned the Gothic buildings arranging them around enclosed quadrangles, providing the university with a sense of importance, place and detachment from the surrounding metropolis. As a coeducational institution modeled on the graduate research universities of the recently formed Germany, women constituted over half of the students by the first decade of the 20th century. The University's first president, William Rainey Harper, envisioned a university "as solid as the ancient hills" - a modern research university, combining an English-style undergraduate college (as found in Oxford) and a German-style graduate research institute. "The question before us", asked Harper, "is how to become one in spirit, not necessarily in opinion." This saying came to embody the work of the Department of Sociology, of the University of Chicago. It was under the leadership and management of Albion W. Small that the world's first Department of Sociology was established.

Harper's vision translated into reality. Distinguished scholars from colleges and universities across the world were enticed to Chicago. John Dewey and George Herbert Mead helped establish the Philosophy Department. Albion Small, and later Ernest Burgess and Robert Park, helped established and develop one of the most internationally influential departments of sociology.

There are many excellent introductions to the history of sociology and in particular the history of the Department of Sociology at the University of

Chicago such as Bulmer (1984), Kurtz (1984) and Deegan (1991)[4]. In this introduction I would like to tease out some of the theoretical traditions and sources that influenced different members of the department. The reason for doing this is that there seems to be a general misconception about the theoretical frameworks used by the members of the department between it's foundation and the mid-1940s. The audience for this introduction is undergraduates not only of sociology but also of applied social studies and professions who increasingly employ insights from across the social sciences in their work, often from the ethnographies done at Chicago. It would be ambitious to have the aspiration that if undergraduates were introduced to more of the methodological traditions in sufficient detail then they would have a better understanding and a more balanced view of historical achievements in the social sciences.

Understanding the Methodological Influences
on and in the Department of Sociology

Chicago Sociology is underpinned and infused by three theoretical trends; aspects of German Idealism, Anglo-French Positivism, and British Anthropology. All of the members of the Department, in this period, had first hand experience of each of these major trends, taking from them, that which would 'fit' into a practical framework, a framework that similarly fitted with their particular conception of social reality and their criterion for social science. We can grasp the essentials of the weltanschauung of the School by initially turning to the stuff that they produced, in particular, Park and Burgess's, *Introduction to the Science of Sociology* (1921)[5] The latter, for example, comprises of some one thousand plus pages of carefully chosen extracts from a very wide range of European and American writers. Included in the one volume are extracts from, for example, Hobbes, Descartes, Darwin, Tonnies, Hobhouse, Durkheim, Bacon, Rousseau, Simmel, Gumplowicz, Max Muller, Adam Smith, A.V. Dicey, V.H.S. Rivers, Louis Leopold, Spencer, Le Eon, Comte, Francis Galton, Schopenhauer, an so on; something of a select 'who's who' of the period. This extensive reading range in the 'Introduction' is mirrored in the wealth of translations of European writings in the American Journal of Sociology. That much of this stuff appears to be unrelated, or in C. Wright-

---

[4] Martin Bulmer, (1984) *The Chicago School of Sociology: Institutionalization, Diversity, and the Rise of Sociological Research*. Chicago: University of Chicago Press. Lester R. Kurtz, (1984) *Evaluating Chicago Sociology: A Guide to the Literature, with an Annotated Bibliography*. Chicago: University of Chicago Press. And for a revealing study of the influence of women in the Department and sociology as a whole see, Mary Jo Deegan (ed.). (1991) *Women in Sociology: A Bio-Bibliographical Sourcebook*. New York: Greenwood Press.
[5] Throughout this introduction the 1969 edition is used for quotations.

Mills[6] words, 'unsystematic' does not entail that it is a reflection of chaotic thinking and a diluted grasp of the relative positions expounded by these European theorists. Far from it. The Park and Burgess text did not set out to germinate some kind of grand systems model, as present some ideas that might be of help for sociologists, especially their students. A modest and deceptively simple aim. A quotation from the text itself might exemplify the use to which Park and Burgess hoped such artefacts might be of help;

> The fundamental problem... is that of social control. How does a mere collection of individuals succeed in acting in a corporate and consistent way? How in the case of specific types of social group... a boys gang, or political party, does the group control its individual members: the whole dominate the parts?
> (Park and Burgess, 1969 edn:27-29)

Park and Burgess propose a deceptive definition of the problem; the same in content and concern as most of their contemporaries, to which they add;

> This gives the problem a name, but not a solution. What the purpose of sociology requires is a description and explanation. What are the mechanisms - physical, physiological, and social - by which a group imposes its control, or what seems to be control, upon the individual members of the group.
> (Park and Burgess, 1969 edn:27-29)

Such unambiguous statements may save the student from the complexities of such problems as theory construction, theory testing and methodology, these problems are, nevertheless addressed throughout the text. The battery of conceptual artefacts presented in the Introduction' for instance, 'assimilation', 'ecology', 'moral regions', 'competition', and so on, are clearly intended to be operationalised by the student in whatever manner is logically applicable to whatever subject is in hand. Two points need to be made about this. Firstly, these conceptual and theoretical positions are loosely interrelated. Secondly, their loose relationship does not preclude the formation of a coherent analytical framework; the main elements of which are discussed below. For now it is important to make clear that Park and Burgess show not only that they are well conversed in the nature of analytic approaches and in what ways they differ from generic and causal explanations, but what the purpose and limitations of analytical frameworks are. The purpose being, to furnish students with the theoretical and conceptual tools with which to conceive, in an ordered manner,

---

[6] Mills, C. Wright. (1963, 1967) 'The Professional Ideology of the Social Pathologists'. In, *Power, Politics and People. The Collective Essays of C. Wright Mills.* Edited by Irving H. Horowitz. New York: Oxford University Press.

the flux of the multitude of interactions that make for the realms of social reality.

That this conceptual, theoretical framework came to be expressed in a loose isomorphic structure should neither be a cause for surprise nor for sever criticism. Isomorphic mental structures abound in all the sciences; some are rigidly systematic, some are not. The analogy proposed in the *Introduction to the Science of Sociology*, the elements of which being the conceptual artefacts such as, succession, assimilation, competition, form and content, accommodation, and so on, is not systematic in the sense of the Parsonian scheme of the 1950s. In part, the reason for this is that systematic theory is not only incommensurable with, but also incommodious for, Park and Burgess's conception of sociology. In other words, while systematic models tend to impose a closed conceptual order upon social reality, Park and Burgess are attempting to avoid such theoretical entity building by constructing an analytical framework that was coherent but spacious enough to adapt to the nature of social reality and not social reality to it.

The word 'science' in the title of this volume is no historic anomaly. It has for Park and Burgess and specific intent. For Park and Burgess science is the work of 'finding out' in a systematic verifiable way, it is a particular cognitive social activity which, though encompassing several approaches, has certain commonly agreed upon characteristics, namely, preciseness and clarity; objectivity and neutrality; that there be, at least in principle, a demonstratable relationship between theoretical assumptions and observable social phenomenon; accountability of data and methods; and, that the whole process of theory construction and testing has a logical consistency (adapted from Kaufmann, 1958)[7]. These basic criterion, in one form or another, are the yardsticks by which a particular application to the scientific enterprise can begin to be assessed. But such criterion tell us nothing about the epistemological and ontological choices, nor processes involved in the fundamental activity of producing a clear conception of the problem, or of the related problems of designing possible contenders for its solution. The original impetus for tackling any of these problems can come from everyday life, for example, problems generated from immigration, or the impetus can come from the scientific enterprise itself, for example, problems of theory construction, use and validation. It is this latter package of problems that must, before science can begin, be addressed first. This is what the *Introduction to the Science of Sociology* is about. Specifically, Park and Burgess are attempting to circumscribe the problem of 'control'. To understand how they went about this task I suggest we use as an organising agent the question posed by Georg Simmel, 'how is society possible?'

---

[7] Kaufmann, F. (1958[1944]) *The Methodology of the Social Sciences*. New Jersey: Humanities Press.

Simmel's Influence

How is Society Possible? is the title and question of an essay by Georg Simmel (Simmel, 1908[8]; Wolf 1955)[9]. Simmel's paper mirrors Kant's, *How is Nature Possible?*[10] This similarity although quite intentional should not be interpreted that Simmel was merely copying Kant. Simmel's use of Kant's ontological and epistemological works is more of a starting point for his own work than a propagation of Kantian philosophy. H.J. Helle puts it, "Simmel was not so much a representative of neo-Kantianism as he was a prominent autonomous authority on the work of Kant" (Helle, 1985:9-10)[11].

Simmel's project was to construct a theoretical framework for the social sciences, a framework that consisted of forging a middle-ground between the two main trends in European thinking, German-Idealism and Anglo-French Positivism. The guiding principles to the formation of this framework were quite revolutionary and have been virtually ignored. Simmel begins by posing the problem of what must social reality be like in order that we can theorise about it, hence the question as to the possibility of society. We can achieve a better grasp of this essential point by comparing Simmel's approach with that of Edmund Husserl[12]. Husserl followed Descartes in attempting to establish where the certainties of reality lie. According to Husserl, not only does proper reliable science require certainties but until some are found scepticism must reign over what is commonly accepted as certain. Simmel, on the other hand, while accepting the idea of there being 'certainties' conceives the problem of certainties in a different way to Husserl. Instead of searching for certainties, Simmel attempts to unravel the nature of what we take as certain. A subtle difference but a major one all the same. Simmel therefore is not looking for some rock-bottom reality but describing the nature of reality construction and just how we can go about describing this construction in the first place. Simmel's social reality is fluid; it can expand through the addition of further 'givens' as well as contract with the redundancy of knowledge: reality is continually being added to, reduced and moved - all at the same time!

How Simmel went about communicating this conception of social reality and developing it, is what I now turn to. Simmel's main sociological and

---

[8] Simmel, G. (1908) 'How is Society Possible?'. In his *Sociologie* (2nd German Edition) Munchen Und Leipzig: Duncker and Humblot.
[9] Wolff, K. H. and Bendix, R. Trans. (1955) *Georg Simmel: Conflict and the Web of Group Affiliations.* Glencoe IL: Free Press.
[10] These notes on Kant refer to the translation of Kant's *Prolegomena,* reproduced in the *Modern Philosophy: An Anthology of Primary Sources,* edited by Eric Watkins and Roger Ariew. Indianapolis: Hackett Publishing Company.
[11] Helle, H.J. (1985) 'The Classical Foundations of the Micro Sociological Paradigm', in Eisenstadt, L.N. and Helle, H.J. *Perspectives on Sociological Theory.* CA: Sage.
[12] Husserl, E. (1913 [1982]) *Ideas Pertaining to a Pure Phenomenology and to a Phenomenological Philosophy: First Book: General Introduction to a Pure Phenomenology.* Trans., Kersten, F. The Hague: Nijhoff.

philosophical writings are widely available in bound editions, for example, Wolff (1950 and 1955),[13] Rosenthal and Oberlaender, K. (1945),[14] and the American Journal of Sociology. The style and ease and which Simmel communicates his ideas makes his essays and papers a positive pleasure to read. What Simmel so stylistically communicates is what we might call a middle-way between the two strains in European thinking. He does this simultaneously upon a number of levels, the ontological, the epistemological, the methodological and, what can be called, the human nature aspect. Both German Idealism and Anglo French Positivism, in their extremes, held quite distinct positions regarding each of these levels. German-Idealism held that there was a fundamental difference between Nature and Culture; the nomothetic (i.e. rule governed and law like) character of the Natural World was not an appropriate assumption to attribute to the Social World which, they argued, was composed of unique events and characterised by the autonomy of the human spirit. Windelband[15], a propagator of this dichotomy, concluded that such a dichotomy entailed that there was no basis for giving 'society' any ontological status above and beyond that of the individual consciousness. Therefore no 'science' of the social was possible because the unique, non-law like character of the Social World. Only ideographic type studies were possible.

At the other end of the pole, the Anglo-French tradition, presumed that there was little substantial difference for the purpose of scientific investigation between nature and Society. Accordingly, natural (mechanical) science approaches were adopted, in particular, evolutionary theories. A scheme of societal development was constructed onto which different cultures could be placed in the belief that the differences indicated a continuum from the 'advanced' to the 'primitive'. For the purpose of scientific investigation 'society' was attributed a concrete ontological status and assumed to be characterised by the operation of laws and tendencies which were in principle were to be uncovered by the methods of investigation used by the natural sciences.

On the level of human nature, the positivists and idealists are also at opposite poles. Durkheim's[16] positivism had a deterministic import. This resulted from Durkheim's concern for the role of the individual in organic type societies and from the problems of integration: rampant individualism was seen as a threat. Durkheim was optimistic that the division of labour would become the embodiment of integration. Park and Burgess's references to Durkheim,

---

[13] Wolff, K.H. (1950) *The Sociology of Georg Simmel* Glencoe IL: Free Press. Wolff, K.H. and Bendix, (1955) op cit.
[14] Rosenthal, E. and Oberlaender, K. (1945) 'Books, Papers, and Essays by Georg Simmel', *American Journal of Sociology*, 3:238-47.
[15] Wilhelm Windelband (1848-1915) is now mainly remembered for the terms *nomothetic* and *idiographic*, which he introduced. Windelband's disciples were not only noted philosophers, but sociologists like Max Weber. See his *A History of Philosophy*, NJ: Paper Tiger. ([1893]2001).
[16] See, Durkheim, E. (1938[1895]) *Rules of Sociological Method*. London: MacMillan, trans., G.E.G. Catlin.

however, should not be seen as signs of general agreement with Durkheim. Rather Park and Burgess believed that it was the normative life of a group that exerted pressures for the integration of the individual and not the economic. A slight shift of emphasis, but a shift all the same. The optimism and determinism of Durkheim was not shared by the Germans, eg, Tonnies[17], Weber[18] or Simmel. With their sense of foreboding and idealized reconstructions of the past, they attempted to counter what they considered the economic determinism of the Marxists and the individual subsuming reification of Durkheim's position. They did so by resurrecting the idea that the individual or local community was a force in its own right. They defended the individual from being reduced to an epiphenomenon and from being crushed by the absolutionist state by giving the subject a place outside the grand public sphere, in primary type involvements, such as the family, neighbourhood and local community. Simmel, using Kant's work, rejects the extreme consequences of both trends and gives us in their place a brilliant reformation of the entire enterprise in which he argues for an analysis of human 'association' and 'interaction' in scientific terms.

A basic understanding of Kant's work is crucial. Kant, like Simmel, attempted to reconcile the better of two theoretical conceptions about the nature of the world. Kant argues against the innatists and the empiricists, two classically opposed views about the nature of reality and our knowledge of it. The innatists argued that our knowledge of the world is fixed by the innate structures of the human mind, while the empiricists argued that our knowledge of the world came solely from experience. The innatists we can represent with Rene Descartes who assumed that the scientific procedure was deductive, i.e. progressed from the general to the particular. The empiricists, on the other hand, can be represented by John Locke[19], who assumed that the scientific procedure was inductive, i.e. from experience of particulars we make generalisations. Kant's problem in creating an alternative but common ground was that of accounting for the ways in which objective knowledge of an independent reality could be attained with the use of sensory *and* mental processes that construct experiences of social reality.

The Unavoidability of Kant

When discussing the methodology of the social sciences, therefore, Kant is a common and unavoidable reference point. Kant's work then, was a project to

---

[17] See, Mitzman, A. (1987) *The Three Sociologists of Imperial Germany: Sociology and Estrangement.* New Brunswick, NJ: Transaction Books. Orig. published 1973 and Aldous, J. (1972) 'Emile Durkheim and Ferdinand Tonnies'. *The American Journal of Sociology*, Vol. 77, No. 6:1191-1200.
[18] See, Smelser, N. (1976) *Comparative Methods in the Social Sciences.* Princeton, NJ: Prentice-Hall. Chapter 3.
[19] See, Ayers, M. R. (1991) *Locke. Epistemology and Ontology.* London: Routledge.

deal with the two theoretical conceptions about the nature of knowledge. One the one hand, was the scepticism of David Hume[20] who regarded it an impossibility to obtain more than mere provisional knowledge of reality. On the other hand, there was what has been called Radical Rationalism (Kaufmann, 1944[1958])[21] that attributes all knowledge and being to the mind of God: that which is not in the creators' mind, is not, and that which is, is. Although this is a rough and ready description of what are, two complex views, it will suffice for our purposes. These two positions are what we have termed the empiricist and the innatists respectively.

Kant found fault in both of these philosophies which made neither acceptable as a sound basis from which to build knowledge. Each position claimed superiority over the other as being the means for unlocking the door to reality (both presuming that there was a door to unlock and that behind it laid some bedrock reality). The Radical Innatists argued that our knowledge of the world is fixed and limited: by virtue of our minds being the creation of the creator and limited by what the creator wished us to know, by his plan. The Empiricists on the other hand, argued that such arguments for the existence of God were unacceptable, that knowledge of reality came solely through experience. The Innatists assumed on the basis of Rationalism that the scientific procedure was deductive, that is, progressed from the general to the particular. The Empiricists assumed that the scientific procedure was largely inductive, that is, a progression from experience of the particular to generalisations.

Having set the scene we can proceed. Kant was a Rationalist until he read the works of David Hume, a Radical Empiricist. Hume's work while undermining Radical Rationalism lead to the undermining of Empiricism itself. Simply put, Hume argued that inductive inference and associated notions of 'cause' – the basis of Rationalism and Empiricism - were non-empirical and therefore render all human knowledge to belief and expectation. Kant realised that Hume's scepticism about the claims to certainty which had been made by Descartes amounted to a philosophical bogyman, a fearful spectre which would jump out and catch philosophers and scientists as soon as they became confident in their expectations. Hume's arguments then, left such highly acclaimed scientific knowledge such as that of Newton's as mere confident expectations and not as certitude as intended. Such a situation, believed Kant, would not do. Hence, Kant set himself the task of countering Hume's scepticism. However, it is an important point to make that Kant did not set himself the task of discovering some rock-bottom reality but attempted to produce a satisfactory epistemological theory which synthesized the more acceptable elements of the Innatists and Empiricists, and which showed the

---

[20] See, Norton. D. F. (1978) *David Hume: Commonsense Moralist, Skeptical Metaphysician.* Princeton: Princeton University Press.
[21] Op cit.

ways in which objective expandable knowledge of an independent reality could be attained. Kant approached the task by making some initial distinctions about the kinds of knowledge possible. This can be schematised as follows.

Table 1 *Kant's distinctions*

	A priori	Aposteriori
Analytic	Logic	
Synthetic	Mathematics Metaphysics	Science, Religion Common-sense

Basically what this amounts is there are two sources of knowledge, that obtained through the senses and that resulting from thinking. The former is available through sensory experience and the latter from human reason. Sensory knowledge is of two types, random and coherent. Random sensory knowledge is that which is external and chaotic; it makes no sense to us, it has no meaning. Coherence can be made of random experience through the intermediate, mostly routine, application of 'forms', for example, space and time are forms. Space and time are, according to Kant, basic 'categories' of reason; the former is external (though ultimately metaphysical) while the latter is an internal organising device contingent upon relevance and succession of experience. Space and time are therefore apriori: they are forms applicable to any experience, thought or felt. Intellectual knowledge, the second kind, is not knowledge of phenomenon experienced by the senses. The metaphysical, God, Soul, are what Kant calls intellectual knowledge, they are apriori forms of knowing: apriori concepts are ones like necessity and substance, they are intellectual concepts with which the empirical as well as mental realms can be categorised, understood and used. Kant set limits to the acceptable use of each kind of knowledge. In his *Critique of Pure Reason* (1871) Kant sets out a complex argument about the criterion for assessing the certitude of statements. Kant argues that propositions that we may make about the world necessarily arise, in the first instance, from a priori knowledge. While this claim by Kant has not as yet been fully understood by anyone apart from Kant, we will leave it as it stands and move on to the next part of his work, the distinction between the Analytic (explicative) and the Synthetic (amplicative).

Analytic statements are a priori, for example, 'triangles have three sides', 'peaceful resisters shun violence', and "husbands are married men' are all analytic because the relative words 'triangle', 'peaceful' and 'husbands' are all predicates and subjects. The predicate concept is included in the subject concept. Therefore judgments about analytic apriori statements can be made without recourse to experience. Analytic a priori statements can only be contradicted. Synthetic statements, on the other hand, do not have the predicate/subject concept, for example, 'peaceful residence is effective' is synthetic and not analytic. Synthetic apriori statements are made in mathematics, natural science, metaphysics and ethics: cases in which the predicate concept is not in the subject concept but the belief is that the statement is universal. An analytic apriori statement is true by virtue of the terms from which it is made up of. The statement 'all bodies have mass' is necessarily true. While, synthetic apriori statements are not necessarily true but can also be judged on the basis of their logic formation. Both kinds of statements therefore have truth-value by virtue of our reasoning and not our experience.

Aposteriori judgments are not, as some think, the opposite of apriori ones. Synthetic *a*posteriori are statements in which the relation between the subject and the predicate is attainable (verifiable) through experience. For example, the statement, 'carrot seeds grow in eight weeks', is *a*posteriori. It is knowledge about 'carrot seeds', which is dependent upon verification by experience, that is, watching and waiting to see if carrot seeds do in fact grow in eight weeks. Synthetic *a*posteriori judgments are not diametrically opposed to apriori ones by the virtue that, according to Kant, all empirical knowledge has more or less been compounded into forms by the basic categories of reason (Kant believed that there were twelve such basic categories).

Thus to summarise what has been said. On the one plane we have the analytic-apriori synthetic-aposteriori, and on the other plane we have the synthetic-aposteriori. It is a distinction based on differences in contingencies: statements which are true by virtue of the meaning of the terms used in their logical presentation and those statements which are contingent-upon-something or other that can be experienced. Kant's typology may be useful but it is neither exclusive nor easy to fully understand. However, this point will be left to philosophy. What we need from Kant is the belief that he left us with which implied that deductive reasoning was the key to acceptable knowledge and explanation: that understanding is of phenomenon and cannot be of the thing-in-itself, moumenon. What this has been taken to imply is that not only should the social sciences follow a deductive approach but should attempt to offer explanations of social - phenomena, leaving the noumenon of social reality where Kant left it, in the realm of the unknowable. The issue was to become, is there an alternative to Kant's view of knowledge and if there is, what would it involve in practice?

Simmel and Kant

It was Simmel who took on this challenge and attempted to provide an alternative to Kant. What Kant did for philosophy Simmel attempted for the social sciences? Simmel's ontological stand although similar to Kant's is closer to Max Weber's, in that the search for ultimate realities or essential cores is regarded as non-sensical. In the same vein Simmel attributes no ontological superiority to either society or the individual: to Simmel, both are synthetic accomplishments in that they are categorisations of qualities experienced. It is from such an approach to Simmel that his so called middle-way between the

Nominalism of the German's and the Realism of the Anglo-French can begin to be appreciated as more than a simple synthesis. Simmel's work is a systematically thought out theory as to what it takes to make society knowable and its operationalisation to show the processes by which social phenomenon are created. This is no small claim to make on behalf of Simmel and must therefore be demonstrated.

Simmel expressed his ideas in his essays and papers. It is from these that Simmel's conception of social reality can be understood. However, from the nature of his essays, that they are usually short and compact but very clear and stylish and often briefly titled, for instance, *The Ruin, The Adventure, The Handle, The Aesthetic Significance of the Face*[22], Simmel's ideas are often found to be relegated to the sociological curiosity shop. In Simmel's works, 'society' is not an entity but a process made of social interactions. In this, Simmel is directing attention to the form-creating processes, which is society. What this amounts to is a distinctive analytical definition of the subject matter of sociology, which incorporates a distinctive analytical approach, which involves empirical procedures for their elucidation. The real, as opposed to the imagined differences between the analytic and synthetic are now becoming clearer. Hence, epistemologically, Simmel's noumena are the unique, unreflecting experiences and drives that once reflected upon, thought about, become phenomena or, to Simmel, social forms. Experience is unique and non-ordered or non-social; however, through the mediation of social forms experience is rendered knowable and understandable. Simmel's forms are what Lewis Coser (1965[23]) called the geometry or grammar of social life, that is, patterns and similarities in life experience that are shared. The social is therefore analysable through formal analysis, through focusing upon patterns of contents. This does two main things, it allows the researcher to advance beyond limited ideographic description of content to a position where the social can be investigated as *if* nomothethically characterised. Secondly, treating social reality as if it were nomothethically characterisable, the researcher therefore sways towards the criteria of the objectivity presumed given by detachment. This is a position that is not too dissimilar to that Weber proposed. Thus, the uniqueness of history and experience has been retained as an object of study in its own right while at the same time it is possible to transcend it so as to allow for the possibility of an objective approach to social reality.

Forms are the common currency of interaction, like the grammar of language they are used by all but do not belong to nor were they created by *any* one individual. Not only do common forms make socially meaningful interaction possible but do so because of their usefulness, they are enablers in that their use enables persons to pursue their needs and wants. Forms are laid

---

[22] In Wolff, K. (1959) Translated and edited, *Georg Simmel, 1858–1918: A Collection of Essays, with Translations and a Bibliography*. Columbus: Ohio State Press.
[23] Coser, L. (1965) *Georg Simmel*. NJ: Prentice-Hall.

down by successive generations; they are not static but fluid, changed and changing, adaptable yet, some appear to remain stable, this is because more efficient forms have not been devised; such "forms are emancipated: they are separate facets of life which confront men as independent realities" (Rock, 1979:43).[24] Surviving forms are not always commonly useful, the recognisable activities as can be observed in ceremony are forms that give a sense of tradition and stability and along with other kinds of forms, are often regarded as natural and immutable and can hence come to be perceived as constraining, humans find themselves inhabiting an environment of objectified forms which they cannot control. Worse, they can barely understand the inner workings of that environment. So abundant and complex are they that they appear as opaque and alien entities which threaten to submerge them (Rock, 1979:43). Simmel's view of human nature therefore is a one of a complex middle-ground characterised by conflict, co-operation, competition and struggle between the natural and the social. The relationship is a "dialectical tension between the individual and society... the individual is determined yet determining, acted upon, yet self-acting" (Coser, 1965:10-11).

Conflict is, according to Simmel, inherent. Conflict of forms, of their usefulness, ambiguosity and redundancy and popularly, all via in the process of interaction. Significantly, conflict to Simmel is not a monolithic term but to be used to describe a dialectical process. For example in his *The Poor* (1908) Simmel investigates the form 'poor' and the forms that are manipulated to be used in conjunction with it. He does so in order to look at the realm of social institutions and of the motives and reasons for such institutions that 'deal' with the poor. The poor are found to be persons confined, constrained, at odds with dominant economic, social and moral forms, they are, outsiders: like strangers, they attract attention, curiosity and fear. The poor, also like the stranger, are groups that are subject to social definitions that become the common forms with which the poor come to be known. For example, the 'lazy', the 'immoral', the 'scrounger' and all forms, that some use, to describe the poor.

The analysis of social forms does not have to have relativistic consequences nor entail *a*structural analysis. The distinction between form and content is a complex one but which nevertheless has a structural aspect. For example, using the example above, we can see how contents refer to those drives, motives and ideas, which lead people to associate with one another in different ways. Forms are the patterns exhibited by the associations people get into. Therefore, to analyse forms means to look at structural aspects of patterned interactions which people create when they associate to achieve their various purposes. Associational forms are then, structural patterns. But once again it needs to be stated that forms are the product of human activity and not some supra-

---

[24] Rock, P. (1979) *The Making of Symbolic Interactionism*. London: Macmillan.

individual entity. In sociological terms Simmel's work provides a comprehensive analytical framework that if taken seriously is an outline programme for synthetic sociology. In his *Saziologie* (1908) Simmel demonstrates his ideas in a number of diverse examples; problems of defining society (ch.1), the quantitative aspects of groups (ch.2), super and subordination (ch.3), conflict (ch.4), secret societies (ch.5), the poor (ch.7), the stranger (ch.9), and group expansion and the development of individuality (ch.10). This collection of essays on various phenomena exemplify the analytical framework and its implication for synthetic sociology in the following way; chapters 1 and 2 give an analytical definition of the subject matter and its antecedent synthetic characteristics; chapter 3 designates a social relation; chapter 4 a type of process; chapter 5 a kind of collectivity; chapter 9 a kind of social role; and chapter 7 alienation; and chapter 10 developmental pattern. These are just examples of the forms of association and their antecedent structural variables (see chapter 2, 1908): any one analytical set or combination of sets can be used for the analysis of any association historically or contemporary.

What Simmel is attempting to demonstrate with these examples is that each can be seen to represent regularities abstracted from actual life. Each has regularities defined analytically and substantiated synthetically. For example, stranger is a status role that concerns the characteristic properties of one party to a relationship with a group while conflict concerns activities that go on between two or more incumbents of those statuses (see Levine, 1981)[25]. What is normally called structural changes and structural variables of a form are aspects of any analysis of any form. To Simmel, these two sets are manifested in six variable characteristics of any form, briefly, they are, size (quantitative aspects of groups); distance (degree of interactional proximity, emotional involvement, cognitive familiarity, cultural similarity): position (vertical and horizontal statuses); valence (amounts of positive or negative sentiment involved in forms of interaction); self-involvement (amount of personal involvement required by different forms of association), and symmetry (some forms entail complete reciprocity or a distinctive reciprocity). Apart from these six characteristics, Coser (1965) draws attention to the use of dialectical analysis of forms in Simmel's work, that is, the idea that for any phenomena to persist as a stable form within, it coexists with diametrically opposed elements. For example, fashion is a form that contains conformity and individualisation. A comprehensive example is needed here.

In *Metropolis and Mental Life* (1903)[26], Simmel turns his attention to the struggle between the individual, attempting to maintain independence against supra-individual forms, forms which in use have real consequences, such prejudice, racism, bias, and stigmatising labels. In such actions as anger,

---

[25] Levine, D. N. (1981) 'Sociologist's Quest for the Classics; The Case of Georg Simmel', in Rhea Burford, *The Future of the Sociological Classics*. London: Allen and Unwin.
[26] *Die Grosstädte und das Geistesleben*, (1903) Dresden: Petermann. [*The Metropolis and Mental Life*]

resentment, violence is such struggle manifested. Of course, conflict is not the only consequence; co-operation, acceptance, passiveness, acquiescence and assimilation are other possible alternatives whether in the singular or in combination. Conflict and co-operation are, as it were, opposite sides of the same spinning coin of social order: chaos is the diametrically opposed to both. Simmel's writings, then, have a modern feel about them; his topics of study, his style and approach are refreshingly non-systematic. Simmel not only theorises about the socially defined character of social reality but through his works such as *The Stranger, The Poor, Fashion*, and so on, he demonstrates how social phenomena are built up and maintained, how from the relativity and reciprocity of association emerges the lebenswelt.

Simmel's social reality is not conceived in terms of a totality or a system or as a machine but is conceived

> as the interweaving of forms, animated by the gaps, the ignorance and the fragmentary nature of social life and knowledge. No human can know all the facets of an individual, a process or a society. When a person focuses on one aspect they must neglect others. A person can tackle only minute sectors of life and then only momentarily. We are always on the interface of countless worldviews and perspectives and cannot incorporate them all. Social reality is accomplished by innumerable people coming and going, meeting and parting, loving and hating, creating social order through their encounters... society... a continually unfolding process... given structure by the routine and ostensibly petty.
> (Rock, 1979:38-44)[27]

To Simmel, Pure Sociology, as he was to call this activity differs from the so-called Cultural Sciences, such as politics and law, that deal mainly with substance and contents in a much more fragmented way failing to transcend to the level of Pure Sociology. However, even with such a status, Simmel does not regard sociology, as did Comte, the Queen of the Sciences, but as a form of knowing. To Simmel sociology is but one form of knowing among a number of others, that is, other ways of understanding and accounting for 'reality'. Hence, according to Simmel, one can adopt the sociological standpoint or not. This is because sociology as one form of knowing among many has no basis to claim supremacy or to be able to give absolute answers, solutions or a total view of what is and what is not. Far from it. To Simmel, as he demonstrates in his essays, sociology is a limited technical exercise.

Although our formulation of the work of Simmel has been brief, it is important grasp Simmel's conception of social reality and of the domain of sociology if we are to understand the roots of the philosophies and

---

[27] Op cit.

methodologies that underpinned the writings and empirical studies by members of the Department during this period.

C. Wright Mills: Tangent to the Story

To Park, the greater influence upon the output of the Department than any other in this period, sociological research involved systematic and detailed observation of social phenomena. While, for Thomas and Znaniecki[28] sociology involved the inductive development of hypotheses and the establishment of the conditions for their possible validation. These founders of the sociology of the Department, were a strong intellectual community by virtue of their overriding concern and dedication to the making of an empirically based sociology and not, as C. Wright-Mills suggests, because of their presumed middle-class origins[29]. The evidence for this is supplied to a large degree by the numerous studies carried out by the students of Park, Burgess, Small and Faris. For C. Wright-Mills, the studies were gross ethnographic descriptions of transient migratory groups. Wright-Mills argues that these studies are objectionable because they lack abstraction, systematic theorising, but most of all they lack an awareness of a Capitalist social class structure from a Marxian framework (Wright-Mills, 1967:535). Notions of class, class conflict and class divisions, Wright-Mills would have us believe are absent from the Chicago studies. However, a reading of even a few of the studies, for example, Zorbaugh's, *The Gold Coast and the Slum* or Anderson's, *The Hobo* reveals Wright-Mills assertions to be unfounded. *The Gold Coast and the Slum*, as the very name suggests, is an account of the gross disparities between the rich and the poor while *The Hobo* describes the way of life of the wage laborer forced into being a wanderer in search of work.

It is also evident that neither class as a concept nor class analysis are the primary approaches to the phenomenon in any of these studies. It is this that Wright-Mills is actually objecting to. Wright-Mills is arguing that 'class' is primary and should be the guiding concept of such studies and should be shown to be so in the final study. But why, we may ask, should 'class' be accorded such a status? Assuming for the moment that 'class' is an important concept and also assuming that 'class' can be a major variable in explanation, we need to ask of these studies, were they intended to be explanations and what part could class analysis have played in them if they were explanatory studies? Again, a reading of the studies reveals that our answer to the former question

---

[28] Thomas, W. I. and Znaniecki, F. (1918-1919) *The Polish Peasant in Europe and America*. 5 volumes. Boston: Badger.

[29] Mills, C. Wright. (1963, 1967) 'The Professional Ideology of the Social Pathologists'. In, *Power, Politics and People. The Collective Essays of C. Wright Mills*. Edited by Irving H. Horowitz. New York: Oxford University Press.

must lean towards a negative answer: these studies are neither argumentative nor explanatory, they are descriptive. Therefore, the problems the Chicago members were attempting to over come were at the level of description in order to become knowledgeable about rather than only explanation. This is not to say that class analysis could not have played a part for it could have but only on a primary basis if the methodology had been deductively oriented and not, as it was, inductively oriented. Secondly, while the concepts of 'conflict', 'struggle' and 'competition' all show that the Chicago members had an acute awareness of social divisions. What the Chicago members were attempting to describe was the order of society when that societal order was, to a large degree, seeming absent in a world of transient populations, numerous ethnic groups and rapidly expanding cities. The Irish, the Germanic, the Poles, the Italians, the Russians and the Jews had successively been the large immigrant groups to the large American cities. As one group was 'incorporated' into the mainstream of American life another took its place as a group of mass strangers. This was a phenomena well worth looking at; it was a Halle's Comet of sociology, a once in a life time occurrence, Wave after wave of different immigrant groups made for a difference in approach to that which had been used in the established industrial nations such as Britain. Class distinctions were to be observed among and between the various immigrant groups but they were not the only nor primary organising features of interaction.

To have used the concept 'class' would have been to impose an abstraction upon the data and resulted in compromising methodological faithfulness. Therefore, the members took the idea of the 'stranger' and asked; What were the cultural difficulties faced by the successive immigrant groups? Was there and observable pattern? What kinds of statuses were the immigrant groups given by the previous wave of immigrants? In what parts of the City did new immigrants first settle? Did they maintain kinship, social and 'old country' communal bonds? In what ways did the immigrants see themselves and the place to which they had come? What effects did this movement have on the 'look' of the City (eg. housing, trade, industries, crime, entertainments and so on)? In what ways did the immigrant regard the host culture as strange and in what ways did the indigenous peoples regard the immigrant way of life? In many ways the Becker, Goffman, Freidson and Kornhauser successors to Chicago School sociology can be seen to be establishing a tradition to make the strange familiar. To Wright-Mills, such sociological industry was at best a missed opportunity to politicise sociology and at worst only serving to obscure structural and class positions.

Far be it for anybody to deny Wright-Mills his political views but his claim to verifiable statements about the Chicago School are, due to the empirical evidence so far looked at, invalid and largely irrelevant. In the previous two sections we have looked at the philosophical environment the members of the Chicago School found around them and at two of the basic texts produced by members in attempts to clarify or overcome some of the classical methodological and philosophical obstacles to their particular preference for the object of study for sociology. In what follows, a similar mode of refutation of Wright-Mills is followed by outlining the third main influence upon the work of the Chicago School, namely the synthesis of ethnography and Pragmatism. This will be presented in the following order. Firstly, we will look at the anthropological teachings of Bronislaw Malinowski followed by an outline of writings of the Pragmatist, William James. In the third section, we will look at the way in which Robert Park synthesised the work of James and Malinowski to provide a sociological framework for the empirical investigation of aspects of social life.

Malinowski and Fieldwork Ethnography

Bronislaw Malinowski's work marked a departure in the method and conception of anthropology. Unlike the contemplative school of ethnocentric desk bound theorists of late Victorian and Edwardian years, Malinowski earned and nurtured the image of a contemporary equivalent of Indiana Jones - a bushwhacking, all daring anthropologists always ready to go, and to give an opinion, not least on himself. Teaching by example (though not exactly always by choice) he was the standard setter of the day for his profession. Malinowski's classic study is *Argonauts of the Western Pacific*, first published in 1922[30], contains the essentials of Malinowski's prescriptions for doing ethnography. First and foremost, Malinowski makes it clear that the object of study is not so much the place, either geographically or historically, but what happens within it, of "the regularities in interaction, in beliefs, customs, opinions, activities" (Malinowski, 1922:11-12). The routine as much as the exotic events and actions that make up daily life are the objects for study; what Malinowski calls the 'imponderabilitia of actual life'. Malinowski's natives were active agents not imprisoned in evolutionary stages or 'redundant' survivals from the past t o be understood by reference to social evolution. Malinowski tells us that the,

> Firm skeleton of tribal life has to be ascertained. This ideal imposes in the first place the fundamental obligation of giving a complete survey of the phenomena, and not of picking out the sensational... still less the funny and quaint. Time when we tolerate accounts presenting the natives as a distorted, childish caricature of a human being are done.
> (Malinowski, 1922:11)

To Malinowski, all societies were on-going affairs lacking neither complexity nor sophistication of organisation to "guide them in their strenuous enterprises

---

[30] Malinowski, B. (1922) *Argonauts of the Western Pacific: An Account of Native Enterprise and Adventure in the Archipelagoes of Melanesian New Guinea.* London: Routledge & Kegan Paul.

and activities" (Malinowski, 1922:10). The science of anthropology had shown, contrary to popular belief, that the peoples of other societies engaged themselves in activities made up of very much the same stuff as all people, talking, making deals, expressing opinions, making transactions, moaning, laughing, the body and blood stuff of actually lived communal life (Malinowski, 1922:18).

Malinowski's conception of the subject matter creates its own difficulties, difficulties he calls the Gordian Knot of social psychology (Malinowski, 1922:22). Malinowski's Gordian knot amounts to much the same philosophical and methodological problems as faced by Thomas and Znaniecki when aiming to capture, in full faithfulness, the subjective element. An essential part of the subjective element to Malinowski is the imponderables of everyday life. As the "real substance of the social fabric, the threads of which keep the community together"(1922:18-19). The imponderables of life are of great analytical importance. But the puzzle (or Gordian Knot) consists in the problems of describing in faithful terms this body and blood of actual interaction. Malinowski states the problem thus,

> The duty before him [the anthropologist] of drawing up all the rules and regularities of tribal life... of giving an anatomy of their culture, of depicting the constitution of their society. But these things though crystallised and set, are nowhere formulated. There is no written or explicitly expressed code of laws, and their whole tribal tradition, the whole structure of their society, are embodied in the most elusive of all materials; the human beings.
> (Malinowski, 1922:11)

Defined as important some means must be devised to record and capture the imponderabilia of everyday life. "But", asks Malinowski, "is this possible? Are these subjective states not too elusive?"(Malinowski, 1922:22). In-stock methods such as compiling genealogies, census plans are all, according to Malinowski, dead material. Nor is direct questioning of the native of much use, adds Malinowski, for "as any humble member of any modern institution... is of it and in it... has no vision of the resulting integral action of the whole, still less could furnish any account of its organisation"(Malinowski, 1922:11). Malinowski therefore concludes passing abstract sociological questions to the native would be futile. However, Malinowski saves us from despondency by claiming to have devised by example the method for overcoming such problems and for producing accurate scientific text. Malinowski distinguishes the three main principles of this method. Firstly, the researcher must possess and espouse scientific aims and values. Secondly, the researcher must live with and amongst the people she or he is studying. Lastly, the researcher must apply a number of special methods for collecting data and special techniques for ordering and presenting findings.

In espousing the values of science the researcher must present all findings in a manner that is absolutely candid and above board (Malinowski, 1922:2). The researcher must also have cleared the mind from pre-conceived values. Malinowski writes on this,

> Good training in theory, and acquaintance with its latest results is not identical with being burdened with 'preconceived ideas'. If a man sets out on an expedition, determined to prove certain hypotheses, if he is incapable of changing his views constantly and casting them off ungrudgingly under the pressure more problems he brings with him into the field, the more he is in the habit of moulding his theories according to facts, and of seeing their bearing upon the theory, the better equipped for the work. Preconceived ideas are pernicious in any scientific work, but foreshadowed problems are the main endowment of a scientific thinker, and these problems are first revealed to the observer by his theoretical studies.
> (Malinowski, 1922:8-9)

Theory is important then to free the researcher from preconceived ideas that may obscure or distort. Secondly, Malinowski makes it clear that there is all the "difference between sporadic plunging into the company of natives and being really in contact with them"(Malinowski, 1922:7). The researcher, as 'stranger' must endeavor to become an 'ordinary member', to become a part of the daily life of the people under study so that his or her presence does not disrupt the natives routines and produce a false picture of their life. Finally, while immersed in the daily life of the community, data must be collected. Idealised answers and opinions are to be avoided, one method by which this can be done is, suggests Malinowski, to engage the native or natives in spontaneous discussion or listen to the discussion of the natives. Discussion can, suggests Malinowski be induced in preference to direct questioning. "It would be vain", Malinowski writes,

> to put to a native a sweeping question such as 'how do you treat and punish a criminal?, But an imaginary case, or still better, a real occurrence, will stimulate a native to express his opinions and to supply plentiful information... talk will contain a wealth of definite views.
> (Malinowski, 1922:12).

In presenting findings the descriptions given and statements made must, according to Malinowski's third principle, be candid and above board; they must be rooted in observations of the imponderabilia of everyday life. However, statements are not to be taken as absolute but as limited to the observations from which they were made and by contemporary knowledge, both of which are open to revision. On the academic battleground Malinowski's prescriptions can be seen as an attack on and rejection of the de-contextualised accounts to be found in the works such as James Frazer. In his attack, Malinowski makes the further recommendation that the researcher concentrate upon the typical events to be observed in a culture or actions or a group. In such he places emphasis upon the researcher not only living daily life amongst those he is studying but upon the researcher understanding the argot of the group: the language, terms, the protocol of the group all have to be grasped and understood in use so as to avail the researcher with the material - observations of interaction that makes for the particular organisation of that groups particular interactions. Familiarity with the native language use and protocol has the added boon in that it can be a technique employed by the researcher as a means for introspection by both the natives and other anthropologists as a semi-autonomous verification.

Malinowski set up a framework by which sociologists and anthropologist could measure standards: all statements to be rooted in actual observations and open to revision by further empirical evidence; clarity of findings; contextualised accounts; empathetic understanding; open mindedness; and concentration upon the routine and everyday actions and events, such prescriptions amounted to a tough framework by which other studies could be assessed.

As Head of the Department of Anthropology, at the London School of Economics, Malinowski's works were internationally influential. Apart from his own lectures and published material Malinowski's work was propagated in Chicago by Alfred Radcliffe-Brown who visited the Department of Sociology several times during the mid-twenties. However, in saying that British anthropology was a major influence upon the work of the members of the Chicago school is not to claim that British and American Sociology were similar. Unlike their British counterparts the Americans were well at home in both anthropology and sociology; it was not, in fact, until 1940 that the University of Chicago established separate departments for the two disciplines. The other great difference between the two was that while the British believed that they could make statements about their own culture by virtue of their membership of it the Americans made no such assumption because of the manifest ethnic differences and diversity around them.

Thus the empirical and empathetic ideas of Malinowski were applicable to the home ground of the Americans. But Malinowski's ideas alone were not enough to overcome the philosophical problems which had been brought into sharp relief by Thomas and Znaniecki. For these, the Chicago sociologists found a solution amongst their own members, Pragmatic Philosophy. Pragmatism was the second influence for the making of an empirical basis of Chicago sociology. The incorporation of Pragmatism into the Department of Sociology at Chicago was, in the main, due to Robert Park. The Pragmatism of the school was that of William James and John Dewey, though in the section that follows it is the particular Pragmatism of James that we will concentrate upon. This is because of all the influences upon the Chicago School none other than the work of William James captures the essence of toleration and accommodation of the School.

William James: *Pragmatism* (1907) and *Essays In Radical Empiricism* (1912)

The works of William James, for example, *Pragmatism* (1907)[31] and *Essays In Radical Empiricism* (1912)[32] are often discussed with apologising respect and said would have been more important if only they were not so obligingly liberal to other philosophers in positions contrary to Pragmatism. In his work James does not mock nor ignore the philosophies with which he disagrees. For James, Pragmatism was the philosophy that had largely resolved the main problems of philosophy while at the same time allowed room for those who found it necessary to believe in the spiritual and metaphysical. To James, the great diversity of opinion and belief in the world was a source of interest and definitely not to be used as the justification of dogma. James was against dogma and the dismissal of the religious and metaphysical as nonsense. In many ways it is James' charity to others that has led to his Pragmatism being misunderstood.

The greatest misunderstanding of James' Pragmatism is that it is often believed to be implying that truth is to be equated with expediency, i.e. that any belief is to be accepted as true if it can be seen to satisfy the needs or interests of those who held it. Nothing could be further from the work of James than this interpretation. James's use of the word is not to be likened to the common usage of the term. To James, truth is a philosophical issue to be discussed as an interactive process synchronously at the philosophical level of epistemology and at the level of practical science. We can illustrate what is meant by this statement by asking a string of questions. How is truth realised? What concrete difference does it make if we grant an idea to be a true idea? Lastly, having deliberated on the above two issues, what experiences will be different from those, which we would obtain if the belief were false? As a process and not something given "true ideas are those", James tells us, "which we can assimilate, validate, corroborate and verify. False ideas are those that we cannot". Ideas are neither given to be true or false:

> truth and false are status's conferred upon ideas by events. An idea becomes true, it is made true by events. Its verify is in fact an event, a process: the process namely of it's verifying itself, it verification. It's validity is the process of its veridational.
> (James, 1907:97).

---

[31] James, W. (1907) *Pragmatism: A New Name for Some Old Ways of Thinking.* New York: Longmans, Green and Company. Full text available from: http://www.gutenberg.org/dirs/etext04/prgmt10.txt.
[32] Originally published posthumously in 1912 by Longmans, Green and Co., New York, and edited by Ralph Barton Perry a more accessible version is *The Works of William James: Essays in Radical Empiricism*, (1976) edited by Frederick Burkhardt and Fredson Bowers, Harvard University Press.

Not all ideas, which are commonly or secretly accepted as true, have been verified. Very few true ideas have been verified but are still accepted, on trust, as being true. Ideas which fall into this majority category have, in James words, greater cash-value by their possible than actual verification. In other words, James is suggesting that while all ideas assumed to be true are accorded truth by a verifying process the status true operates on differing levels of generality: differentiation can be seen between the accepted, taken-for-granted or uncontested and the verified or contested. Ideas which have been contested have had their truth value put to a testing process of validation. If that idea is found to be unfulfilled it is not, as one might expect, labeled as false. It is only labeled as false when majority trust has been withdrawn (a contemporary discussion of similar processes is of course to be found in Kuhn's *The Structure of Scientific Revolutions*, 1962). Trust therefore plays an important part in the process of truth. James puts this suggestion about the nature of truth in the following

> Truth lives, in fact, for the most part on a credit system. Our thoughts and beliefs 'pass' so long as nothing challenges them just as bank notes pass so long as nobody refuses them. But this all points to face-to-face verification, without which the fabric of truth collapses like a financial system with no cash basis whatever. We trade each other's truth. But beliefs, verified concretely by somebody are the posts of the whole superstructure.
> (James, 1907:100)

James 'theory of truth' is one of two intertwined aspects of his Pragmatism. The second aspect is his 'theory of method', which we will come to in a moment. But first a deeper grasp on the nature of Pragmatism is required if we are to understand its use by Park. Returning to the earlier epistemological discussion in this introduction we can cast the work of James into the philosophical map that was constructed. James himself makes much use of the dichotomy of the Rationalist and the Empiricist, the former he regards as tender-minded and the latter as tough minded. In the category of tender-minded James includes the Idealistic, Optimistic, Religious, Free-willist, Monistic, and Dogmatical; while among the tough-minded he includes the Sensationalistic, Materialistic, Pessimistic, Irreligious, Fatalistic, Pluralistic, and Sceptical (James, 1907:7-12). David Hume and John Stuart Mill can be seen as among James's tough-minded and Hegel and his followers among the tender-minded. To decide where James stood in this mix we need to elucidate more about the predominant strains of this dichotomy, and of the Pragmatic response to it. We can begin by attributing to the Pragmatists a basic postulate: knowledge is drawn, in the first instance, from the realm of concrete experience. This simply stated postulate is deceptively radical. It is a radical departure from the Kantian divide and the responses and reactions to it. Kant and the Neo-Kantians had created the great Gordian Knot of philosophy: the puzzle of a seemingly impassable divide between the subject and the object, between the knower and the known. The philosophical industry followed in the wake of Kant only managed, at best, to create fragile bridges, at worst, absurd rejections of the void. The former, the Rationalists, took as their starting point to knowledge the 'rational properties of the mind'. Mind, for the Rationalists was primary; it was the determining factor of all knowledge and action. Taken to one of its logical conclusions some Rationalists argued that since Mind is a mystery to Human kind, an entity with no referent within the body, it must be some supra-individual entity, possibly God.

The second, main reaction to the mind-body divide was that by those whom we called the Empiricists. Among the Empiricists the Positivists emerged to declare that the search for 'mind' was a quark hunt. The existence of a supre-individual was said to be beyond empirical proof while mind since it could not be accounted for in observational language is to be counted as a primitive belief. Instead of searching for the nature of true reality or what some of their ranks regarded as the non-existent, the positivists turned their attentions to scrupulous empirical inquiry, dismissing many of the classical epistemological questions as being insoluble, metaphysical or absurdly meaningless for practical purposes. All that exist is the material world. Mind was an illusion of the nervous system or created by theology or by nation states to control its subjects. Everything, including human action could, in principle be explained by reference to the mechanics of the body and its relationship to its environment. The point the Pragmatists noted about both these positions was that not only are both reactions or replies to Kant, in that they are just different sides of the same coin as it were, but that both place human action in a derivative and determined position. The Materialists regard action as the outcome of mechanical, physiological processes while the Rationalists regard human action as the outcome a supra-individual entity: either way action is derivative and determined. In the midst of all this philosophical banter, the Pragmatists arrived, swept it aside and set up an alternative for themselves. The whole issue of dualism, they argued was simply misplaced. Language, myth and other forms of knowledge had overlapped or had become dogmatical creating reactions which became in their turn just as dogmatical: as each form of knowledge declared itself to be the form of knowledge, the battlefield took shape with the differing camps becoming entrenched continually sparing for space and making alliances.

The result of all of this was that they created the image of there being a dualism between mind and body, so much so, that this dualism had become the in-stock knowledge in both the realm of common-sense and philosophical knowledge. To the Pragmatists the question of Rationalists or Empiricists made, whichever choice was made, for no practical difference. No matter which choice was made absurdities and barriers to practical empirical science emerged, therefore a difference that makes no difference is no difference. The difference is made when one declares that there is no divide between mind and body. To the Pragmatists, mind and body are of the same substances: experience is neither physical nor mental for both mind and matter can be constructed out of it.

Instead of the word 'mind' the Pragmatists prefer the word 'consciousness'. This is because the very word mind connotes images of soul and spirit; meanings entrenched in the common knowledge stock to be displaced using the same term. The Pragmatist theory therefore is that consciousness is of 'things' that are constructed out of experience. Consciousness becomes a process initiated by experience; it is the difference between merely being 'acquainted with something' (Plato's *anamnesisor*) and having 'explicit knowledge about something'. Being in a state of *doctra ignorantia* is to be in a state of low consciousness, in a state where instinct and biological drives determine behaviour (in an animal state). Humans however, make their doctra ignorantia clear: they come to know their impulses and learn recipes for controlling their responses, to a level where they can initiate actions from others for the fulfillment of their own ends. But, how does one make ones' doctra ignorantia clear? First and foremost we do not make a choice between reflection and experience. To do so would lead us straight back into the absurdities of the traditional philosophical battlefield. Instead, James suggests that consciousness comes about as an emergent property from experience; knowledge is derived in working living experience. Knowledge is work involving a methodological approach and process.

> To attain clearness in our thoughts of an object... we need only to consider what conceivable effects of a practical kind the object may involve - what sensations we may expect from it, and what reactions we must prepare, our conception of these effects, whether immediate or remote, is then for us the whole of our conception of the object, so far as that conception has significance at all.
> (James, 1907:29)

An object, be it human or not, is brought into consciousness if we regard that object as having relevance to us. Consciousness is not a separate entity, but as can now be grasped, a process of becoming aware of experience through its relevance to our projects for ourselves. It is from the awareness of the value of being aware of the relationship between experiences and our capacity to control and even direct actions and courses of events that consciousness and knowledge result. Therefore, knowledge is to be sought (synthetic apriori /aposteriori) among the details of interactions between people. James is not denying apriori knowledge nor is he taking a reductionist line. What James is doing is stepping outside the Rationalist-Empiricist paradigm to look upon that knot and suggest it was made with false beliefs. James recommends an alternative approach, which pays its dues to both Rationalism and Empiricism because of the use-value inherent in both. An example might clarify what is meant here. Mathematics is often regarded as the apex of abstract thinking. Equations are apriori. When we are presented with an equation that is unfamiliar to us we employ our capacity for reasoned thought to clarify, to work out, what the logic of the equation is. In other words, we clarify our doctra ignorantia via the use of our reason and not by counting on our fingers. This is no argument for the traditionalist Rationalist: it is just an observation of the current state of mathematics. In the current state of mathematics counting on fingers is not the essential method to grasping the logical relationship between the parts of the equation. The point to note, however, is that mathematical work had its origin in counting on fingers, which is of course, an empirical experience. Concrete thinking therefore precedes abstract thinking: to believe otherwise is to commit one to the Rationalist-Empiricist 'either - or' divide.

Before we leave this section it is worth formulating what has been attributed to the work of James. James appears to be saying that experience is the initial stuff from which consciousness and apriori thinking develops. Idealised frameworks are ready made for us into which we can understand the meanings of objects. Conceptual frameworks are learned by virtue of communal membership. These frameworks are real in that we cannot ignore them, play fast and loose with them any more than we can do so with our sense experience. We are coerced by these frameworks whether we like it or not (James, 1907:210-211). However, the current primacy given to apriori propositions does not entail that they will be eternally true: apart from the fact that apriori truths are self-defining the mental objects that make up the idealised framework are liable to change in the light of further experience. It might be revealed the current apriori framework was built upon gaps in consciousness which were hidden by the tendency for consciousness to make affinities between experiences for the sake of coherence and continuity.

Therefore, even the trust endowed in the apriori may turn out to be an unintended deception of 'reality'. This view is neither sceptical nor dogmatic; James is simply being charitable to other philosophies and forms of knowledge out not at any cost to his tough-minded attitude to intellectual standards. The awareness of the nature of truth as a process of verification acts for James as a tough barrier against pretenders to the status of scientific knowledge.

Robert Park's take on Malinowski and Pragmatism

It was Robert Park, with Ernest Burgess, who synthesised the anthropology Malinowski with the pragmatism of James. They did so in order to create a framework of assumptions about and which define the domain of sociology, the nature of society and the development of appropriate conceptual tools and methodological approaches in order that sociology could be done. For Park the domain of sociology is the investigation of the interactions of humans in their natural environment by detailed observation. Methodologically techniques were developed including observation to describe and explain the processes of social interaction and the places in which they occurred and what control them. This emphasis upon process was directed by a concern for what controlled interaction. In their book *The City* Park and Burgess make a set of recommendations and suggestions about topics to research, and attempt to deal with the problems created by the acceptance of pragmatism.

The City (1925)[33]: Synthesis of Malinowski and James

Park was selective in what he took from pragmatism. He did not dismiss or ignore the methodological problems created by the conception pragmatism had of the nature of the relationship between the individual and society and of the nature of the genesis of human action. Pragmatism had generally rejected the mind / body divide and in the same rejected the question of whether it was individual or society that had the primacy of action. Parks' reading of the Pragmatist's ideas was that there was no meaningful distinction to be made between the individual and society. To choose society was to demote the individual to a rarefied society, to choose the individual give manipulated freedoms to the individual that they do not generally have. Such notions as group mind, collective consciousness, historical dialectics, and Machiavellian free will were similarly, misplaced abstract constructs to the Pragmatists. Instead, Parks' reading of the pragmatists, resulted in a conception of society as one consisting of individuals learning and becoming conscious of the frameworks and forms into which objects of experience and thought could be known, categorised and rendered meaningful and used in the production and direction of interactional episodes. Membership of the group, for Park, allowed the individual to become acquainted with and use of idealised frameworks for the living of their life and as such it is the use of these frameworks in individual or group action that make society what it is. The problem is, if action is not to be counted for by recourse to neither external nor internal determinants how does one describe the ways in which a persons actions are constrained while at the same time that same person manipulates and directs their own interaction and interaction with others? Although James recognised this is a major problem it was Park who suggested that it could be circumvented by practical means. Park outlines these means in *The City* (1915 / 1925).

In a nutshell, Park says that while conventional sociology, based upon dualist assumptions, has found such methods as the survey and theorising and other abstract approaches - expressed in such phrases as collective consciousness, stimulus response, instincts and so on - as applicable to their meta-theoretical assumptions these will not do for him. For Park with his take on the pragmatist conception of action the only way to understand the why and how of action is a matter of gaining direct understanding of what people experience themselves. The essential prescription is understanding what the people being observed are

---

[33] Park, Robert, E. (1915) 'The City: Suggestions for the Study of Human Nature in the Urban Environment', American Journal of Sociology, 20:557-612. Also in, Park, Robert, E. and Burgess, Ernest, W. (1925) *The City: Suggestions for the Study of Human Nature in the Urban Environment*. Chicago: University of Chicago Press. With contributions from, R. D. McKenzie and Louis Wirth.

doing and understanding what meanings they attach to their actions and the actions of others.

With this notion in mind the Pragmatist problem of 'how action' could be tackled via empirical investigation Park and Burgess formulate a proposal for a research programme into the plurality of life to be found in the urban environment. The city was to be the natural laboratory of the sociologist. "Research work in sociology", Park says, "should be orientated with reference to the utilisation of the city of Chicago as the social logical laboratory. This means the collection of material upon which the social life of the city; the organisation of these materials; and their social analysis" (quoted in Bulmer, 1984:93). According to Park, behaviour in all its varieties is to be found in the city. In part this follows James' criteria that the naturalness of city life has to be studied naturally so as to preserve what it is about this type of life that makes it distinguishable as this type and not another. Park had no doubts about what method would fulfill this enterprise. He points to the work of anthropologist's and other social investigators. The work of Franz Boase, R.H. Lowrie and Charles Booth are held up as examples.

> The same patient methods of observation which anthropologists like Boas and Lowrie have expended on the study of the life and manners of the North American Indian might, be even more fruitfully employed in the investigation of the customs, beliefs, social practices, and general conceptions of life prevalent in Little Italy on the Lower North Side in Chicago.
> (Park and Burgess, 1925:3)

Elsewhere Park and Burgess refer with admiration to the work of the English social investigators, in particular, Booth. Although Booth's[34] work is ostensibly a survey it is also according to McKenzie a,

> realistic description of the actual life of the occupational classes - the conditions under which they lived and laboured, their passions, past times, domestic tragedies, and the life philosophies with which each class met the crisis peculiar to it... makes these studies... a permanent contribution to our knowledge.
> (R.D. McKenzie in, Park and Burgess, 1952:77)

Rigour, precision – in description - and first-hand experience have no equal according to Park. The influence of William James is clear here. Park argues,

---

[34] Charles Booth (1889-1891) *Life and Labour of the People*. Also see, Albert Fried and Richard Ellman (eds.). (1969) *Charles Booth's London*. London: Hutchinson.

The 'blindness' of which James spoke is the blindness each of us is likely to have for the meaning of other people's lives. At any rate, what sociologists most need to know is what goes on behind the faces of men, what is it that makes life for each of us either dull or thrilling... in every single case, has to be discovered. Otherwise we do not know the world in which we actually live.
(quoted in Bulmer, 1984:93)[35]

The cure of the social blindness was, according to Park, a succession of detailed definitions of subjects and situations followed by in-depth observational studies of actual social life. The what is and what do we mean by a question was often asked by Park when a student talked of some particular way of life - Park extracted from the student long definitions of acquainted ways of life with the aim of showing the complexities and diverging nature of conceptions and definitions of a subject matter.

As a guide for empirical research, Park arranges the contents of *The City* as if it were to be used as a reference of knowledge to be used, questions to be asked and the type of topics to be chosen that might satisfy such curiosities. Park is not offering a theoretical package but a set of ideas and constructs which relate to one another and which might have value. Ten years later work was well underway in fulfilling part this ambitious programme. By this time Park and Burgess had published *The Introduction to the Science of Sociology*. In *The Introduction* many of the concepts and constructs that were to become the trademarks of the Chicago School were laid out, in particular, Burgess's notion of city zones. By the early 1920s students from the Department were beginning to produce publications. Nels Anderson had published the *Hobo* (1923), Frederick Thrasher had begun work on what was to become *The Gang* (1927) and Louis Wirth's study of the ghetto was well underway. A dozen or so studies were to follow as well as numerous articles in the American Journal of Sociology.

Substantively, the topics investigated were amazingly broad given the their genesis from one department; race, immigration, media, crime and delinquency, the law, suicide, marital conflict, entertainments, prostitution, age structures, ghetto life, high society life, gang cultures, hotel life, a multitude of occupations including shop girls, peddlers, vaudeville performers, all and more became the topics of student observational studies. Park's influence (alongside that of others such as Burgess, McKenzie and Palmer) was therefore very powerful. His suggestion for a rigorous ethnographic approach was as radical as James' empiricism, not only in the wealth of studies produced by students but in the manner in which in seemingly contradictory theories of Culture and

---

[35] Bulmer, M. (1984) *The Chicago School of Sociology: Institutionalization, Diversity, and the Rise of Sociological Research.* Chicago: University of Chicago Press.

philosophies were incorporated into a framework for sociological action. The Kantian forms and the verstehen of Simmel and Pragmatism of James, with the anthropology of Malinowski were mixed by Park into a recipe for empirical sociology: a sociology that paid little heed to the rear-guard defenses against psychology that had been fought by Durkheim nor to calls for grand deductivism. Instead, a radical break was made with the sociology of the 'old masters', the concerns over the moral and ethical effects of the great transformation and the fear of societal breakdown and the mould of entity thinking were replaced by investigations of life in industrialised urban environments as topics in their own right. Social reality was now thought of as a process and not some given situation.

Introduction to the Science of Sociology (1921)[36]

Although the *Introduction to the Science of Sociology* (1921) was published over ninety years ago its aims are still pertinent. Its aim was to give a lead to students and instruction in the skills of sociological description, investigation and analysis, so that they could produce clear, rigorous and verifiable studies within a framework committed to interpretivist sociology. Thus, first and foremost the Introduction is a manual for the production of sociological studies. The Introduction is a compendium of thought comprising some one hundred and seventy six extracts, fourteen chapters on over one thousand pages:

> it is a framework for the sociological treatment of human nature and personality, group formation, interactive processes, organisation, social forces, social changes... in fact all of the range of interests that may be found among sociology today.
> (Faris, 1967:38)[37].

Janowitz tells us that "the text is unrepresentative... of the intellectual interests subsumed under the Chicago School sociology"(Janowitz, 1969:vi). Even so, the Introduction is a remarkably comprehensive piece of work in its range of theories, thinkers and in its direction for sociological work. The recommendations in the Introduction are two fold; to conceive of social reality in Simmelian terms, as a process and to do sociology as a practical activity. Thus, the Introduction sets out a framework with which to conceive and approach the social world and gives strong recommendations that students should engage themselves in empirical studies.

The origins of the Introduction are worthy of brief mention as they give some insight into the type of personalities the members of the department had.

---

[36] Park, Robert. E. and Burgess, Ernest, W. (1921) *Introduction to the Science of Sociology.* Chicago: University of Chicago Press.
[37] Faris, Robert. E. L. (1967) *The Chicago School, 1920-1932.* Chicago: University of Chicago Press.

Unlike many sociological texts today, personal gain either in terms of fame or royalties was not the reason. The book was written to fulfill the need felt and expressed by students and staff alike.

> The income derived from royalties was not viewed by Park and especially by Burgess as a regular part of their income. In the case of... Burgess it was carefully husbanded in order to underwrite research and ultimately after his death turned over to the Department of Sociology to make possible a generous scholarship fund.
> (Janowitz, 1969:vii)

The organisation of the book is often said to be loose, however, it is logical and consistent with the authors' intentions. Before looking at the actual contents of the book it is interesting to note that it has a format similar to W.I. Thomas's book, *A Source Book for Social Origins* (1909)[38]:

SOCIAL ORIGINS (1909)	THE INTRODUCTION (1921)
Ethnological Materials	Introduction and Materials
Psychological Standpoint	Psychological Standpoint
Classified and Annotated Bibliography	Investigation and Problems
	Topics for Written Themes
	Questions for Discussion

While the format replicates Thomas's *Source Book* the concern of the contents reflects those of Simmel: the chapters have the following headings,

1. Sociology and the Social Sciences.
2. Human Nature.
3. Society and the Group.
4. Isolation.
5. Social Contacts.
6. Social Interaction.
7. Social forces.
8. Competition.
9. Conflict.
10. Accommodation.
11. Assimilation.

---

[38] Thomas, W.I. (1909) *Source Book for Social Origins: Ethnographical Materials, Psychological Standpoint, Classified and Annotated Bibliographies for the Interpretation of Savage Society.* Chicago: University of Chicago.

12. Social Control.
13. Collective Behaviour .
14. Progress.

There are obvious similarities between Simmel's *Sociology* (1908) and Park and Burgess's *The Introduction to the Science of Sociology* (1969edn.), but saying what these similarities are is quite another thing for in doing we have to introduce a degree of order to Simmel's work not provided by Simmel himself. The chapters that contain selections from Simmel fall into two sets. Chapters 4 to 7, and chapters 8 to 11. Chapters 4 - 7 treat the ways in which individuals move from isolation into contact with others and then move into interaction and conceptualise and use the concept of 'social distance' along lateral and vertical dimensions. Chapters 8 - 11 discuss the major interaction processes which underlie four main types of social order identified by Park (Park and Burgess, 1969:504-510). These are, competition (economic equilibrium), conflict (the political order), accommodation (social organisation) and assimilation (personality and the cultural heritage). Various attempts were made by students of Park's to implement this programme, for example, Kelvin Vincent's, *A Study of Accommodation as a Conscious Social Process Reflected in Employer and Employee Relationships* (Chicago, unpublished thesis, 1928). From the Introduction and student research we can see that Park and Burgess accepted Simmel's basic assumptions, though some more than others, especially the assumptions that the particular forms are identifiable and that forms entail structural aspects. Given such a clear influence of Simmel, which can also be seen in the fact that his works are reproduced and referred to in the Introduction more than any other single thinker it is surprising to find Janowitz echoing a criticism of Wright-Mills when he claims,

> The [the Chicago Sociologists]... concern with social processes limited their identifications of the essential stratification features... and weakened their analysis of social structure. Instead of examining the macrostructures of society... they used such vague formulations as 'social forces', (Janowitz, 1969:viii)[39]

Like Wright-Mills' observations[40], Janowitz's criticisms here are both misleading and based on attributing incorrect ontological assumptions to the work of the members of the School. Janowitz's mistake is to assume that because the members of the department make few direct references to structural influences such as class, wealth inequalities, race, gender and the like and instead preferred

---

[39] Janowitz, M, (1969) 'Introduction' to *The Introduction to the Science of Sociology*, by Park, Robert, E. and Burgess, Ernest W. Chicago: University of Chicago Press.
[40] Op cit.

the use of concepts denoting process and cognation they were demoting structural analysis. Far from it. The Formalist influence of Simmel and his conception of social reality as a dialectical process between the individual and objectified social forms the question of structural analysis or individual self-determination, as proposed in the classical dualist paradigm is simply not an applicable frame of reference for an evaluation. Since Park, Burgess and Thomas did not think within the dualist paradigm their work cannot be judged within it, that is, knowing that they conceived social reality as a process and hence attributed no ontological status to the concepts 'society' or 'individual' it makes no philosophical sense to criticise them for not being classical structuralists. The consequence of assuming, as the Chicago School did, that the person acted upon and was also acted on by their social environment was manifested in their terminology and concepts. Hence, if the members of the School had given primacy to structuralist concepts such as class, race, and gender determination, they would have been misplaced by not being in accord with the initial assumptions about the nature of the relationship between the subject and their social environment. However, it does make political sense to do just this if one wishes to promote ones' own sociological or political preferences.

What is at issue here is the implications of the ontological and epistemological choices a thinker makes. Thinkers who work within the classical paradigm regard the situation as if it were a choice between either a 'subjectivist cum relativist cum individualistic' position and 'objectivist cum scientific cum structural' position and that any position which is clearly not one of these must be conceived as if it were and categorised as being individualist or structural according to the terminology it employs. Hence, even though Simmel's Formalism was removed from this classical paradigm because it was created in the shadow of Kant, it was assumed that it and any subsequent developments of it could be categorised according to terminology and labeled subjectivist or objectivist.

Thus, such criticisms that their work was 'loose', 'lacked explicit systematisation' and 'paid insufficient attention to social structure' while preferring 'detailed descriptions of fragments of social life' to explanations in terms of totalities, is literally ironic. That is, from the structuralist preference these consequences are criticism while from the Simmelian point of view of the Chicago School they are manifestations of success. Therefore, the point is, one cannot legitimately criticise one theoretical framework from an entirely different frame of reference. To criticise the work of an interpretivist from the intentions of a structuralist position without taking into consideration the intentions and aims of such a choice, is, for all practical sociological purposes – an act of bad faith. The differences between different conceptions of social reality and of the relationship between the person and their social environment is not only a difference in forms of knowledge but as Simmel appears to show in his essays there is little difference in the consequences in which ever position one chooses within the classic paradigm, that is, whether one chooses an empiricist or rationalist view of action the consequence remains the same, human action is deemed to be by either physiological or mental determined. William James made this observation clear and like Simmel attempted to develop an alternative conception of the relationship between the person and the social so that the consequences were radically different from those of the traditional paradigm.

The practices of the Chicago School, for example, gross description, participation and social acquaintance with the subject, are implications of their theoretical position. They are logical implications and not illogical ones as proposed by the critics. But, why are they logical implications? They are logical implications given the commitment to the verstehen criteria and the elections made about what the domain of sociology should be. This is to return to the point made above, that is, if one conceives of the domain of sociology to be the identification of forms in use and a conception of social reality as a dynamic process then one does not attempt to portray social realities as entity like in static deductive approaches; that would fly in the face of common sense. Louis Wirth said of Park, "he was rarely sympathetic with attempts to develop deductive sociological theory, speaking of such endeavours as 'mere exercises' in theory construction', that "most sociological theories", he writes, "ignore the most obvious and obscure... human beings...". (Wirth, 1964:xii)[41].

This comment echoes Bronislaw Malinowski. Both have in common their objections to hypothetical models taking the place of actual living with the groups one wishes to study. According to Park, if hypothetical models became the norm for sociological work then contact with actual social realities would be sacrificed for theorising and speculation: a void would open and increase between the world of lived experience and the world of hypothetical entities and happenings. Thus, describing the social world, albeit whatever small part of it, is a tricky business, fraught with almost impassable difficulties. The work of the Chicago School, therefore, is to be seen as attempting to fulfill a Simmelian conception of social reality, which attempts to engage at the level of description and not so much at the level of causal explanation. This is an important point. Park and Burgess state it thus,

> The first thing that students in sociology need to learn is to observe and record their own observations; to read, and then to select and record the materials which are the fruits of their reading; to organise and use, in short, their own experience. The whole organisation of this volume may be taken as an illustration of the method, at once tentative... for the collection, classification, and interpretation of materials, and should be used by students from the very outset.
> (Park and Burgess, 1967:40)[42].

---

[41] Wirth, L. (1964) *On Cities and Social Life.* (edited by Albert Reiss Jr.) Chicago: University of Chicago Press.
[42] Op cit.

One of the implications of this aim is that if social reality is not conceived as a system it cannot be accounted for in holistic terms but in terms of limited descriptions. Limited to the description of particular forms observable in association. It is in this sense, that Simmel meant that sociology was a technically limited activity; limited to what can be described at any one point in time and place and limited by the techniques it employs to produce descriptions. The difficulties arise from the self imposed criteria of providing descriptions that are faithful to the social phenomena described, that is, the gap between the description and the described must be as narrow as possible while at the same time revealing the use of forms so as to display the socially created nature of that social reality. The description must, in a symmetrical fashion, relate clearly to that aspect of the social world in much the same way as a painter of portraits 'captures' the essential subject, so sociological description must capture the essential dynamics of that slice of social life. The dynamics of social life are what W.I. Thomas called the 'process of becoming', others, the 'emergent properties' of everyday life.

How does one go about producing authentic descriptions of social realities? This is the question Park asked himself and his students. His answer was another, clearer question, from where does one obtain first hand descriptions? Although this limits the problem, it still remains a problem. However, Park had already expressed his ideas about where and how researchers might obtain first hand descriptions in *The City* (1925). Parks suggestion to his students was straight forward,

> Go and sit in the lounges of luxury hotels and on the door steps of flop houses; sit on the Gold Coast settees and on the slum shake downs; sit in the orchestra hall... in short; get the seats of yours pants dirty in real research.
> (Quoted in Bulmer, 1984:97)[43]

As an experienced investigative reporter, Park knew what he was talking about. In an autobiographical note, Park recalled, that when he was a journalist (1905-1914) that he,

> wrote about all sorts of things and became in this way intimately acquainted with many different aspects of city life. I expect that I have actually covered more ground, tramping about in city streets than any other living man. Out of all of this, I gained, among other things, a conception of the city, the community, and the region, not as a geographical phenomenon merely but as a kind of social organism.
> (Park, 1950:viii)

---

[43] Op cit.

Park's suggestion then, is that first hand descriptions can be obtained from observation of a particular aspect of social reality, for example, hobo life. This involves becoming acquainted with the descriptions the subjects themselves use to describe their own social world and their perceptions of the ways in which non-hobos, that is, such people as officials, are experienced by the hobo. Such a programme was to produce some very detailed descriptions of social life.

In attempting to obtain first hand descriptions of aspects of social reality, one can not observe everything that goes on in the life of a group of subjects: one is limited to observing episodes of interaction. As episodes of interaction are, like the social world of which they are a part, in a state of constant flux, the methods one brings to bare must meet the particulars of that episode so as to reveal the essentials of that episode. Therefore, researchers' using such assumptions must keep their wits about them, being alert for descriptions. This necessarily involves an openness to approach and not the imposition of vertical deductive logics.

The two main analogous constructs often referred to by the critics are 'ecology' and 'natural area'. Obviously borrowed from biology these two constructs are not descriptions of observed phenomena of sociology. Briefly, what they refer to in biology, is the study of the relationship of organisms to their environment. Used by Park and Burgess, these constructs furnished the idea that the city of Chicago could be used as a laboratory in which various types of relationships between persons and their environment could be observed and used as possible sources for descriptions of social reality.

Ernest Burgess probably deserves credit for turning these ideas into a concrete research project. As a part of a course in field research studies, which he taught with Park, Burgess influenced the employment of Vivien Palmer as a senior research worker. Palmer, under Burgess's supervision, amassed an enormous amount of descriptive data on the city. Apart from creating an archive for the Department she was instrumental in the production of student theses, for instance, "she put Paul. G. Cressey in touch with Franciso Roque, who was interested in taxi-dance halls" (Bulmer, 1984:118)[44]. Palmer's achievements, like Burgess' were foundational in that they collected and organised material for students to use in their field projects. Palmer's main achievement, however, during her five years at Chicago (1925-30) was the identification of seventy five community areas or natural areas which "not only formed the basis for the subsequent urban sociology of Chicago, but was widely used by city organisations as a means of distinguishing sub-divisions within the city". Bulmer adds to this comment that not only do local telephone directories still bear the names of these classifications but that they are now used by inhabitants to describe their local areas.

---

[44] Op cit.

Palmer's definitions and identification of so many natural areas was not simply an exercise in social geography or data gathering, it was crouched in terms a reader of Simmel would be familiar with; constructs such as symbiosis, assimilation, contacts, isolation, and succession, "evoke a picture of Chicago as a complex metropolis, a mosaic of residential villages, industrial suburbs, immigrant areas, business and commercial zones, and hotel and apartment house areas" (Bulmer, 1984:119). Further, in her book, *Field Studies in Sociology: A Manual for Students* (1928)[45] Palmer in a clear and concise style (if somewhat lacking actual examples) lists the pros and cons of the various methods available to the researcher, emphasising above all others the benefits of participant observation, informal interviewing and life history approaches for obtaining first hand descriptions of episodes of social life.

Returning back to the connections between Simmel and Park it can now be seen that the problem of obtaining first hand descriptions is crouched in the questions of where and how can such descriptions be obtained is a consequential implication of a commitment to verstehen, and the analytical tools for fulfilling this commitment were to be found in Simmel's work. Simmel wrote,

> The structure of every 'verstehen' is, from the beginning, intrinsically a synthesis... Given... a factual appearance, which as such is not understood. And added to it from inside the subject, to whom this appearance is given, something else, which either emerges directly from the subject or is applied by it: the recognition of meaning, which in a way penetrates the initially given factual appearance and transforms it into something that is 'understood'.
> (Simmel, 1918, quoted in Helle, 1985:4)[46]

To understand, is therefore a process which can be achieved, in the view of Park, by the researcher becoming thoroughly immersed in the social scenes that give rise to and in which various meanings or forms are used. However, as we have seen students were not sent into the social world blind without any ideas and nor were they allowed to do research without an understanding of the awkwardness's involved in distinguishing form from content. Harold Laswell remembered Park's "sagacious insight and my appreciation of his respect for creative interplay between hours of high abstraction and days of patient contact with humble detail' (quoted in, Bulmer, 1984:125)[47]. While Norman Hayner remembered that he once spent a seminar discussing the logical problems of defining a hotel. "What is a Gang? What is a public? What is a nationality? What

---

[45] Palmer, V. (1928) *Field Studies in Sociology: A Students Manual.* Chicago: University of Chicago Press.
[46] Op cit.
[47] Op cit.

is a graft?," Park asked Hayner, this was because Park believed that "we could not have anything like scientific research unless we... could sort out and describe in general terms the things we were attempting to investigate". (Odum, 1951:132)[48].

As a conclusion to this section we can say that as beneficial to Park's biography, as these memories are, it is of greater credit to Park that the essentials of what is being attributed to him be spelled out. Park took Simmel's notion of a verstehen approach to social forms to be apriori and not aposteriori as many assume from reading such quotes above. That is, the objectivity of forms in everyday life is not given directly to the senses nor is it a property solely of reason: rather it is, Simmel suggests, that experience is known through forms, forms being descriptions of experience. Hence, objective reality is social in genesis (Simmel, 1922:21-30)[49].

What is of real interest here is the ways in which such notions were used and developed by the Chicago School. The School took it upon themselves to develop techniques that would capture the use of forms in episodes of life and to develop standards on how adequate descriptions could be produced. Park, as it has been seen, tended to concentrate on the former advocating that to be able to describe the use of forms by persons, involves social closeness with those persons. This is the way in which his work and the work of his students is rendered logical and complementary. This recommendation as practice is not bland empiricism but a means of rooting statements in actually observed processes of phenomena. The subsequent production of studies of social realities, for example, Anderson's, *The Hobo*, Zorbaugh's, *The Gold Coast and the Slum*, Cressey's, *The Taxi-Dance Hall* or Shaw's, *The Jack-Roller*, are not prescriptions about the domain of sociology or conceptions of social reality. They are quite simply sociological descriptions of different forms of social reality the like of which set high standards for contemporaries and successors alike.

The contents of this volume

It is with sincere honour I present the following papers in this collection for you, the readers', pleasure.

The Art of Comparison: Lessons from the Master, Everett C. Hughes, by Professor Howard S. Becker.
Howard's concern is with Everett Hughes' paper on industrialization, 'Queries Concerning Industry and Society Based on the Study of Race Relations in

---

[48] Odum, Howard, W. (1951) *American Sociology: The Story of Sociology in the United States through 1950.* New York: Longmans.
[49] Op cit.

Industry'. He argues that this paper is a model of the use of the comparative method as it has suffused Chicago-style research since the days of Robert E. Park. The basic moves of a Hughesian comparative analysis, from the choice of cases to the linking up of seemingly disparate phenomena, allow researchers to gain maximum theoretical reach form the findings of a single study.

The Ethnographic Mosaic' of the Chicago School: Critically Locating Vivien Palmer, Clifford Shaw and Frederic Thrasher's Research Methods in Contemporary Reflexive Sociological Interpretation, by Dr Shane Blackman.

Contemporary accounts of ethnography as a research method usually cite the Chicago School of Sociology as the starting point for urban participant observation, the use of life history and the gathering of personal documents as valid sources of data (O'Reilly, 2005, Brewer, 2000). Shane suggests that rather than just triggering the development of new qualitative research procedures, the different and diverse sociological researchers from the Chicago School were experimentally defining and employing some of the key empathetic strategies which would later define contemporary ethnographic practice, through the use of narrative, biography, autobiography, 'pocket ethnography', personal documents, dialogue, life stories, exchange and voice. Shane argues that Clifford Shaw's (1930) application of the 'delinquent boy's own story' in *The Jack-Roller* marks the beginning of modern sociological life history narrative and reflexive ethnography which seeks to advance the voice of the research participant. Initially Shane looks at the influences shaping Shaw's take-up of these research methods and then moves on to explore some of his own ethnographic work, to demonstrate that the concepts elaborated by members of the Chicago School have explanatory value in interpreting current sociological ethnography.

'All Life is Experimentation': The Chicago School and the Experimenting Society, by Dr Matthias Gross.

Experimentation is generally regarded as a constitutive element of modern science and is understood as its distinguishing characteristic when compared with methods of discovery prior to the 17th century. Its predominant features are the artificial set-up of an experimental system, the inducement of changes by external control of certain parameters and the measurements of observable effects. Mattias argues that the notion of experiment needs to be discussed that does not model itself along the natural scientific idea of laboratory experiment. Instead what is needs, argues Matthias, is a sociological perspective of experiment beyond the realm of the laboratory that was outlined by some of the classical authors of the Chicago School of Sociology. The sociological notion of experiment used by Albion W. Small, Robert E. Park, and George Vincent – among other early Chicago sociologists – implies a process of societal self-experimentation especially in the big cities without a fixed setting of a sociological experimenter. Matthias highlights some of the Chicago sociologists' ideas of a self-experimental society as a sociological means to understand and analyze contemporary societies focusing (1) on general aspects of the study of society and experimentation in social science research, (2) the Chicagoans notion of experiments in every field of social life, and (3) finally the idea of cities as societal self experiments in the development of modern society. Matthias concludes that the Chicago School's notion of experiment today can serve as a means to understand modern societies' social practices that increasingly present themselves as experiments via a willingness to remain open to new forms of experience.

Mind, Self and Society: The Overlooked Potential of G.H. Mead's Legacy, Dr Julie L. Arthur Kirby.
The depth and richness brought to our understanding of sociality within G.H. Mead's thought remains under-utilised. Perhaps Herbert Blumer's legacy in developing 'symbolic interactionism' (SI) to describe Mead's approach has created barriers to appreciating the scope, richness and radical potential of Mead's original thought and intention; SI has been criticised for its 'reductionism" and neglect of social structure (Meltzer, 1975, Rock 1979, Layder 1994, Joas, 1980). However, Mead explicitly drew attention to the impact of organising structures within society on its members throughout Mind, Self and Society. Mead adopts an 'in flux' process philosophy to 'becoming' wherein situated cognition is a central organizing process within a dynamic, materialist and reflexive approach to the self/society relationship. It brings together concrete (material) and abstract (ideas) dimensions of social experience by retaining a situated mind and body link through the cognitive (social) act of thinking. In this approach there is no absolute separation between nature and culture, body and mind, materiality and knowledge, they are all interconnected dimensions of social experience (Burkitt, 1998). Additionally, for Mead, persons act habitually, non-consciously in the absence of 'problematic' social situations/encounters. This chapter reports on an application of Mead's framework within a qualitative doctoral study exploring the 'problematic' phenomenon of voice-hearing, or in medical terms 'auditory hallucination', from the perspective of those who experience it. Participants included mental health care service users and non-users; social contexts framed both their commonality and differences. A diagrammatic model was constructed that has wide application across the social and psychological sciences.

Human Ecology and the Emergence of Global Society: The Theoretical Insights of Roderick D. McKenzie, by Dennis W. MacDonald.
In this chapter Dennis examines one of the most unusual and insightful aspects of the work of Chicago sociologist, Roderick D. McKenzie. Although urban sociologists and ecologists may be somewhat familiar with McKenzie's work, most know of him as a sort of footnote to Park and Burgess and co-author with them of *The City*. In fact, despite an academic career cut short by an illness that claimed his life at a young age, McKenzie's contributions to the development of sociology were numerous and quite significant. Dennis highlights three of

McKenzie's contributions. Firstly, the *idea of ecology*. The evidence suggests that the idea of human ecology originated with McKenzie, not with Park and Burgess. Further, in McKenzie's conception of it, ecology represented an alternative conception of society, one emphasizing "the physical basis of social relations." (1968:4) Secondly the suggestion of the *centrality of institutions*. In his 'Ecology of Institutions', McKenzie argued that the institution "has become the fundamental unit in modern society...." (1968:115) Thirdly, the recognition of the *emergence of World Society*. Long before 'globalization' became a household word, McKenzie offered detailed description, informed by his ecological insights, of the 'great integrated unity', which the world had become. Although his writings on this subject raise some of the central issues in today's debate over globalization, Dennis shows that his major contribution is the detailed description of 'world organization'.

'Ahead of its Time?': The legacy and relevance of W.I. Thomas and F. Znaniecki (1918-20) The Polish Peasant in Europe and America, by Professor Brian Roberts.
Brian argues that this 'neglected classic' is noted as an early, major study at Chicago – pioneering the study of migration, social disorganisation and the use of the life story (and other materials – letters, formal records) but rarely read. The study, Brian points out, attempts to trace the changes in personality and communal life/organisation due to migration from one society to another. It employs a range of concepts to study the social personality – including character, temperament, lines of genesis, personality types – to follow the effects of migration and changes in attitudes and values. Despite questions on theorisation and methodological uncertainties the overall intention and scope remains important. The study, Brian argues, attempts to understand the 'evolution' of an individual's social personality due to the biographical experience of migration and how groups 'adapt' to a new a social environment. *The Polish Peasant*, Brian shows, was instructive in the use of life histories and letters alongside organisational and press records (a 'mixed methodology'.) Brian's key point is that it has an increasing relevance at a time of mass migration (e.g. c600,000 Polish migrant workers in Britain) and academic discussions of local-global relations. Brian concludes that the contemporary relevance of the *Polish Peasant* study is it's 'translocal/transnational' dimension operating at a number of interrelated 'levels' – each one employing relevant source materials: Individual, Family, Communal, Organisational.

Ernest Burgess: Exploring Urban Marginality, by Professor Roger A. Salerno.
Roger points out that very little has been written on Ernest Burgess who was in some ways the cornerstone of Chicago school sociology. While Robert Park has been the subject of extensive biographies, Burgess has remained a somewhat shadowy figure - both personally and professionally. Nevertheless, he was instrumental in the production of a wide range of graduate student monographs that have become the hallmark of the Chicago school. Active on the editorial board of the University of Chicago Press he herded many of his students works

into print. Roger's chapter is a thoughtful examination of Burgess's career. It looks at his life as a university professor, his relationship with his students and his work with Albion Small, Charles Merriam, and Robert Park. It examines his place in the history of Chicago school sociology and in establishing its legacy in the social sciences. Burgess is seen here as both an astute student of urban life and an architect of the Chicago school tradition. Above all Roger views Burgess as an advocate and promoter of his students. While primarily known for his concentric zone theory that he produced with Roderick McKenzie and his structuralist approach to sociology, this chapter draws particular attention to his interactionist sensibilities, his interest in human sexuality and marginality and some of the groundbreaking research he conducted on the seamier side of urban life. Burgess is reassessed here as a central operative having launched Nels Anderson's *The Hobo*, Cressey's *Taxi Dance Hall* and a host of other studies of urban low-life. Roger concludes with a reassessment of his venture into the study of human sexuality.

An Unresolved Legacy of the Chicago School, by Professor Ian Shaw.
In this chapter Ian starts with an historical sketch of the early-shared path and subsequent divergence of sociology and social work at Chicago. Ian takes this as emblematic of the subsequent relationships between the two disciplines/fields of study, and the continuing themes that remain today. These are the methodological character of each which informs the wider debates about discipline relations in the social sciences in the USA and the UK. Ian's intention is to provoke conversation among both social work academics and sociologists. Casting doubt on the distinctions implied in the phrase 'practice oriented disciplines' (Mills, et. al, 2006), arguing that it says too much both by way of assertion and denial. Ian proposes their dual identities as fields of academic research and areas of professional practice should be seen as a strength rather than a weakness. At the same time, these distinctions makes the development of autonomous disciplinary research traditions and intellectual debates all the more vital (Mills et al, 2006: 38). Ian seeks to provisionally theorise these relationships, while respecting Howard Becker's remark that while we have to do theoretical work, 'we needn't think we are being especially virtuous when we do it' (Becker, 1993: 221).

Communication: an Inheritance of the Chicago School of Social Thought, by Dr Filipa Subtil and José Luís Garcia (Translated by Richard Wall).
Although the communication issue has won intellectual status in modern thought and in social research through Chicago sociology, communication and media studies have tended to neglect, with some exceptions, that crucial contribution. Filipa and José focus on the way James Carey, one of the most influent American theorists of media and journalism in the second half of 20th century, considered, discussed, and critically embodied the reflection about communication in the Chicago School of sociology. By questioning the 'standard' history of mass communication research confined to the functionalist

and empiricist paradigm of mass communication, Carey points out the importance of reconsidering an argumentative, civic and universalistic conception of communication, which was a legacy of Dewey, Cooley, Mead, and Park. Filipa and José show how Carey recovers and re-elaborates this notion to argue that communication is more than transmission of signals and signs. Supported by the Chicago tradition, he defines communication as a life experience found on human quality of intimacy, conversation, and on the understanding that comes from shared experience. Filipa and José then present Carey's critique to the utopic features of this tradition, especially to the excessive expectations on communication technologies to improve the quality of culture and civic life. Finally, they discusses how Carey brings back the sociological communication concept of Chicago to confront it with a technical conception of communication that distinguishes the present media industry, showing how communication has lost its dimension of communion and sharing, and definitively tangled in a world of sophisticated economical and political strategies.

Blumer's Dilemma Revisited: Is Social Science Possible?, by Professor Martyn Hammersley.
Herbert Blumer was, of course, one of the key figures in what has come to be identified as the Chicago School of Sociology: he invented the term 'symbolic interactionism' to label an approach to understanding the social world that derived from the work of G. H. Mead and from other Chicago sources. In his evaluation of Thomas and Znaniecki's *The Polish Peasant* he identified a dilemma facing social science: the problem of how to use science to understand human social life without violating the latter's nature. Martyn argues that at the heart of this problem is the issue of causality: exactly how are people's interpretations and actions shaped by socio-cultural processes or structures? And what are the implications of this for the task of sociological explanation? Martyn's aim is to try to clarify the nature of social causality, against the background of Mead's and Blumer's ideas about sociality, Znaniecki's notion of analytic induction, more recent debates about constructionism, and current philosophical analyses of causation.

CHAPTER 1

Sociology and Social Work: An Unresolved Legacy of the Chicago School

Ian Shaw
University of York, England

Introduction

Unfashionable though it may be, this story has two heroes. One, a sociologist, may need no introduction – though I would hazard that readers may not anticipate the grounds for the ascription. The other – once a part time Chicago lecturer in social statistics – is known today, if at all, for her social work rather than her sociology. But I will leave them to play their part in the story and make their voice heard – 'voice', not 'voices', because from diverging locations they share the accolade of challenging their own and the other discipline to fresh constructions of identity and direction.

It is my theme - that the tales of sociology and social work at Chicago are ones of rich and complex inter-relationships that promised much. But the establishment of the School of Social Service Administration (hereafter SSSA) in 1920, and the associated shift of (women) sociology faculty into that school, while welcomed to some extent on both sides, led directly to the eventual – but not as we will see, immediate - closure of conversation that worked against the interests of both fields of study. Mirrored to this day across those countries where both social work and sociology find their domiciles in universities, this continues, if I may be so bold, to hobble both sociology and social work. It may not need to be so.

> All social work practises are deeply embedded in historical and cultural habits from which we cannot detach ourselves at will'. Lorenz aptly infers from this that we should be practising history 'in the dual sense of positioning ourselves in a historical context and of giving our interventions a historical dimension. (Lorenz, 2007:601)

Not that Chicago sociology – still less, social work – were microcosms of their respective disciplines; for, as Clifford Geertz remarked in some context, that is 'an idea which only someone too long in the bush could possibly entertain' (Geertz, 1973:22). For many years social work research and training in the Chicago SSSA has taken a distinct, almost unique line in the USA. But it is interesting because it exemplifies in stark and sometimes innovative ways how a tension between scholarly objectivity and the desire for advocacy has been present throughout the history of social work. I want to revisit this moment in the history of these respective disciplines with the intention, if I may echo Geertz once more, to enhance 'the precision with which we vex ourselves' (Geertz, 1973:29).

'Sociology' and 'Social Work' at Chicago

In inverted commas, for neither term carried its present meaning, nor was either recognisable as itself. 'Sociology' and 'social science' were often interchangeable expressions, hence part of Albion Small's efforts were devoted to establishing sociology as a definable field of study within the social sciences (eg Small, 1903).

Chicago University was founded in 1890 as a Baptist institution by William Harper, its first president. He wanted the university to be marked by fundamental research/training and the improvement of society.[50] Hence he set out to appoint outstanding people rather than to build disciplines as such. For example, he added Charles Henderson, an expert in charity administration, to the nascent sociology department. This ensured that welfare work was part of the department. Henderson, who died in 1915, was central in the reform of social services. Involved in many bodies – he was part of the then independent School of Civics and Philanthropy (forerunner of the SSSA) and President of the National Conference of Charities and Corrections (the predecessor of the National Association of Social Workers). He brought a conviction of first hand observation and the importance of the intimate experience of everyday life.

The city of Chicago was central to much of this development. 'All of social life was here and being investigated by sociologists' (Plummer, 1997:8). Plummer expresses it nicely as a place where 'a world of strangers and danger merges with a world of diversity and innovation. Here was the pathos of modernity' (Plummer, 1997:7). Yet in the subsequent intellectual staking of claims this was too little recognized. Sociological history tends still to take the modernist view that wider work in the city was simply the precursor to sophisticated social science.

Accounts written from within sociology, as history of sociology, generally treat both other disciplines and groups outside the academy as parts of the

---

[50] I am indebted here to Stephen Diner's work.

background. They are seen as instrumental to the main aims of sociologists, or as introducing distortions into the...course of pure sociological development. (Platt, 1996:264)

The work of Jane Addams and the Hull-House Settlement is a case in point. The Hull-House Settlement was collecting systematic data before the sociology department.

...those methods and indeed topics, which were characteristic of the 'Chicago School' were equally characteristic of social workers and voluntary activists who were in the field somewhat sooner. (Platt, 1996:263)

The point is not original (cf Plummer, 1997:8), but Deegan has developed this argument with force, commitment and in great detail (e.g. Deegan, 1991; 1997a; 1997b). Informed by the work of Charles Booth, Addams and her colleagues at Hull-House such as the 'outstanding' Florence Kelly mapped the structure of the whole city in ways that were subsequently adopted by Chicago sociologists. Published in 1893, the 'Hull-House Maps and Papers' are seen by Deegan as methodologically and substantively central to, yet subsequently 'erased from the annals of sociology' (Deegan, 1997b:5) and evidence of the hostility of male sociologists. The intention of the writers of the papers was to 'combine scientific and objective observation with ethical and moral values to generate a just and liberated society' (Deegan, 1991:39). Platt (1996) concludes that it was only by doing so that the university sociology department could be made to appear pioneering. Sociology was, in Platt's view, original in its theorization of methods and not in the practicalities. But at the time, the borders were more fluid. Indeed, Albion Small wrote to Addams offering her a half time sociology appointment in 1913, saying that one line of development being considered was 'to shift our emphasis more in the line of social service' (Diner, 1997:40), through lecturing, training and supervision. There is no record of her reply and of course she never took up the post.

Sociology was embedded in the ameliorative mission of the university. 'Fundamental scientific understanding of immediately present events, directly observed, and all on behalf of the improvement of society' (Diner, 1997:55) lay at the heart of Small's programme. There is much evidence that early sociology did not view theorizing and an ameliorative mission in dualist terms. For Small, 'scientism and moralism were integrally connected' (Bulmer, 1984:35). To continue Diner's argument, it was the 'ravages of theological doubt' that prompted a turn to 'sociology as a "scientific" reinforcement of the social gospel' and the university was 'in the forefront of the movement to marry Christianity, science and social improvement' (Diner, 1997:55). This led to a sociology whose 'main feature was vivid description coupled with theoretical commentary' (Diner, 1997:56).[51] The debt Chicago sociology owed in this regard to the philosophy of Dewey and Mead has been carefully documented (e.g. Bulmer, 1984; Deegan, 1997a; Diner, 1997; Plummer, 1997). Mead's philosophy, for example, was directly tied to his engagement in social reform movements, and his links to the network of women sociologists. Thomas may have been less reform minded than his colleagues, though his research was funded by two women philanthropists associated with Hull-House.

Social work education and research were proceeding in rough parallel to sociology. In 1893 there was a call for training schools that would cover the 'alphabet of charitable science' with 'laboratory practice' to supplement course work. In 1897 Mary Richmond called for professional standards and training, and in the following year the New York Charity Organization Society established a summer school in philanthropy, which became a full time one year course in 1904. In 1903-4 the Institute of Social Science was set up in the Extension Division of Chicago University, emerging from Graham Taylor's work with the Chicago Commons and Julia Lathrop at Hull-House. In 1907 the Institute received a grant from Russell Sage to set up a research department through the efforts of Lathrop and Sophia Breckinridge, and in the following year it became the Chicago School of Civics and Philanthropy. The first Bulletin of the School, in 1910 concluded optimistically that relief had become scientific, and that social work had 'attained recognized professional status and those who lead it are rightly regarded as scientific specialists' (Lubove, 1965:143).

There was a tension from the first between scholarly aspirations and employer demands for training, specialisms and practical curricula – this remains social work's 'troublesome legacy' (Lubove, 1965:143) to the present. Chicago social work took a distinctive line both then and now, in that social research, reform, public welfare administration and broader professional education were strongly emphasized, and Edith Abbott and Sophia Breckinridge resisted agency demands for specialized techniques.

The SSSA was established as a professional graduate school in 1920, replacing the School of Civics and Philanthropy. The reasons are difficult to disentangle[52]. They were partly financial, and there was an important mutuality in the separation of the two fields. Secularising tendencies, reinforced perhaps by the death of Henderson in 1915, were associated with growing confidence among faculty in both fields. With an over-simplification of hindsight, Ruth Cavan, a student in the sociology department from 1922 to 1926, remarked that 'the department also separated itself from courses in social work and thus

---

[51] An interesting brief historical account of science and practice in early American social work is given by Kirk and Reid (2002). Timms provided an early and thoughtful discussion of historical stances on social work as science and/or art (Timms, 1968). I have sketched the relationship of social work, Christianity and science elsewhere (Shaw, forthcoming).
[52] I do not intend to discuss the reasons for the parting of the ways. It is important but not central to this chapter.

strengthened its objective approach'[53] (Cavan, 1997:46). She remembered that for Small, 'the purpose of sociology was not humanitarian or social reform, but an understanding of human behaviour' (Cavan, 1997:47). This is better seen as a vision for sociology that crystallized during the later 1920s primarily through the work of Burgess (who took over some of Henderson's courses) and especially Park. Yet at the time the parting of the ways was probably not seen in such binary terms. The changes were more complex and Coghlan may be correct when she concludes that

> (I)t is not likely that permanent, full-time positions in a university affiliated program were seen by Abbott and Breckinridge as banishment from sociology. Rather, it was the culmination of their efforts to that point to define and professionalize the discipline of social work. (Coghlan)[54]

Sociology had 'become closely connected to welfare work (obliquely through Hull-House, specifically through the Chicago Area Project)' (Plummer, 1997: 32). I will explore the interplay of social work and sociology before and after 1920. I will briefly revisit two fairly familiar arguments about gender and methodology at Chicago, whose import is insufficiently weighed, and move to a more extended presentation of a hidden history of an intellectual case for reciprocity between the two disciples as seen in some barely noticed work of Burgess.

Sociology, Social Work and Gender

The 1920 establishment of the SSSA was a gendered division. Deegan sees this as a step by step segregation with the net result 'that by 1920 the women faculty were administratively and professionally separated into the School of Social Service Administration'. The women were defined as social workers and the men as sociologists. 'Women's place in sociology was first established through special qualities of mind and action and later removed from the field to another profession' (Deegan, 1997a:203).

Yet Deegan herself recognizes that the events of 1920 were not imposed or allocated in the way this complaint suggests. Her reference to 'special qualities of mind and action' is an allusion to the doctrine of the separate spheres.[55] Women "managed" the home, emotions, morality and children. Men "governed" the family, social and political institutions, especially the economy, and were more rational than women' (Deegan, 1997a:201). Jane Addams also thought women were different, but superior. Her 'cultural feminism' took the

---

[53] In the context, 'objective' appears to roughly approximate 'empirical' and is set against 'philosophical'.
[54] Catherine Coghlan, (2005) Unpublished Paper. See references for full citation.
[55] I am following Deegan's exposition at this point.

stance that 'traditionally defined feminine values are superior to traditionally defined male values' (Deegan, 1991:16). The women who ended up in social work saw their distinctiveness as based on strengths. Small's position as Head of Department was crucial. He held to the separate natures but equal ability, but it led him to see women's work as being in social settlements and women's institutions. He wanted equal pay but an absence of competition between men and women. He greatly admired Addams and treated her as a colleague sociologist. The university's position was equivocal. The early years were founded on a commitment to co-education – a radical position for its day – but moved to a segregationist position early in the last century[56].

The subsequent paths of sociology and social work following 1920 would need a paper in their own right. Addams and most of her colleagues did not resist the change. She worked in other fields and did not cultivate her sociological base. 'Now they entered a new professional arena with psychological adherents, new professional networks, and different ideologies and practices'. Deegan's position is perhaps contestable, when she reflects that Addams changed little, but her contemporaries were often obliged to change considerably. 'Addams' sociology moreover, was buried in these professional realignments' (Deegan, 1997a:225)[57].

Edith Abbott's contribution may, in fact, be of more interest. We have met her already when, with Breckinridge, she resisted agency pressure to produce specialist technicians. Abbott, a Hull-House resident, was appointed in 1913 as lecturer in social statistics. With the advent of the SSSA she became Professor of Social Economy, and by 1924 she was dean of the School - a post she held until 1942. She 'mastered the most advanced statistical and survey methods of the day' (Diner, 1997:36). She had previously visited London (the LSE) in 1906, and on her return reproduced Beatrice Webb's course in 'Methods of Social Investigation' in Chicago. She became Director of Social Research at the School of Civics and Philanthropy in 1908. Statistical work was considered women's work. Mathematics was thought 'technical' and defined as repetitive and not creative. Man's work required creativity and the power to analyse patterns of social action (Deegan, 1991).

Across the States, efforts to develop a scientifically grounded method of modifying individual behaviour were the central social work concern of the 1920s. Following the separation of the Department of Sociology and the School of Social Service Administration in 1920, Edith Abbott and Sophonisba Breckinridge formed the *Social Service Review* in 1927 with the aspiration of

---

[56] For an interesting account of the response of the men sociologists to the segregation issue, see Deegan, 1997a.
[57] Deegan is probably too set upon making her case about the role of women in early sociology. This leads her on occasion to perpetuate an anachronistic sociology/social work divide. Thus, when she is defending the sociological contribution of the *Hull-House Maps and Papers*, she objects on one occasion that they were not about social work.

undertaking important work that would combine intellectual challenge with social usefulness. These remarkably able and influential women were exceptional in their commitment to research (cf essays on them in Deegan, 1991). In fact, the flavour of their intellectual commitment set them somewhat apart from the other influential women at Chicago, some of whom opposed the merger of the social work training with the university, fearing that a practical orientation would not be maintained in the university. However, Abbott and Breckinridge had clear views about the kind of research that was needed.

1. It should solve welfare problems and not simply advance the frontiers of human knowledge. They 'established a tradition of sound research and political advocacy on behalf of the powerless' (Deegan and Hill, 1991:31).
2. It had to be good research. Abbott complained that 'some of our social science friends are afraid that we cannot be scientific because we really care about what we are doing...' (Diner, 1977:11). She retorted that 'the social worker may care very genuinely about what happens to the unfortunate child or the broken family for whom she is temporarily responsible without being less scientific' (Diner, 1977:11).
3. They believed that practitioners must have the skills to contribute to research. Research could not be carried out solely by social scientists. 'Social workers must be so trained scientifically that they belong in the social science group' (Abbott, quoted by Diner, 1977:11).

Unlike some typical sociology courses for social workers today, Abbott was opposed to sociology being taught in a 'tamed' or instrumental way. She distinguished the idea that courses like research, law and government should be construed as 'background' for social workers. She saw them as 'foundation' (Lubove, 1965: 149). Abbott and Breckinridge held the interesting view that 'such training is needed for the sake of social research itself, which so often demands a competent understanding of the field of social treatment... and should be carried out by social workers, who are also trained in social research' (Diner, 1977:12).

Viewing her arguments as a whole, they have enduring interest. They face both ways, in that they challenge both social work and sociology – a stance I find compellingly attractive (c.f. Shaw and Gould, 2001, Chapter 1; Shaw, 2005). Hence, asking whether she was a sociologist *or* social work scholar illustrates the intellectual anachronisms of our own time[58], as well as the tendency to see professional courses as standing in a client relationship to sociology, psychology and so on. Not surprisingly, Abbott and Breckinridge came under fire in return

---

[58] To refer to this network of women as 'The Chicago Women's School of Sociology' is a stark instance of such anachronistic rhetoric. I am indebted to Javier Treviño for this reference.

from both 'sides'. In addition to the doubts of their 'social science friends' they famously refer to 'our eastern colleagues' (the social work programmes at Boston and New York) who 'told us we could not have casework and fieldwork in a university' (Diner, 1977:7; c.f. Lubove, 1965:265). Stephen Diner concludes that,

> Contemporary sociologists are not likely to regard Edith Abbott as an intellectual ancestress. Yet the combination of rigorous methods of collecting and analysing information...is one of the most distinctive features of modern sociology... Her contribution...no longer bears her name. But without those contributions the tradition would not be what it is. (Diner, 1997:36-37)

Method, Sociology and Social Work

Method at Chicago finds a place in this chapter for much the same reason as gender. Both have been the subject of extensive and justified attention in their own right, but they illuminate the creatively shadowy interplay of intellectual and welfare elements that were part and parcel of early sociology and social work. Take, to start with, Diner's remark that Abbott was at ease with the most advanced survey methods of the day. Platt has pointed out that the term 'survey' was used very early, but not to refer in the current sense to a method of data collection.[59] Rather, the term laid 'emphasis on the purpose (which was social reform and local community improvement), and on the coverage of a limited geographical area' (Platt, 1996:45). In the USA the social survey movement was a reform-minded one, and had some similarities to post-war Fabian social policy research in Britain, aiming to provide unbiased data that would stimulate action[60].

The case has been made, perhaps incontrovertibly, that the explicit or didactic emphasis on methodology in Chicago was slight in the period before the Second World War. Plummer quotes Park as saying (presumably in the context of a gradual contrary shift) that methodology is 'distinctively secondary... Science is not a ceremonial matter as some reverent souls seem to think' (Plummer, 1997:30). Cavan later recalled that 'no courses on methods of research were offered. Students learned how to do research by following their

---

[59] I am aware, of course, that surveys are also categorized as a research design, and not only a data collection method (Hakim, 2000).
[60] The reader is often struck in the sociology and social work sources of the period how similar they read to left-leaning social policy research in the UK. Abbott, to quote one of a number, seemed closer to social policy research as it was understood in post 2nd World War UK than to either later sociology or social work. As Deegan and Hill express it, she 'typically explored institutional inequities that could be documented statistically' and had a vision of social work as 'an aggressive, policy-making and controversial profession' (Deegan and Hill, 1991:33).

professors' suggestions for the writing of term papers, and later by a kind of informal apprenticeship' for the Masters or PhD (Cavan, 1997:49).

Survey, statistical method and the case study were the central terms of the period. The point I want to emphasize is that sociology had deep debts to social work when it came to methodology, in that the case study almost certainly had much to do with the borrowings of ideas of 'case history' and 'case work' from social work. We can perhaps infer as much from the origins of social work in the USA:

> Professional social work in the United States developed from an imperfect union between the late nineteenth-century "scientific charity" movement ... on the one hand and the slightly younger social settlement movement, with its strong orientation towards social reform and social survey on the other. (Diner, 1977:3)

It is possible that social workers were first in the field in this regard. Cavan (1997) remembers Burgess using psychiatric case histories in class, side by side with statistics. Despite Small's joking aside that 'a great many people have the notion that sociology is merely a pretentious name for slumming' (Small, 1903:471), Diner remarks that American university teachers – 'generally a sedate class of men' – 'stayed away from low life, from the poor, and from noisy, drunken, brawling conduct'. They 'did the next best thing: they associated with social workers who knew them first hand, and they encouraged their students to study them' (Diner, 1997:54).

The interpretive problem for us lies in part in the subsequent construction of a sociological meta-narrative that downplays any counter-claims. There are hints of this even in Platt's work in her remark that 'sociology and social work took a long time to become disentangled' (Platt, 1996:46).

How Chicago Sociologists Saw Social Work: The Case of Ernest Burgess

It is doubtless indicative of buried discipline histories that I stumbled with surprise upon a citation of a paper by Burgess in an early issue of a social work journal when reading for another paper. I had never, to my best memory, previously heard any serious social work discussion of the aspects of his work in relation to social work. In the sociology literature, any reference to Burgess in this connection is either as a passing mention that he took over part of Charles Henderson's social welfare teaching, or as part of an early pre-history of sociology when it was still 'entangled' (Platt, 1996) with social work or prior to sociology's male hegemony (Deegan, 1991). Apart from the brief accounts of sociology's methodological indebtedness to social work, already outlined in this paper, there are no hints in the literature of any significant intellectual interaction after the 1920 divide. Yet a preliminary analysis of Burgess' writing and work in the decade following the establishment of the SSSA will help open up a different history and an alternative view of the possible promise of reciprocal work between sociology and social work. I should come clean, as by now you will have divined my heroes – Edith Abbott and Ernest Burgess – and will have realized the sense in which from diverging locations they share the accolade of challenging their own and the other discipline to fresh constructions of identity and direction.

We can encapsulate the argument as follows. Right through the 1920s Burgess pursued a preoccupation with the identity and historical development of sociology and social work in relation to one another. This led him to an early position (Burgess, 1923) that there is an essential interdependence between the two, and that their separate disciplinary developments had converged on a mutual while still distinguishable set of linked research interests. This essentially egalitarian view of their relationship prompted him to a view that there are reciprocal gains to be had, the one from the other. It also enabled him to voice positive criticisms of his own discipline and of social work. In the earlier part of this period he expounded the primary contribution of sociology to social work in terms of emerging conceptualizations of the city and community from leading sociologists across North America. In the later years of the decade he gave closer attention to spelling out the benefits for social work of empirical work carried out in Chicago. His primary application of the contribution social work could make to sociology was in seeing agency records as a radical resource for sociology, and, to a less developed degree, reflecting on the implications of seeing social work as a 'concrete experiment' that gradually focused his mind on the potential for what today we would call 'outcomes research' and on the possibility of predictive judgments. However, by the later years of his career, for reasons I have yet to fully understand, he appears to have lost this cluster of interests, and to be speaking to social work, if at all, only from a distance.[61] I will try to tease out and give substance to these threads. In doing so, it is not my intention wholly to own or assess the details of Burgess' position[62], but rather to engage with his intention to place the interdependence of the two fields at the centre of their respective discipline-health. It should cause us serious disquiet that the majority in both my discipline and yours no longer believe this. I will allow Burgess to speak largely in his own voice.

---

[61] I am aware of the various arguments in the sociology literature regarding gender; secularized abandonment of the social gospel inspired ameliorative mission in favor of objective science; the scholarly dynamics of the intellectual hostility that developed between the two disciplines and departments; and the significance of external world events such as the First World War. Yet none of these seems to provide sufficient texture and anchor points. For example, in the earliest paper discussed here, Burgess is categorical that sociology is not about amelioration, yet he is forceful in his case for its 'necessary interdependence' with social work (Burgess, 1923:370).
[62] For example, there are difficulties with his starkly different creation stories for the two fields.

Distinct and Interdependent

It was common in the early years of the last century to view social work as a branch of sociology – as applied sociology. Burgess expressed his response to this view without equivocation.

> It is a fallacy, widely current, that social work has been, and is, applied sociology. As things are, nothing could be farther from the truth. The origins of sociology and social work go back to different motives, they have pursued independent paths, each has upon occasion been indifferent, hostile, or even contemptuous of the other. (Burgess, 1923:366)

As to their respective aims he expands as follows:

> The aim of social work is and will continue to be the maintenance and the raising of the standards of economic, social and civic life. The aim of sociology, in the future as in the past, will be the increase of knowledge of the behaviour of the person and of society. (Burgess, 1923:370)

He traces the beginnings of sociology to the philosophy of history in the work of Comte, Spencer and Ward, and detects a transition from philosophy to science moving from Comte and Spencer's 'sociology, conceived in the grand style' (Burgess, 1923:367), through a period of various sociological 'schools' to what he describes – significantly for our interests - as 'the period of investigation and research into which sociology is just now entering' (Burgess, 1923:367).

In contrast, social work 'had its origin in attempts to organize and systematize the giving of relief to individuals and families in distress' (Burgess, 1923:367). He is more tentative about periods in social service history, but suggests an initial period of philanthropy, followed by a period of social reform, social politics and the launching of social movements, and leading to,

> The period of social work as a profession, applied social science, with a technique of personal and social adjustment, the period social service is now entering. (Burgess, 1923:367)

His later schematizing varies in language. He suggests in 1927 a period 'based upon experience and common sense', succeeded by a stage in which the influence of social economics and its application to social work became dominant.

> The third stage has been marked by the invasion or introduction into social work of the psychiatric point of view and the technique of the psychiatric social worker. (Burgess, 1927:191)

Yet he still believes by 1927 that 'the central current of the development of social work has remained in the channels of social economics and social politics' (Burgess, 1927:191) through the influence of books by Richmond (1917) and Breckinridge (part of what he describes as a 'small but promising' social work literature, Burgess, 1923:367).

I can imagine under-collar heat rising by the moment with a suppressed wish to contest these periodizing interpretations! But their interest for us lies in Burgess' wish to see an historical convergence and congruence of interest. He suggests that both fields of enterprise had been too immersed in immediate preoccupations of development and survival to engage in actual field research in the case of sociology or 'have much energy left to deal with the relation of human nature and social forces to problems of case work with individuals and families' (Burgess, 1927:191) in the case of social work. But

> The inexorable logic of a common social situation, however, is now forcing sociology and social work to recognize and act upon their necessary interdependence. (Burgess, 1923:366)

The interdependence circles around their respective research interests. As sociology, at Chicago at least, entered a period of investigation, so 'there can be no doubt that social work is moving with increasing momentum toward research' (Burgess, 1923:367). He detects within this a shift of emphasis, yet in its infancy, to seeing case work 'as a pragmatic art based upon the experimental study of behaviour' (Burgess,1923:368).

Contributions of Sociology to Social Work

I suggested that in the earlier part of this period he expounded the primary contribution of sociology to social work in terms of emerging conceptualizations of the city and community from leading sociologists across North America. He refers to the way that the notion of social forces 'arose independently both in social work and in sociology' (Burgess, 1923:368), and in both 'the motive...has been to secure an explanation of human behaviour' (p. 368). He illustrates this from Thomas and Znaniecki's 'Polish Peasant' research on social attitudes and human wishes. He suggests also the relevance of Sumner's work of folkways.

> One can hardly overestimate the extent to which the lack of knowledge of European customs and cultural backgrounds has been responsible for the failure of social workers to secure cooperation of immigrant families. (Burgess, 1923: 368)

His third suggestion draws on the work of Charles Cooley regarding human nature as a product of social life, such that the person is an individual with status. 'Insights such as these terms suggest are helpful alike to the social theorist and the social worker' (Burgess, 1923:369). By 1928 he expresses the connection more forcefully and optimistically. 'The perception that "the relation of the individual to the group" is the basic problem both of research in sociology and of treatment in social work is at last becoming clearly recognized' (Burgess, 1928:525). In a way I find fascinating, he goes on in this subsequent paper to evidence his wide reading and reflection on the social work literature, and his extending convictions regarding the interdependence of the two disciplines. For example, he cites Mary Richmond in her *Social Diagnosis* who in turn is drawing on Octavia Hill, the major English 19th century housing reformer. Richmond credits Hill in a paper in 1869 to the Social Science Association, with 'the first description we have been able to find of inquiry with social reinstatement as its motive and aim' (Burgess, 1928:525). Hill is quoted as saying that

> By character is meant...knowledge of the passions, hopes and history of people; where the temptation will touch them, what is the little scheme they have made of their lives, or would make, if they had encouragement; that training long past phases of their lives may have afforded; how to move, touch and teach them. (Hill, in Burgess, 1928:525)

While he sees neither sociology nor social work as having adequately based their work on the implications of Cooley and Hill's insights, he remains optimistic that 'both sociology and social work have taken long strides in this common (*sic*) direction' (Hill, in Burgess, 1928:525).[63]

As the Chicago programme of research became embodied in the major research studies of the 1920s, Burgess took a more research-led stance as he developed his interest in the application of sociology to social work. He states this most fully in two papers published at the end of the twenties and at the opening of the next decade (Burgess, 1929, 1930). His 1929 paper is a detailed report and application of an early study of the potential of parole records to provide a predictive framework in social work. He picks up on early social work intervention studies by Healy and Karpf, and reports a straight quantitative study, (without any obvious statistical calculation), of the records of 3000 parolees in three Chicago institutions. He prepares expectancy tables, and suggests the application of the basic approach to social work with various child and family risks, and as a stimulus to intervention development.

---

[63] He goes on to extol in similar terms and at some length the social work writing of Ada Sheffield in her book on *Case Study Possibilities*, for presenting a social view of the individual over against the 'atomic view of the individual' adopted by 'most medical men' (Burgess, 1928:526), saying that 'with her theoretic statement I find myself in complete agreement' (525).

> In my judgment this same method and variations of it may with profit be widely used wherever a social agency or other organization keeps relatively full records of significant traits of personality and of behaviour. (Burgess, 1929:545)

Consistent with his assumptions regarding the reciprocity of relationships between sociology and social work, he concludes that the study of prediction in human behaviour 'opens up a new avenue of cooperation between sociology and social work' (Burgess, 1929:545).

His 1930 paper is rather different, and offers a crystallized sense of the relevance of Chicago sociology to social work. His optimism and efforts over the decade seem to have yielded limited reward. He wishes to,

> Throw the question open for general discussion why at present these materials on the basic facts of community life have had but little effect upon the policies and practices of social agencies. (Burgess, 1930:481)

Drawing on the work of Anderson, Thrasher, Shaw, Wirth, Zorbaugh and others, he discusses the relevance of research in three groups, *viz* the growth and structure of the city, basic social data, and the description and analysis of the groups and institutions of the local community. On the growth of the city, he sketches the main strands of Chicago research, from his own work and that of Clifford Shaw, and argues,

> ...both for purposes of research and for the practical work of social agencies, it is only possible to get a grasp of the form and trends of city life by setting up such an ideal construction. (Burgess, 1930:482)

He suggests the kind of theoretically and empirically informed application he has in mind when he asks,

> ...if the city has, like an organism, a structure that is closely correlated with its functioning, why should this not be taken into account in any plan of districting by social agencies? What is the justification of treating the city not as a living organism, but as if it were a corpse which can be cut up arbitrarily into unrelated parts? (Burgess, 1930:486)[64]

His reflections on the importance of basic social data stem largely from the Chicago study of local communities, funded in part by the Chicago Council of Social Agencies. In accord with Chicago theorizing, he advocates gaining community level material on the social forces and trends of local community

---

[64] Mainstream social work, at least in the UK, still largely ignores this perspective.

life, and draws on Vivien Palmer's work, in which she placed special reliance on interviewing older community residents and real estate men, in addition to more conventional small-area data from the Census. Once again he pleads the relevance for social work, and the value of such data to enable social agencies to 'check the effectiveness of their case work processes' (Burgess, 1930:488).

> It should be feasible to note the effect of the modification of one factor as for example the introduction of a new method of treatment of poverty or of juvenile delinquency. (Burgess, 1930:488)

As with other of his proposals he is not fully confident they will be adopted. He recognizes that 'many social agencies may not wish to subject their work to so impersonal and external a test, but no doubt some agency will have the courage required for experimentation' (Burgess, 1930:488-89). He does not pull his punches and sets out implications as he sees them for social work training.

> These local community studies point unmistakably to the systematic inclusion in training for social work and in the practice of social work of the cultural, or the community or the group treatment of problems of personality, of the family or of the neighbourhood. (Burgess, 1930:490)

He details Clifford Shaw's work on juvenile delinquency as offering methods of intervention that, while developed for research, are in his view fully susceptible to transfer to social intervention[65], and advocates the formation of conference groups of social workers organized around the discussion of community factors for each of the districts of the city, as promoting an alternative to what he sees as the existing 'haphazard and unsystematic' approach where 'even the most successful demonstrations of group treatment are ascribed to the "personality" of the worker' (Burgess, 1930:490).

Contributions of Social Work to Sociology

His work is marked by depth, range and specificity in engaging with social work. This is equally evident when he considers the obverse case – perhaps mirror image is a better metaphor - of social work's contribution to sociology. The main argument he develops over three papers (Burgess, 1923, 1927, 1928) is the value of agency case records, especially regarding families, as sources of 'data of distinct value for sociological investigation' (Burgess, 1923:369). He quotes as the 'proverbial grain of truth' writers saying that 'The student of social work... is himself recording facts that will go to make up new sociological text-books of the future' (Burgess, 1923:370). His interest is far from instrumental or naive,

---

[65] For a more recent text that adopts a similar logic, see Shaw 1996.

and reflects the facing-both-ways stance that was prominent in Edith Abbott's stance. I will rehearse his argument and tone in summary.

He consistently sets his hearers/readers readers back on their heels. Here are two examples of opening sentences from his papers.

> What I am about to say will be astounding and probably disquieting to you all and especially to my fellow sociologists. For I propose to explode the current and soothing convention that because sociology is a required subject for social work...therefore sociology has made a contribution to family social case work... Sociology as I see it has made little or no direct contribution to family social case work. (Burgess, 1927:191)[66]

> What should social case records contain to be useful for sociological interpretation? They should contain what will render them valuable for social case work, that and no more. This answer will, I know, perplex and astonish many social workers and sociologists. (Burgess, 1928:524).

Having set expectations on their heads, he goes on to reframe 'the question of the joint interest of social workers and sociologists in the content and form of social case records' (Burgess, 1928:524). He clears the ground by saying of current literature that 'there is not a single volume – good, bad or indifferent – on the application of sociology to social work' (Burgess, 1927:191).

His perspective rests, we now realize, on the assumption of a convergence of interest. It is in this light that we need to read his elaborations of the gains sociology brings to social work. Reflecting on the fact that such research had 'not as yet been integrated into the general scheme of training and practice in family social work', he concludes that

> The full value of sociological research for social workers will only come through experimental procedure involving the co-operation of sociologists and social workers (Burgess, 1927:192).

His specific proposal is enticing, even at this distance.

> My proposal is actually quite simple and I think, entirely feasible and reasonable, in spite of the fact that I do not anticipate its immediate and general adoption. It is to enter into the case record statements made by all

---

[66] His paper was given to the National Conference of Social Work, Division on the Family, earlier in 1927. In the light of his opening sentences we note that sociologists are assumed to be present in a social work conference audience; that the majority of schools of social work were integrally linked to sociology departments; that social workers of the time got more sociology teaching than from any other social science discipline; and that he places himself as challenging sociological (and presumably social work) convention.

persons visited in nearly as humanly possible the language which they used. (Burgess, 1927:192)

He immediately glosses this with the complaint that he is

> strongly opposed to having the language of the father and the mother in the home, of the landlord, or the teacher, or of the employer, translated into the language of the social worker on the case. The translation invariably and inevitably distorts the point of view and the attitude of the person interviewed. Each informant has a right[67] to have himself appear in the record in his own language. (Burgess, 1927:192-93)

He foresees this plan as giving 'a human document in place of a routine report' and candidly acknowledges 'How invaluable for case work and, I am frank to admit, for sociological research, would be the case records entirely in the first person' (Burgess, 1927:193).

Having made the case in brief in 1927, he devoted the majority of his 1928 paper to developing his argument. We noted some moments ago his reference to Octavia Hill. He draws the chastened conclusion that

> Existing case records seldom, or never, picture people in the language of Octavia Hill, with their "passions, hopes, and history" or their "temptations", or "the little scheme they have made of their lives, or would make if they had encouragement". The characters in case records do not move, and act, and have their being as persons. They are depersonalized, they become Robots, or mere cases undifferentiated except by the recurring problems they present. (Burgess, 1928:526-27)

He explains this by reiterating the point of his 1927 paper, that the 'characters...do not speak for themselves. They obtain a hearing only in the translation provided by the language of the social worker' (Burgess, 1928:527). He reflects his nascent interactionist sociology and social psychology[68] by setting the choice as one between a legalistic conception of the interview and a personal one.

> To enter the interview in the words of the person signifies a revolutionary change. It is a change from the interview conceived in legal terms to the interview as an opportunity to participate in the life history of the person, in

---

[67] This remark about human rights is not accidental. It is repeated in his 1928 paper, page 527.
[68] Herbert Blumer invented the term symbolic interactionism. His doctoral dissertation was published in 1928. Not everyone would regard Burgess as an interactionist. Robert Prus remarks that Burgess 'was really more interested, I think, in family relations from any perspective, rather than being an interactionist, per se' (Kleinknecht, 2007, 233)

his memories, in his hopes, in his attitudes, in his own plans, in his philosophy of life. (Burgess, 1928:527)

He continues to be alert to points of common ground with social work writing and cites a then recent paper by a leading social work scholar, Gordon Hamilton. She had suggested a distinction between the natural and the social sciences, where the latter 'are inevitably concerned with preferences and values' (Burgess, 1928:527). He reiterates his appreciation of the work of Clifford Shaw at the Institute for Juvenile Research who had 'as far as I know more consciously developed the method of first person reporting and carried it further than anyone else in the country' (Burgess, 1928:529).[69]

Conclusions

I have been unable to locate any further engagement with the relationship of the two fields. Deegan observes, for example, that Burgess in the earlier period was supportive of 'practical sociology' (a quote from 1916) and in 1924 was speaking approvingly of women's 'neighbourhood work', but in his late career writing was downplaying it as 'isolated', and not scientific or objective, and referring to its 'social work' orientation (Deegan, 1997b:13). Speculatively, this may have been due to an expanding preoccupation of each field with its own development. There is little evidence of critical engagement of social work with the creative challenge posed by Burgess, Clifford Shaw and others. For sociology, Burgess was playing a central role in this with Park, eg in the publication of their benchmark text on sociology in the later twenties. It may – though I am but guessing – have been connected with wider intellectual hostilities between the two disciplines that marked the decade. Burgess himself developed a strand of interest in the relationship between sociology and Freudian psychoanalysis – psychoanalysis and socioanalysis as he somewhere expresses it (Burgess, 1939:263).

In papers where his earlier interests seemed opportune for further development (e.g. Burgess, 1939, 1947) he makes no mention at all of social work. His 1939 paper is a very interesting discussion of Freud's influence on sociology in which, within his characteristic periodizing of sociology's development, he argues the point that the central methodological problem of the two disciplines is the same. Exploring the reasons as he sees them for divergences between the fields, he moves to discussing the potential for a

---

[69] He addresses and counters likely objections to his plea, *viz.* that such verbatim remarks are trivial; that they are not objective; that it would render records unduly lengthy; and that it would require new social work skills. He also suggests other ways that case records could be improved. The controversial character of proposals is implicitly acknowledged in that his paper is immediately followed in the same issue by a response from Bruno on the limitations of verbatim recording.

combination of methods between sociology and psychoanalysis. The underling logic has obvious but unspoken points of connection with his approach to the relationship between sociology and social work, thus tacitly implying how he might have further developed his earlier thinking. The issues lie fairly close to the surface.

1. The nature of the unresolved legacy, and my sense that it might have been otherwise.
2. The relationship between the applied, the ameliorative, and what Mills *et al* (2006) have recently, in a somewhat invidious comparison, contrasted as 'practice oriented' and 'research-based' social science disciplines.
3. The social contingencies of discipline recognition (Shaw, Arksey and Mullender, 2006).
4. The institutional shaping of fields of study.
5. The hard won gains and easy losses of inter-disciplinary collaboration.
6. The continued prevalence of 'friendly fire' actions among the social sciences.

Several disclaimers are in order. I do not, for a moment, want to claim that sociology and social work are part of one and the same enterprise. Small, of course, was correct, at least in principle, when he remarked on the existence of 'practical social workers who have but a vague notion of society in general, and who consequently cannot properly be called sociologists' (Small, 1903:472). Nor do I believe we should aspire to a circumstance in which sociology and social work coexist in perfect amity. Neither should we wish to draw a line from 80 or 90 years ago and teleport Edith Abbott or Ernest Burgess to the present.

What I would plead for, however, is a relationship between social work and sociology of intellectual reciprocity based on egalitarian respect. Yet this is all too rare. It is as if we are 'too embarrassed to look seriously at our history, afraid of the disorder we might find, too eager to distance ourselves from the pre-professional beginnings' and are, in consequence, homeless and 'disembedded' (Lorenz, 2007:599). Whatever we may conclude from these *leitmotifs*, Diner is surely correct when he says that above all university departments (sociology or social work) need 'teachers and investigators who are learned, imaginative, curious, scrupulous, patient and tireless in their exertion' (Diner, 1997:56).

References

Bulmer, M. (1984) *The Chicago School of Sociology*. Chicago: Chicago University Press.
Burgess, Ernest, W. (1923) 'The Interdependence of Sociology and Social Work', *Journal of Social Forces*, 1 (4):366-370.

-----.(1927) 'The Contribution of Sociology to Family Social Work', *The Family*, October, 1927:191-193.

-----.(1928) 'What Social Case Records Should Contain to be Useful for Sociological Interpretation', *Social Forces*, 6 (4):524-532.

-----.(1929) 'Is Prediction Feasible In Social Work? An Inquiry Based Upon A Sociological Study of Parole Records', *Social Forces*, 7 (4):533-545.

-----.(1930) 'The Value Of Sociological Community Studies For The Work of Social Agencies', *Social Forces*, 8 (4):481-491.

-----.(1939) 'The Influence of Sigmund Freud Upon Sociology in the United States', *The American Journal of Sociology*, 45 (3):356-374.

-----.(1947) 'The Family and Sociological Research', *Social Forces*, 26 (1):1-6.

Cavan, R. (1997) 'The Chicago School of Sociology, 1918-1933', in Plummer, K (ed.). *The Chicago School: Critical Assessments, Vol I, A Chicago Canon?* London: Routledge.

Coghlan, C.L. (2005) 'The Graduate School of Social Service Administration: Beginning or End of the Differentiation Process between Chicago Sociology and Social Work?' Paper presented at the annual meeting of the American Sociological Association, Marriott Hotel, Loews Philadelphia Hotel, Philadelphia, Unpublished Paper.

Deegan, M.J. (1991) *Women in Sociology: a Bio-bibliographical Sourcebook*. New York: Greenwood Press.

-----.(1997a) 'The Chicago Men and the Sociology of Women', Plummer, K. (ed.). *The Chicago School: Critical Assessments, Vol I, A Chicago Canon?* London: Routledge.

-----.(1997b) 'Hull-House Maps and Papers: the Birth of Chicago Sociology', in Plummer, K. (ed.). *The Chicago School: Critical Assessments, Vol II, Theory, History and Foundations* London: Routledge.

Deegan, M.J. and Hill, M. R. (1991) 'Edith Abbott (1876-1957)', in Deegan, M.J. (ed.). *Women in Sociology: a Bio-bibliographical Sourcebook*. New York: Greenwood Press.

Diner, S. J. (1977) 'Scholarship in the Quest for Social Welfare: a Fifty-Year History of the *Social Service Review*', *Social Service Review*, 51 (1):1-66.

-----.(1997) 'Department and Discipline: the Development of Sociology at the University of Chicago, 1892-1920', in Plummer, K, (ed.). *The Chicago School: Critical Assessments*. London: Routledge.

Fine, W.F. (1979) *Progressive Evolutionism and American Sociology, 1890-1920*. Ann Arbor: UMi Research Press.

Geertz, C. (1973) *The Interpretation of Cultures*. New York: Basic Books.

Hakim, C. (2000) *Research Design* London: Routledge.

Kirk, S. and Reid, W.J. (2002) *Science and Social Work*. New York: Columbia University Press.

Kleinknacht, S. (2007) 'An Interview with Robert Prus: His Career, Contributions, and Legacy as an Interactionist Ethnographer and Social Theorist', *Qualitative Sociology Review*, 3 (2):221-288.

Lorenz, W. (2007) 'Practising History: Memory and Contemporary Professional Practice', *International Social Work*, 50 (5):597-612.

Lubove, R. (1965) *The Professional Altruist*. Cambridge: Harvard University Press.

Mills, D., Jepson, A., Coxon, T., Easterby-Smith, M., Hawkins, P. and Spencer, J. (2006) *Demographic Review of the UK Social Sciences*. Swindon: ESRC. Available at http://www.esrc.ac.uk/ESRCInfoCentre.

Platt, J. (1996) *A History of Sociological Research Methods in America*. Cambridge: CUP.

Plummer, K. (1997) 'Introducing Chicago Sociology', Plummer, K. (ed.). *The Chicago School: Critical Assessments, Vol I, A Chicago Canon?* London: Routledge.

Richmond, M. (1917) *Social Diagnosis*. New York: Russell Sage.

Shaw, I. (1996) *Evaluating in Practice*. Aldershot: Ashgate

-----.(2005) 'Practitioner Research: Evidence or Critique?', British Journal of *Social Work*, 35 (8): 1231-1248.

-----.(forthcoming), 'Merely Experts? Reflections on the History of Social Work, Science and Research', *Research, Policy and Planning*.

Shaw, I., Arksey. H. and Mullender, A. (2006), 'Recognizing Social Work', *British Journal of Social Work*, 36 (2):227-246.

Shaw, I. and Gould, N. (2001) *Qualitative Research in Social Work*. London: Sage Publications.

Small, Albion W. (1903) 'What is a sociologist?', *American Journal of Sociology*, 8:468-477.

Timms, N. (1968) *The Language of Social Casework*. London: Routledge and Kegan Paul.

Webb, B. (1929) *My Apprenticeship*. London: Longmans Green.

Acknowledgements

I am grateful for the comments of sociology colleagues at a conference on the legacy of the Chicago School at Manchester, England, 2007, and to observations made by social work colleagues at the 2007 Bielefeld meeting of INTSOCEVAL (an international network of social work evaluation centres). The editor of *Social Service Review* kindly drew my attention to Stephen Diner's 50 year anniversary essay on the journal.

CHAPTER 2

Ernest Burgess: Exploring Urban Marginality

Roger A. Salerno
Pace University, New York City, USA

Introduction

One of the essential problems in researching Ernest W. Burgess's life is that although he was an exceedingly public sociologist, he was by far a remarkably private person. And according to some critics a personally colorless one (Cottrell, 1973; Faris, 1967). It is this personal privacy and blandness that has led to speculations about the man who wrote of personal intimacy, marital relations and romantic love, yet lived his entire life, or a considerable portion of his adult years, either alone or with his father or sister in an apartment not far from his university's campus.

Ernest Watson Burgess was born in Tilbury, Ontario, Canada on May 16, 1886. Often referred to as "the little professor" in grade school because of his proclivity to study, he was to become one of the most important sociologists in the United States in his early thirties. His family was comprised of civic-minded people. His father Edmund J. Burgess was a teacher and a minister in the Congregational Church. His mother, Mary Anne Jane Watson was the daughter of a Canadian farmer. She was described as quite domineering in her bearing and "not given to overt manifestations of personal warmth" (Bouge, 1974: xii). He had one younger sibling, a sister Roberta, who attended the same schools he did and was to remain his life-long live-in companion.

Ernest Burgess was sent to boarding school in his formative years. His family later moved to Kingfisher, Okalahoma and he and his sister attended Kingfisher College - a four-year institution founded by the Congregational Church. There he came under the influence of one of his professors who had been trained in sociology at the University of Chicago, Julius Temple Howe. There Burgess received his B.A. degree in 1908. That same year he entered the sociology program at the University of Chicago on a fellowship (Goldman, 1973). His sister was to later attend the university's school of music.

Burgess's graduate teachers were the primary founders of Chicago sociology: Albion Small, the department chair and dean of the graduate school of arts and sciences, Charles Henderson who taught urban sociology and served as university chaplain, George Vincent, also a dean and a co-author with Small of one of the first American sociology texts, *An Introduction to the Study of Society* published in 1894, and of course W.I. Thomas, flamboyant scholar and the fount of much Chicago school inspiration and folklore. They were often referred to as "the big four." All of these men with the exception of Thomas had deep religious affiliations and were considered men of the Social Gospel. Yet to some extent each was radical in his own way. While Burgess was close to Henderson and worked as Vincent's research assistant, it was Thomas who seemingly had the most lasting influence on him (Burgess, 1948).

Burgess wrote a rather uninspiring doctoral thesis entitled *The Function of Socialization in Social Evolution* and completed his graduate studies at Chicago in 1913. Still the thesis was primarily social psychological, and influenced to some extent by Thomas' work. It attempted to establish the critical importance of socialization as a product of group forces rather than physical environment and heredity. After leaving Chicago, he taught sociology as an assistant professor at Toledo University in Ohio (1912-1913), and followed this with teaching stints at the University of Kansas (1913-1915) and then Ohio State (1915-1916). Having applied himself to social survey work during that time, he came back to Chicago as an assistant professor in 1916, just two years prior Thomas' dismissal from the university. Burgess had been hired by Albion Small to fill Henderson's post after his death. It was Henderson who was the quintessential urban sociologist - a man connected to the settlement houses as well as the social survey movement. While Robert Park was teaching a few courses at Chicago at Thomas' behest, it wasn't until his full-time hire - after Thomas' ouster - that the department regained a sense of stability and momentum. It wasn't until Burgess joined the department that things settled down.

Burgess and Chicago

Burgess' dress and manner gave the more conservative elements at the university confidence. Park was very much an outsider and had a minimal background as an academic. Though well educated, extremely well traveled, and in possession of a doctorate he had worked both as a news reporter and as the personal secretary to Booker T. Washington, one of the country's most renowned race leaders. This would have been enough for some to cast doubt on his steadiness. Burgess was a man much younger than his aging departmental colleagues. When Park began his full-time position in the department in 1919 he was already 54. Burgess was his junior by more than twenty years. Yet despite their age difference and Park's lack of university teaching experience Burgess afforded him the utmost of respect and admiration. They shared an office together in the east tower of the Harper Library. Park remained much more of a gentleman-scholar with Ivy-league academic credentials, great whit and a relatively wealthy family background. He was also, by contrast, a man of style with a love of great literature and artistic sensibilities - in some ways a bohemian of the 1920s (Raushenbush, 1979). And while Burgess generously gave Park the credit for the development of the direction of Chicago sociology, he most certainly provided an important share. Yet his lack of charisma led to his often being overlooked for leadership roles. The following is a description of Burgess taken from Robert E. L. Faris' history of the department.

Slight of stature, Burgess had the pallor of a man who spent most of his time indoors, in spite of an occasional round of golf on a holiday. Frequently he had a somewhat worn look, well justified by his pace of activity, and a harried appearance, reinforced by a transparent green eyeshade which he wore at his desk and sometimes in the corridors. But he moved quickly and energetically and spoke to his classes in adequate volume. His voice was high and his sentences broken with hesitations, but the knowledge was well-organized and authoritative and students seldom complained about the style of his lectures (Faris, 1967:27).

While such a description is not the most flattering, it does point to Burgess' vast energy and his dedication to work. Burgess virtually lived at the university. He worked closely with students from a variety of backgrounds on a vast number of research projects. He was trusted by Small and assisted him and Charles Merriam from Political Science in developing and managing a vast funding base for a variety of research programs and represented the sociology department on the Local Social Science Research Committee established with Rockefeller funding. He developed close ties with community-based institutions and was able to connect research projects to foundation and local civic agency revenue sources.

Scholarly Interests

In many ways Ernest Burgess was a unique individual. While influenced by Thomas' work on human sexuality and social psychology he understood the taboo nature of such study. Thomas was dismissed from the university not only for his hotel indiscretion but also for bringing embarrassment to an institution because of what he studied and what he professed. The Chicago *Tribune* battered the university as much as it attacked Thomas for teaching what it claimed bordered on "sexual perversions". He was forced to leave the university shortly after Burgess' arrival. If anything this dismissal was to have a chilling effect on the course of Chicago research at the time.

Since Burgess had been engaged in community survey work after completing his doctoral course work, and in fact had served on an important survey of the town of Lawrence, Kansas with Frank W. Blackmar, it was viewed as natural for him to assume Henderson's classes. These were courses that stressed urban community and research. Yet, despite his involvement in cities and urban affairs, Burgess retained a strong interest in the social psychological dynamics of human interpersonal relations and particularly human sexuality.

But the beginnings of Burgess' work are rooted in the reform orientations of his teachers particularly Vincent and Henderson. In some of his earlier writings, he grapples with the need for a more "scientific" sociology that is distinct from social reform and particularly social work. At heart, however, he appeared to have remained a reformer his entire life. Prior to his co-authorship of *Introduction to the Science of Sociology*, which he assembled with Park in 1921, and *The City*, which they published together in 1925, Burgess had written about sociology as a means to achieve social betterment. More than Park, he was interested in policy and planning - something that the social survey movement emphasized. In fact Park's position was primarily dismissive of those he referred to as "do-gooders." He was rarely engaged in such projects himself and did little in the way of field work. He won a position in academia because he impressed W.I. Thomas who in turn introduced him to Small. Thomas and Park were men who shared much in common, a love of art and literature, an enriched social life, an interest in issues of race, and a proclivity for theory-building and sociological rumination. What the Chicago school would have looked like, what it could have produced if both men had worked together, is fascinating speculation. Instead, Park was settled in with the young Burgess - a man with whom he shared little in common - at least personally if not intellectually.

But Thomas' loss was Burgess' gain. And so, while this young assistant professor was thrown in with a man of the world he did his best to make the relationship work by taking on much of the administrative labor and leaving Park free to write and explore. It was Burgess, not Park, who did the heavy lifting on their text *Introduction to the Science of Sociology*. This was their first joint venture. And while chapter one was Park's doing, Burgess wrote the introduction as well as the drafts that went into chapters two to eleven. Park was primarily responsible for the introductory pieces on social control most of which were edited by Burgess. While Park also did a lot of editing and good bit of writing, Burgess did at least an equal amount and got the manuscript to the printer on time (Janowitz, 1969).

Burgess' work cannot be as easily characterized as Park's. Park made much of his German experience, his study with Georg Simmel and his familiarity with the work of Max Weber and other German theorists. The notion of academic reportage was primarily his venture and transferring this to sociology in Chicago was his alone. While Thomas had much to do with some of the Chicago emphasis on social psychology, Park was influenced by a very strong philosophy department at Harvard, where he was taught by William James and George Santayna (Matthews, 1977:31). Pragmatism of Chicago sociology was centrally his doing.

Burgess must be given credit for popularizing the concepts of time and space in American urban sociological theory. While mapping was used before, he helped connect maps to dynamic human interaction. He was very familiar with the social survey movement, with the use of census data and its mapping and with the mapping work of the settlement house movement, especially Hull House. Burgess was one of the first American urban sociologists to use ecological modeling. If anyone one deserves credit for the success of urban ecology at Chicago it was Burgess and his students. And although he made considerable use of descriptive statistics, he was also an important influence on translating case study presentation from social work and medicine into the realm of social research. As a student in the classroom of W. I. Thomas he came to understand sociological importance of qualitative tools and used them generously.

On the other hand Park was a sophisticated thinker and journalist. His brilliant essay, "The City: Suggestions for the Investigation of Human Behavior in the Urban Environment," which was originally published in the *American Journal of Sociology* in March, 1915 (ten years before the publication of the book *The City*), was a clarion call for a new urban sociology. By putting *The City* volume together, Park (with Burgess) was able to provide a showcase for this urban acuity and reach out to others to joint him. Here was the first Chicago theoretical enterprise. It was one quite different than that imagined by Thomas. Here Park conceptualizes the city and translates urban investigation into a creative science. And while Park loved exploring the city, he rarely did what might be considered expansive urban research.

Human Relationships

Unlike Park, much of Burgess' focus was on the interpersonal - the social psychological - what Park might have termed "touchy-feely" stuff. This interest emerged from his studies with Thomas as well as from his studies with George Herbert Mead. His early interest in socialization never really waned. While it was the subject of his dissertation, it also served his understanding of families and juvenile delinquency later on. While he understood the ecological dynamics of city growth, he never disassociated urban social ecology from those dynamics that were more intimate. It became the basis for his so-called area studies in which he viewed the neighborhood as an important agent of socialization in the lives of delinquent boys. While Park dismissed Freud almost out of hand, Burgess (1939) embraced much of what he saw in psychoanalysis as contributions to a science of society - something that complimented the work of Mead, Cooley and Thomas. He was also known to have assigned Freud to his students, something Park was adverse to do. He promoted case study and even had his students write autobiographical sketches of themselves and frequently collected their dreams and had them write reports on their sexual experiences. The sexual autobiography was something that Thomas had required of his students (Bierstedt, 1969:12); and it is likely that Burgess was himself was assigned to write one.

But there was something important about intimacy in the work of Burgess - something that he must have taken from Thomas, but something Park did not focus on very much. It was something he transmitted to his students who researched the urban margins and created beautiful and poignant ethnographies - tales of taxi dancers and hobos, stories of delinquents abandoned to the streets. According to one of his biographers, it was as though Burgess himself was possessed of "an affection-starved soul" (Bogue, 1974:ix). One can only speculate about the reasons for his life-long bachelorhood.

There was an *up closeness* in the data he collected - a prying into the innermost lives of others - an intimate acquaintance with the flotsam and jetsam of urban back alleys. If he wasn't the one actually speaking to the people on the street, it was his students regaling him with personal stories from the urban underground - perhaps their own stories. He not only openly encouraged such interviews, but he also interviewed his own students - often in the confines of his office. These stories became part of a massive personal collection of vignettes on sexual escapades, drug use and the like. From all outward appearances it appeared that their lives were certainly more exciting than his own. The same, however, could never be said about Thomas.

Thomas was of course influenced by anthropology and often considered himself a descendant of those engaged in folk psychology (Salerno, 2007). Somehow there was a very strong voyeuristic element to his work as well from his finding a letter in the back alley trash bin from a Polish immigrant girl and reading into it the beginning of *The Polish Peasant* (or so the tale is told) to his use of intimate letters of confession directed to the love advice editor in the Jewish Daily Forward that he scattered throughout *The Unadjusted Girl*. Much of this stuff was titillating, especially for the time. Thomas was sure to know this.

Burgess began his venture into social theory as both a structuralist and interactionist. He viewed people as establishing institutions that could condition and determine social outcomes for themselves and others. The family was such an institution. But such institutions were also made up of interacting individuals who could negotiate their positions within these frameworks. In the changing American landscape of the 1920s, he and Park understood that people in the same family lived in different worlds.

Above all he was a humanist. He believed in the basic goodness of people and saw tragedy in their personal lives affecting socio-behavioral outcomes. He viewed the criminal as first and foremost a person and believed that it was most essential to see him or her in this light. Only then could one understand why one engaged in delinquent behavior (1923).

Methodologically, he could easily go from quantitative to qualitative study. Therefore he might be viewed either as eclectic or inconsistent. Nevertheless Bulmer (1984:94) has seen him as more of an "original thinker" in regard to methods and certainly much more involved with the actual research projects themselves and capable of giving Park's creative flights of research fancy to empirical or case analysis. He helped make Park's work more scientific, more academic. His ability to fuse the micro and macro order was passed along to his students. He frequently took classes in statistics, sat in on William Orburn's class at Chicago, to sharpen his skills.

Kinsey was still collecting bugs when Burgess was collecting stories of people's sexual escapades (See EWB-A, Box 128, Folders 7, 8, 9). The tradition of such "collecting" at Chicago was handed down from Thomas whose career was later destroyed when he was charged with an adulterous affair in 1918. Thomas had collected intimate details from his students of their sex lives by requiring them to write explicit sexual autobiographies (Bierstedt, 1969:12). But Burgess continued in the Thomas tradition. Life histories (including sexual histories) became important sources of urban narratives, and Burgess' students were recruited into their authorship (DSI, Box I, Folder 5).

Burgess worked very closely with Nels Anderson on *The Hobo* and with Paul Cressey on *The Taxi Dance Hall*. He was instrumental in helping Clifford Shaw develop the resources and methodology for *The Jack-Roller* (Salerno, 2007). These tales were mild in comparison to the histories he collected and remain in his Collected Papers housed at the University of Chicago's Special Collections Division.

It was a very few years ago that Chad Heap (2003), a graduate students working with George Chauncey at the University of Chicago's Center for Gender Studies, initiated research for this dissertation that unearthed a vast array of sexual histories, photographs and sexual surveys. He later published some of his important findings from what is now referred to at the Regenstein Library as the Burgess Addenda. Heap also helped organize an exhibit at the Regenstein in September of 2000 using some of his findings. The exhibit was called "Homosexuality in the City: A Century of Research at the University of Chicago." It's been only within the past ten years or so that the Addenda has been organized, boxed and categorized and according to Dan Meyer, Associate Director of Special Collections, has recently received an upsurge of interest. While Burgess seemed to collect everything, he left little about his own personal life.

Overall, it was Heap's contention that these sociological studies of sexuality were largely overlooked by researchers in the past. And while a wealth of raw data fills the Burgess files, little use seems to have been made of this. Burgess had engaged in a long-term project of collecting personal narratives on people's sex lives. He seemed particularly interested in what Heap terms "non-normative" sexuality of that time, particularly homosexuality, prostitution, transvestiteism, cross-racial sexuality. There are stories of mastrubation, and sexual compulsions. According to Heap's optimistic conclusion: "these studies provided the foundation for a radical new understanding of sexuality that emphasized the social context and meaning of sexual practices and types, rather than their biological or psychological determination. (Heap, 2003:457).

That Burgess collected this material with the enthusiastic participation of some of his students is quite undeniable. Some were more reluctant and refused to participate (Interview with Mr. Carter, March 17, 1972 in DSI, Box I Folder 5). Interestingly, here is Burgess working with frequently stodgy social reformers and at the same peering into the most private aspects of human sexuality not only in his own classroom, but in the darkest recesses of the city. According to Heap (2003), Burgess himself ventured into female impersonator clubs to collect photographs and information. Much of this was done under the umbrella of his family research agenda and some of it collected in the course of his investigations into marital success and couple pairing. There is no indication in the Burgess Papers, however, that there was any intention for this "non-normative" sexual research to see the light of day in publication.

Earl Bruce, who wrote his MA thesis on homosexuality, did so under Burgess' supervision. But Burgess required Bruce to make use of personality tests in his research and to supplement this with interviews of more than fifty gay men living in Chicago's Near North Side (Heap, 2003:467). But there was little in the way of formal publication of such research.

It is the area of Series VII of the Addenda entitled "Field Notes" that we find a wealth of these materials, aside from those sprinkled into the boxes on marriage and engagement. And there is evidence that WPA money was used for some of this work. One of Burgess' research assistants, Paul Oien, supplied him with a wealth of field research on the gambling, sexual promiscuity, prostitution, homosexual practices taking place on Chicago's South Side (EWBP-A, Box 209). Oien writes to Burgess on letterhead of The National Conference on Family Relations of which Burgess was Secretary/Treasurer.

There is a wealth of autobiographical material dealing with sexuality that Burgess never integrated into his work on marriage and relationships and likely never intended to use. Still in some respects Chicago was far ahead of other places that began collecting such information for more formal study much later than Thomas and Burgess.

Conclusion

For some Ernest Burgess appears to be a mere research appendage of Robert Park. But nothing could be further from the truth. Much of Park's success at Chicago was due in large part to the work of Burgess. They worked well together. They complemented each other's work, each other's strengths. While Park was frequently away from Chicago, Burgess took on the bulk of administrative and research work. He worked closely with graduate students, secured jobs for them at local agencies and helped them map-out their research proposals. If it were not for Burgess some of these classic ethnographic studies would never have been done. His career was one that spanned several generations of students from the 1920s to the early 1960s. Much of what the Chicago school was (if it was indeed a school) it owed to Burgess. And when he died he left behind an array of community ventures he helped to build (such as the Chicago Area Project) that survive today and continue to work for social betterment.

Burgess stood up against what he viewed to be the forces of oppression. For this he was settled with a fat FBI dossier that takes up an entire chapter in Mike

Keen's *Stalking the Sociological Imagination* (1999). He was openly accused of being a communist as were other members in his department at Chicago. While not a communist, his concern ran deep for those who were oppressed - those who he saw as relegated to the margins. He died in a Chicago nursing home on December 27, 1966.

References

Bierstedt, R. (1969) *Introduction in On Humanistic Sociology*, by Florian Znaniecki. Chicago: University of Chicago Press.

Bogue, D.J. (1974) *Introduction in The Basic Writings of Ernest W. Burgess*. Chicago: Community and Family Study Center, University of Chicago.

Bulmer, M. (1984) *The Chicago School of Sociology, Institutionalization, Diversity and the Rise of Sociological Research*. Chicago. The University of Chicago Press.

Burgess, Ernest W. (1948) 'William I. Thomas as a Teacher', *Sociology and Social Research*, 32.

-----.(1939) 'The Influence of Sigmund Freud Upon Sociology in the United States', *American Journal of Sociology*, 45.

-----.(1923) 'The Delinquent as a Person', *American Journal of Sociology*, 28.

Cottrell, L.Jr. (1973) 'Introduction', in *Ernest Burgess On Community, Family and Delinquency*, (ed.). by L. Cottrell, A. Hunter and J. Short, Jr. Chicago: University of Chicago Press.

Faris, R.E.L. (1967) *Chicago Sociology 1920-1932*. San Francisco: Chandler Publishing.

Goldman, N. (1973) 'Biographical Sketch', in *Ernest Burgess on Community, Family and Delinquency*, (ed.). by L. Cottrell, Jr., A. Hunter and J. Short, Jr. Chicago: University of Chicago Press.

Heap, C. (2003) *The City as a Sexual Laboratory: The Queer Heritage of the Chicago School*. Qualitative Sociology, 26.

Janowitz, M. (1969) Foreword to *Chicago Sociology 1920-1932*, by R.E.L. Faris. Chicago: University of Chicago Press.

Matthews, F. H. (1977) *Quest for an American Sociology: Robert E. Park and the Chicago School*. Montreal: McGill-Queens University Press).

Raushenbush, W. (1979) *Robert E. Park: Biography of a Sociologist*. Durham, NC: Duke University Press.

Salerno, R. (2007) *Sociology Noir: Studies at the University of Chicago in Loneliness Marginality and Deviance, 1915-1935*. Jefferson, NC: McFarland & Co.

From Special Collections, Regenstein Library, University of Chicago. EWB-A Ernest W. Burgess Addenda DSI Department of Sociology Interviews.

CHAPTER 3

'Ahead of its Time?': The Legacy and Relevance of W.I. Thomas and F. Znaniecki (1918-20) The Polish Peasant in Europe and America.

Brian Roberts
University of Glamorgan, Pontypridd, Wales

Introduction

This examination of W.I Thomas and Florian Znaniecki's monumental, classic investigation *The Polish Peasant in Europe and America* (1918-20)[70] is not primarily concerned with the methodological aspects of the study, rather it concentrates on its relatively more neglected conceptual areas and its overall approach and intent. The focus is on the social issues the authors identified arising from migration and the related battery of ideas they employed. The study may be deemed 'Ahead of its time' in that its general conception was not fully recognised and developed – it is an investigation not merely of the culture and structure of the Polish-American community in the U.S. but also of Polish society and the transition of individuals, groups and families between the two.

There are a number of important lessons and relevances of the study: first, it is a pioneering account of 'local' processes within transnational connections – examining life in rural communities, city groupings and organisations, and migration within and between countries. It also reminds us that that forms of mass migration are not new. The study also called for comparative work of other migrant communities. Thomas's subsequent study *Old World Traits Transplanted* published in 1921 (Thomas, 1975) can be seen as following this injunction. (The publication was originally accredited to Robert E. Park and

---

[70] *The Polish Peasant* was originally published in five volumes 1918-20. A two volume edition was published in 1927 which corrected some minor errors, gave an index, made a repagination, and moved 'The life-record of an immigrant' (formerly the middle, third volume) to the end of volume 2. In 1958, the second edition was republished.

Herbert A. Hiller but Thomas is now recognised as the main author, see Young, 1975). Secondly, it anticipated multi-sited research rather than a more limited focus on a single location (Marcus, 1995). Thirdly, it was innovative in employing multiple research materials/techniques, e.g. letters, a 'life record' and various kinds of organisational documents (and reference to a wide range of sources) – some of these have only more recently become 'acceptable' in sociology. Further, the study's use of such materials can still provide useful lessons, for example, in terms of the application of autobiographical accounts – the need to contextualise, theorise and interrelate individual personality with culture. Fourthly, the work can not only be understood as an attempt to understand the complexities of 'personal life' of 'migrant others' within a discussion of the major social issue of immigration. Of course, Thomas and Znaniecki were also 'migrants'. It can be argued that Thomas's interest in migration was stimulated by thoughts on his own early life and career, including his studies and travels in Europe (e.g. Germany and Poland), as shown in his own short autobiographical account (Thomas in Baker, 1973). Similarly, Znaniecki reflected on his own migratory experiences, for instance, he is credited with a short, reflective account of his life as a 'European intellectual' in America in Thomas's *Old World Traits Transplanted* (Thomas, 1975:107-12).[71]

The Origins and Stance

The Polish Peasant study was undertaken in the early years of the 20th century when immigration was a major social and political concern in America. As Thomas reflected:

> At that time immigration was a burning question. About a million immigrants were coming here annually, and this was mainly the newer immigration, from southern and eastern Europe... I decided to study an immigrant group in Europe and America to determine as far as possible what relation their home mores and norms had to their adjustment and maladjustment in America' (Thomas, in Blumer, 1979:103)

In particular, the scale of migration from Poland was considerable:

> In 1913 there were 130,000 Polish immigrants into the United States; another 800,000 Poles, while still nominally domiciled in Poland, were each year moving seasonally into Germany in search of work. This was therefore

---

[71] According to the Mead Project the autobiography of an anonymous Polish intellectual (Thomas, 1975: 107-112) was an excerpt from a previously published article by 'A European' in The Atlantic Monthly (1920) but identifiable as Znaniecki (http://www.brocku.ca/MeadProject/Znaniecki?Znaniecki_1920.html) (see also, Smith, 1988: 109).

a massive movement, and it was associated with very rapid social and economic changes of all kinds in Poland itself (Madge, 1963:52)

In the US, there was widespread debate on the effects of immigration (especially from eastern and southern Europe) on levels of crime, poverty and other problems. Arguments included prevalent eugenicist ideas alongside notions of American 'fitness', and drew on a rising sense of American 'national character'.

During 1908, Thomas discussed research possibilities with Helen Culver (the benefactor of the famous Hull House Settlement in Chicago) who agreed to a support an investigation with the large sum of $50,000. He says that after a year of 'exploration' he decided to investigate the Poles because he had found 'abundant materials, of a kind' and because of their behaviour as 'the most incomprehensible and perhaps the most disorganized of all immigrant the groups' (Thomas in Blumer, 1979:103-4).

The ambitious conception of the research by Thomas and Znaniecki can be indicated by the Preface to the first edition of *The Polish Peasant*:

> The work consists of five volumes, largely documentary in their character. Volumes I and II comprise a study of the organization of the peasant primary groups (family and community), and of the partial evolution of this system of organization under the influence of the new industrial system and of immigration to America and Germany. Volume III is the autobiography (with critical treatment) of an immigrant of peasant origin but belonging by occupation to the lower city class, and illustrates the tendency to disorganization of the individual under the conditions involved in a rapid transition from one type of social organization to another. Volume IV treats the dissolution of the primary group and the social and political reorganization and unification of peasant communities in Poland on the new ground of rational co-operation. Volume V is based on studies of the Polish immigrant in America and shows the degrees and forms of disorganization associated with a too-rapid and inadequately mediated individualization, with a sketch of the beginnings of reorganization. (Thomas and Znaniecki, 1958, I:viii)

The intellectual starting point of *The Polish Peasant* is the exploration of individual and group adaptation to changing social contexts:

> We must put ourselves in the position of the subject who tries to find his way in this world, and we must remember, first of all, that the environment by which he is influenced and to which he adapts himself, is his world, not the objective world of science.... (Thomas and Znaniecki, 1958: II:1846-47)

For Thomas and Znaniecki, their investigation should be judged on its 'ultimate practical applicability' and, accordingly, it drew upon a 'pragmatist' social philosophy: 'One of the most significant features of social evolution is the growing importance which a conscious and rational technique tends to assume in social life' (Thomas and Znaniecki, 1958, 1: 1:19-20). For instance, as in the 'life record' presented of Wladek Wiszniewski, we learn:

> the disorganizing effect which the passage from an old to a new form of social organization has upon an individual if not consciously and rationally directed. (Thomas and Znaniecki, 1958, II:1909-10)

Thomas and Znaniecki point to two basic practical problems in 'reflective social practice': fostering both 'desirable mental and moral characteristics' of the individual in the social group, and a 'desirable type of social organization and culture' with the contribution of individuals. If social theory is to meet these problems it must draw on 'objective cultural elements' and 'subjective characteristics of the members'. These materials, i.e. on social values and individual attitudes, must be 'correlated' (Thomas and Znaniecki, 1958, I:20-1). The underlying pragmatist position is clear in Thomas and Znaniecki's contention that people become dissatisfied with social intervention which is based on 'mere whim of an individual or a social body, or upon preconceived philosophical, religious, or moral generalizations' rather than applying one 'rational technique'. They argue that an 'objective attitude' towards 'social reality' is recent a phenomenon – as the 'demand for a rational control results from the increasing rapidity of social evolution' (Thomas and Znaniecki, 1958, 1:1).

For Polish society, the immediate issue is one of control in social life in the face of transformation and crisis. In the traditional Polish peasant community, beliefs and rules are unable to control problems in a 'more complex and fluid world' where there is a 'rapid' 'social evolution'. In these circumstances, instead of a 'half-conscious routine' a fully 'conscious technique' becomes a 'social necessity' (Thomas and Znaniecki, 1958, I:2). Again, a practical intent is demonstrated by the authors. The work of a range of voluntary and other organisations within the Polish-American community is employed to show the 'other side of this evolution' and 'the positive and constructive results which can be attained by a planful and conscious reorganizing activity' and the role of 'individual efficiency' - where the 'national state-system giving a permanent and stable frame-work' is lacking (Thomas and Znaniecki, 1958, II: 1910).

Broadly, Thomas and Znaniecki transform a notion of individual biological adaptation to the constraints of the social environment to a more dynamic, conscious and progressive idea of an emerging dependence/independence between individual/society.

Theoretical Considerations: Mutual Dependence Between
the Individual and Social Organisation

Within the 'pragmatist' approach of *The Polish Peasant* there is an associated 'symbolic interactionism' underpinning much of the study's theorisation. As Martindale says, commenting on the investigation:

> The individual is thus a product of interaction. In order to become a social personality in any domain, the individual must not only learn the social meanings which objects possess but also learn now to adapt himself to the demands which society puts upon him. Since meanings imply conscious thought, he must do this by conscious reflection, not by mere instinctive adaptation of reflexes. (Martindale, 1961:352)

The interconnection between personality and culture is a central theme in Thomas and Znaniecki's theorization.

Wishes

The idea of 'wishes' is prominent in *The Polish Peasant*: 'Every individual has a vast variety of wishes which can be satisfied only by his incorporation in a society'. An individual's general pattern of wishes may include:

> (1) the desire for new experience, for fresh stimulations;
> (2) the desire for recognition, including for example, sexual response and general social appreciation, and secured by devices ranging from the display of ornament to the demonstration of worth through scientific attainment;
> (3) the desire for mastery, or the 'will to power,' exemplified by ownership, domestic tyranny, political despotism, based on the instinct of hate, but capable of being sublimated to laudable ambition;
> (4) the desire for security, based on the instinct of fear and exemplified negatively by the wretchedness of the individual in perpetual solitude or under social taboo. (Thomas and Znaniecki, 1958, I:72-3)

Society represses many of the wishes held by the individual which are incompatible with group interests; at the same time society is the arena through which wishes and schemes can be met. In a later formulation, in *The Polish Peasant*, the four wishes seem to be reduced to 'two universal traits' or 'powerful tendencies' – the 'desire for new experience' and the 'desire for stability'. These provide 'the condition of both development and conservatism' (Thomas and Znaniecki, 1958: II:1859-61).

The first phase of these 'traits' is manifested in curiosity and fear (e.g. as in the search for food and security). As 'permanent tendencies' they become parts of the 'character' in the social formation of the personality (as the 'desire for new experience' and the 'desire for stability'). The 'alternation' between these desires, it is held, is a 'fundamental principle of personal evolution, as including both the development of a character and of a life-organization' (Thomas and Znaniecki, 1958, II: 1859-60). The authors distinguish between the 'character' and the 'temperament' - character is the 'organized and fixed groups' of attitudes produced by social influences acting upon the temperament (which are intellectual, given by conscious reflection). The 'temperament' is 'the fundamental original group of attitudes of the individual as existing independently of any social influences' (Thomas and Znaniecki, 1958, II:1844). Thomas and Znaniecki state that it is 'relatively easy' to identify temperaments and character but this 'classification' is merely a 'preparation for the study of their evolution, where the aim is to determine human types as dynamic types, as types of development' (Thomas and Znaniecki, 1958, II:1843).

The 'life-organisation' is the connecting link between attitudes and social values ('the existence, within the sphere of experience of an individual, of a limited number of selected and organized groups of social values which play a predominant part in his life both as partial causes and partial effects of his more or less organized attitudes'). In terms of the formation of life organization, they say that in society there are 'ready models of organization with which individuals are expected to comply' – but again these are only a starting point in study of personalities (Thomas and Znaniecki, 1958, II:1843-4). Socially the individual has to find a place within the range group pursuits – economic, political, religious, aesthetic and so on (Thomas and Znaniecki, 1958, II:1860).

Thomas and Znaniecki argue that the individual personality moves along 'typical' 'lines of genesis' or a series of experiences in which attitudes develop. These 'lines' are seen as of great importance for understanding problems of individual development in any area, e.g. economic, religious, intellectual, moral. While the variety of lines of genesis are theoretically open, they are few in number; for instance, society 'imposes' on the individual by giving a 'determined frame of organized activities' which are influenced by the individual's background in family education, career and patterns of living and 'economic, legal and moral sanctions' which regulate behaviour (Thomas and Znaniecki, 1958, II: 1841-2).

In summary, as Martindale argues, Thomas and Znaniecki constructed a view of the personality 'as manifesting itself, as a whole, only in the course of its total life' (Martindale, 1961:351).

Personal Evolution and Personality

The idea of 'personal evolution' includes a recognition that the individual is part of a 'pre-existing social world' – 'the hedonistic, economic, political, religious, moral, aesthetic, intellectual activities of the group' or 'objective systems' that are 'organized either by traditional association or with a conscious regard to the greatest possible efficiency of the result'. Thomas and Znaniecki argue that the interconnection between these systems and the 'progressive formation' of the individual's character and life-organisation is 'the central problem of the social control of personal evolution' (Thomas and Znaniecki, 1958, II:1860-1).

The pursuit of 'social education' has to take account of a 'duality of two opposite tendencies' – the 'suppression' of attitudes or values in 'dis-harmony' with current social organisation and the influencing of personal evolution by the development of features in the character and 'schemes of situations' required by existing social systems (Thomas and Znaniecki, 1958, II: 1861). Suppression involves the destruction of possibilities hence it is associated with limitations of personality (e.g. the adventurous spirit on children). The 'mechanism' of suppression, therefore, has two aspects - temperamental possibility is suppressed where no opportunity is manifest in situations (e.g. suppression of sexual or free-thought attitudes) or where attitudes are already manifested but further development is thwarted by negative sanctions of punishment or blame. In both cases the mechanisms only delay the formation of an 'undesirable attitude' until the character is established (Thomas and Znaniecki, 1958, II:1865).

Thomas and Znaniecki produce a complex notion of individual adaptation to social life by arguing that within a particular group at a given moment there are upper and lower limits to change and stability that are possible – the process is not simply by adaptation or non-adaptation. In summary, Thomas and Znaniecki's notion of individual adaptation including a number of 'parallel and interdependent processes':

> Thus, the whole process of development of the personality as ruled in various proportions by the desire for new experience and the desire for stability on the individual side, by the tendency to suppress and the tendency to develop personal possibilities on the social side, includes the following parallel and the interdependent processes: 1. Determination of the character on the ground of the temperament; 2. Constitution of a life-organization which permits a more or less complete objective expression of the various attitudes included in the character; 3. Adaptation of the character to social demands put upon the personality; 4. Adaptation of individual life-organization to social organization. (Thomas and Znaniecki, 1958, II:1862-3)

The rapidity of modern social change, they argue, has an important effect on these processes, and the personality types that result:

> It was Thomas' and Znaniecki's judgment that the development of the modern world, particularly the forces bringing the primary group rapidly into contact with the outside world with its new and rival schemes, tends to shatter the old organization, increasing the numbers of Philistines and Bohemians. (Martindale, 1961:352)

In fact, Thomas and Znaniecki provide three general types of 'personal determination'– the 'Philistine', the 'Bohemian' and, also, the 'Creative Man'';

while social personalities tend towards these in their evolution, none of these is 'ever completely and absolutely realized by a human individual in all lines of activity' (Thomas and Znaniecki, 1958, II:1856; Coser, 1977:516). Finally, Thomas and Znaniecki claimed:

> The study of human personalities, both as factors and as products of social evolution, serves first of all the same purpose as the study of any other social data – the determination of social laws. (Thomas and Znaniecki, 1958, II:1831)

When applied to the 'practical' problems of immigration and 'Americanization' of individual adaptation, Thomas and Znaniecki conclude that popular conceptions are too simple. The question of individual assimilation or non-assimilation is not the main issue. Instead, the 'fundamental process' is the formation of a new Polish-American society from 'those fragments separated from Polish society and embedded in American society' (Thomas and Znaniecki, 1958, II:1468-9). In this view, 'adaptation' is not simply a new pattern of behaviour due to new external circumstance or merely a 'state' achieved at a given time. Rather, it is to be regarded as a 'process of the widening or narrowing of the sphere of adaptation', regardless of whether there is satisfaction with particular conditions or the desire for stability is stronger than that for new experience (Thomas and Znaniecki, 1958, II:1876-8).

Social Situations

The important notion of the 'definition of the situation' is influenced by a broadly 'pragmatist' (as in Dewey) conception of action in which 'Every concrete activity is the solution of a situation' (Thomas and Znaniecki, 1958, I:68; see Martindale, 1961:349; also Mills, 1964, 1970a, 1970b). Although the term has become famous and is often cited, perhaps its complexity has not always been fully recognised - since it relates to three areas. First, there are 'objective conditions' of action or the 'totality of values', e.g. economic, social, intellectual, which at a given time 'affect directly or indirectly the conscious status of the individual or the group'. Secondly, there are the already held attitudes of an individual or group which have an immediate influence at a certain time. Thirdly, there is 'the definition of the situation' itself – 'the more or less clear conception of the conditions and consciousness of the attitudes'. It is required prior to 'any act of the will', commonly using a 'process of reflection' followed by either the application by conscious definition of a 'ready social definition' (as similar to a previous situation) or a 'new personal definition worked out' (Thomas and Znaniecki, 1958, I:68-9). Therefore, the individual is active in defining situations:

> this is what society expects him to do when it requires of him a stable life-organization... The uniformity of behavior it tends to impose upon the

individual is not a uniformity of organic habits but of consciously followed rules. The individual, in order to control social reality for his needs, must develop not series of uniform reactions, but general schemes of situations; his life-organization is a set of rules for definite situations, which may be even expressed in abstract formulas. Moral principles, legal prescription, economic forms, religious rites, social customs, etc. are examples of schemes. (Thomas and Znaniecki, 1958: II:1852-3)

Social Disorganisation and Social Re-organisation

Central to *The Polish Peasant* investigation is an identification of the destabilising factors acting upon social organisation – so readily witnessed in migration. Thomas and Znaniecki conceive social disorganisation as a loss of influence of current social rules on the behaviour of group members and distinguish between its effects on the younger and older generations (Thomas and Znaniecki, 1958, II: 1206-7). It is not an unusual phenomenon but the breaking of rules influencing group institutions, if not 'counteracted', can become widespread. The stability of organisation depends upon the dynamic between disorganisation and a re-organisation brought by constructive efforts. In emigration - movement from the countryside to the city, and to other countries - new attitudes can arise due to new social values which interact with existing attitudes and erode family organisation (to varying extents) in both rural and urban areas (Thomas and Znaniecki, 1958, II: 1135). Re-organisation and stability is made possible where new attitudes are formed which support new values and match changed circumstances.

The authors argue that the social disorganisation or 'decay' of the economic solidarity of the peasant family is influenced by 'new personal needs' - 'hedonistic' individual pleasures (e.g. new foods and drink) or a 'demand for social recognition' separate from the family (e.g. the 'showing off' of clothes etc.). In Poland, there had been growth in individual interests of advancement and rather than the family's investment in land and farming income. Finally, the shifts in individual attitudes are related to the general changes affecting even remote villages – the pace of communication bringing a greater number, variety and depth of wider contacts, with industrialisation making possible the spread of new attitudes. Peasant traditional values, while allowing for some change, were being met by deeper challenges. A greater adaptation to the disorganising influences on communal solidarity, moral control, standards and opinion of the new context was required, hence the importance of new institutions and new attitudes to social re-organisation (Thomas and Znaniecki, 1958, II:1139, 1303-6; Madge, 1963:78-9).

At the end of their 'Methodological Note', Thomas and Znaniecki hold that their study of *The Polish Peasant* had given 'a good starting-point' for addressing a number of important problems:- the extent that 'individualization' is possible with 'social cohesion'; efficiency between individual and society according to individual attitudes and types of social organization; how far 'abnormality', such as crime, is due to 'inborn tendencies' of 'social conditions'; the increasing number of occupations of little stimulation and interest brought by the modern division of labour; relations between the sexes; 'social happiness'; 'the fight of races (nationalities) and cultures'; and, related to the latter, the 'ideal organization of culture' (Thomas and Znaniecki, 1958, I:78-86). Such conflicts could be tackled not by the 'destruction of historical differences' but by 'recognition of their value' and by greater 'reciprocal acquaintance and estimation'. This list demonstrates the great ambition and scope of the study – how migration highlights major societal and sociological issues. They end by a call for 'systematic sociological study of various cultures' to help solve conflicts (Thomas and Znaniecki, 1958, I: 86).

Source Materials

An outstanding feature of *The Polish Peasant* is the variety and extensive nature of source materials:

Letters

Thomas and Znaniecki made immense use of letters sent between immigrants in America and their families and others in Poland. The more than 700 separate letters presented were divided under fifty family names. The letters were gathered were from different parts of Poland and, in fact, from a wide strata of 'peasants': 'from the nobility – not quite the aristocracy, but landed farming families – at one end to the manor peasants, who were only slightly higher than serfs, at the other'; and also the 'peasant proletariat' who did waged seasonal work from farm to farm and some letters between peasants now resident in towns (Madge, 1963:56). Thomas and Znaniecki believed that these letters were the 'concrete materials' upon which their description and analysis of peasant life was founded.

The letters were obtained by an advertisement in American Polish émigré newspapers and 20 cents per item was apparently offered - this was not clearly stated in the study (although mentioned in a letter and by Wladek) or how many letters were gathered and (so) how a selection was made (Thomas and Znaniecki, 1958, I:400; II: 2223; Madge, 1963:56). The editors introduce each series of letters, with an interpretation on members' outlook, familial relations and culture, and social position – there are also detailed footnotes.

Newspapers

A second source of materials was numerous documents and the records of a Polish newspaper bought by Thomas during a visit to Poland. It was only during the later conference in 1938 on the book that some of the background of these materials, including how they were gained, was given. Even so:

> ... we do not know how many original documents there were, but Thomas mentioned that all together these and certain other documents he had brought back totaled 8,000... Most of the other material was from published sources, such as copies of newspapers. (Madge, 1963:57)

A mass of documents were also obtained by Thomas's assistant Mr. Kulikowski but these were left behind as he hurriedly left Poland with the outbreak of WWI (Thomas in Blumer, 1979:105).

Organisational Documents

A further set of materials came from various organisations. Znaniecki was Director of the Emigrants Protective Society in Warsaw (1911-14) which dealt with people seeking to leave Poland and information was collected from this source. Other materials were from Polish organisations in America (termed 'superterritorial organizations'), various parishes, a Legal Aid Society, charities, Cook County Criminal Court and the Coroner's Office.

The Life-Record of the Immigrant

The authors used both existing documents as well as a requested (311 page) 'Life- Record of an Immigrant', by Wladek Wiszniewski.[72] The life-record is given a substantial introduction that outlines a series of theoretical ideas, has detailed comments in footnotes throughout, and a summary of 17 pages. The use of the 'life-record' approach is used overall to demonstrate the disorganizing effects of social change on the individual, as in the case Wladek's transition from peasant society in Poland to lower class life in America.

Wladek is described as a 'typical representative of the culturally passive mass' – while aspects of his personal evolution have an importance 'far beyond his milieu and his time' (Thomas and Znaniecki, 1958, II:1907, 1911). Wladek describes his village, travels in search for work, and relations with women and family. The account is generally about his life before his migration to America, but towards the end he outlines more recent work and housing difficulties, family problems and the birth of his son. Thomas and Znaniecki summarised Wladek's life as 'an alternation of periods during which he drifts into Bohemianism with periods of Philistinization, and shows a gradual increase of Philistine tendencies in the total curve of its evolution'. He is someone who has broken with the 'old forms of social life without being able to construct any new personal life-organization' (Thomas and Znaniecki, 1958, II:1908, 1910-11). More prosaically, Madge, says:

---

[72] Interestingly, the 'The Life-Record of an Immigrant' is moved from the middle (3rd) volume in the 5 volume edition to the end of the second volume in the 2 volume edition. An extensive review of Wladek's life-record is given by Dollard (1935).

He makes himself out to be at times a somewhat doubtful character... At the same time most of the events he describes are presented as ending in his favor, though in practice it is clear that economically and socially he is actually drifting down. (Madge, 1963:60)

Thomas and Znaniecki gave a number of specific interrelated purposes of Wladek's personal life record. First, the authors regard the life record as being superior in characterising attitudes and values. Secondly, because it can show clearly the processes associated with attitudes and values, it can enable the formation of abstract generalisations or social laws. Thirdly, in outlining 'single facts,' the life-record can show the 'evolution' of the personality as a whole. Fourthly, the life-record can showe the emergence of an 'attitude' within an individual's evolution or 'typical lines of genesis' (Thomas and Znaniecki, 1958, II: 1832-39). The tracing of this individual 'evolutionary process' provides the basis for the construction of types and a theory of personality. Broadly, Thomas and Znaniecki held that as the life-record can demonstrate the emergence of new individual attitudes and new social values and their interplay – it has use for scientific generalisation and can contribute to the solution of a widespread social problem (Thomas and Znaniecki, 1958, II:1834).

Research Techniques and Substantive Concerns

Bulmer (1983) usefully outlines the connection between the 'research techniques' used and the corresponding 'substantive concerns' of *The Polish Peasant*. First, the substantive concern with the organisation of the primary groups of family and community and the changes (i.e. marriage and the peasant family, religion, the class system and the socio-economic context) brought by migration and industrial isolation are considered through the private letters. Secondly, the life-record of Wladek, as a peasant immigrant to America now in 'lower class' Chicago, is reproduced to outline individual disorganisation and the experience of transition. Thirdly, Bulmer says the substantive concern with the 'strains and tensions within the primary group in Poland, and its social and political re-organisation on modern rather than traditional lines' is discussed according to five problems: '(1) leadership (2) education of the peasants (3) the press (4) co-operative organisations (5) role of the peasant class in the nation'. Here, the 'third-person' materials on Polish life are used (i.e. records of Polish newspapers, and the Bureau for the Protection of Emigrants). Finally, the type and degree of social disorganisation experienced by the immigrant - 'demoralisation, economic dependency, breakdown of the conjugal relation, crime, etc.' - is investigated by 'third-person' materials from court and social work agencies and Polish-American organisations Included here is the emergence of communal self-help in the creation of Polish-American organisations (Bulmer, 1983:472, see Bulmer, 1984).

It is important, not to take the various extensive materials and their substantive concerns as separate elements of the study - they are part of a general conception. For example, Wladek's life-record should not be understood simply in its own terms but within the wider analysis of society given in *The Polish Peasant*:

> All of the five volumes of their study are related to Wladek's autobiography, at least in the sense that they constitute a monumental definition of the society into which Wladek came. Without reference to the cultural background thus delineated, his life would seem very strange indeed and must seem so to readers who study it alone. This background is not defined, point for point, in following the autobiography of Wladek, but it swings like a massive frame to the document, and one finds constantly that one can bring to bear on the document itself one's knowledge of the Polish culture as defined from the other materials. Shifts in the social picture, such as the realignment of classes or break-up of older forms, are also indicated; indeed Wladek himself is a resultant and partly a victim of such changes. (Dollard, 1935:147-8)

Evaluation

The impact of *The Polish Peasant* is indicated by the detailed assessment undertaken for the SSRC by Herbert Blumer (1939, 1979) and the subsequent conference to discuss his commentary. Herbert Blumer's (1939) 'appraisal' of *The Polish Peasant* was part of a wider evaluation of life or personal documents in the social sciences in the 1930s and 1940s, notably by Dollard (1935), Allport (1942) and Gottschalk et al., (1945). Earlier, Burgess (1928) had discussed the usefulness of social case records by social workers for sociological research. The development of both life-record or case record methods and statistical techniques during the inter-war period led to an important debate on their respective qualities (Plummer, 2001:108-9).

Blumer's Critique

Blumer, despite his criticisms, gives a number of 'important contributions' of *The Polish Peasant* accounting for its 'profound influence': it showed the 'need' for the study of the 'subjective factor' in social life, the use of 'human documents' as sources, and introduced the 'life history technique'. Thomas and Znaniecki also gave a theoretical 'framework' of social psychology and sociology and a 'statement' which contributed to sociology as a scientific discipline. Blumer noted that the study had important theorisation in areas such as personality, social control, disorganisation, and the 'four wishes'. He stated the study had a 'rich content of insights, provocative generalizations, and shrewd observations' and the portrait of 'Polish peasant society'. Finally, he noted that perhaps the main importance of the study was its 'stimulation' to social research

(Blumer, 1979: 81-2). He gave particular attention to conceptualisation – the relation between the concepts used and the data – how much arose from the data and how much was pre-existing. For example, on the letters presented in *The Polish Peasant*, he argued that that while it appeared the authors considered them very carefully and gained ideas that were theoretically helpful, even so, they had a pre-existing broad theoretical framework which often shaped ('coerced') interpretation. Thus, while the letters were not simply 'inductive materials' neither were they simply illustrative of a theoretical approach – the relationship remains 'exceedingly ambiguous' (Blumer, 1979:37-8). Blumer says that the use of human documents did not pass scientific principles (i.e. representativeness, adequacy, reliability, decisiveness). It seemed that documents could not 'prove' or 'disprove' theoretical statements but helped to 'support' them, while in turn theory 'illuminated' and 'clarified' data (Blumer, 1979:xii).

Later, Blumer (in 1979) summarised his Critique by saying that the authors had shown very clearly that 'subjective dispositions' lay behind social action and should be part of sociological analysis – even if the definitions of the concepts of 'attitude' and 'value' and the attempt to formulate 'laws of social becoming' could be questioned:

> The Polish Peasant set a series of methodological problems of the gravest import to sociology… These methodological problems remain even though sociologists in the pursuit of new interests are disposed to ignore them. The problems remain because they inevitably arise as soon as one recognizes that human beings in either their individual or collective capacity act by confronting and defining the situations in which their action takes place. The recognition forces scholars to bring 'subjective' factors into consideration. Once this is done, the methodological problems have to be faced. (Blumer, 1979:xxxvii)

Blumer's assessment has been revisited in recent years due the wider development of qualitative methods. For instance, Plummer has questioned Blumer's approach:

> so stringent were his criteria that in general he found the report to be a scientific failure… the representativeness of each document was not established; that the adequacy of each document for the purposes for which they were employed was not proved; that their reliability was not checked by independent sources; and, finally, that the validity of the interpretation drawn from any single document was not demonstrated… 'these may not be the best criteria for evaluating such documents. (Plummer, 2001:110)

In fact, the basis on which to 'evaluate' personal documents has been a central part of discussions within recent qualitative research.

The Life-Record

The methodological and theoretical issues, raised by *The Polish Peasant*, can be seen in detail, for example, in relation to the use of the life-record. Thomas and Znaniecki argued (famously) for the use of 'life-records':

> We are safe in saying that personal life-records, as complete as possible, constitute the perfect type of sociological material, and that if social science has to use other materials at all it is only because of the practical difficulty of obtaining at the moment a sufficient number of such records to cover the totality of sociological problems, and of the enormous amount of work demanded for an adequate analysis of all the personal materials necessary to characterize the life of a social group. (Thomas and Znaniecki, 1958, II:1832-3)

Madge helpfully gives a concise summary of Wladek's life and some of the main issues:

> Wladek had lived in Poland until shortly before the end of his story, which is essentially about his experiences in Poland. He was induced to write this story by Thomas' offer of payment. He became so enthusiastic when he began to write that he set about his task very rapidly, and about three months later he delivered an immensely long but well-constructed story of his life. The authors themselves admit that they could use only half of what Wladek had written, and as the printed version is 300 pages long, it was quite a novel, Here again there are considerable difficulties about the truthfulness of what Wladek writes, so his story has to be considered a variety of levels. The first question is, Was he sincere? (Madge, 1963:60)

The authors stated regarding Wladek's document that while he was asked to write for money, the 'main motives' became 'ambition', 'literary interest' and 'interest in his own life' (Thomas and Znaniecki, 1958, II:1912). It was held to be 'representative' of immigrant transition and was possibly part of a number collected (Madge, 1963:61). Thomas and Znaniecki say that they did not make any additions except the ones noted and that Wladek has a degree of 'real literary talent'. The 'sincerity' of the document is 'unmistakable' as shown in the 'self-complacency of the author' who 'thought everything about him as interesting to others as it was to himself' (Thomas and Znaniecki, 1958, II:1912). Letters were also received from Wladek (and some from his sister) but only a few short extracts of these are given at the end of the life-record.

Again, Blumer's Critique, questioned the document according to 'scientific criteria' (e.g. the reliability and truthfulness of the document) (Blumer, 1979:44-5). Even so, he concluded (in his new Introduction) that Thomas and Znaniecki's use of life histories 'exemplifies abundantly' their possibilities as an 'instrument of naturalistic studies'; they 'permit one to identify the lines of formation which lead over time to the emergence of given personality types among individuals and given cultural patterns and social arrangements in group life' (Blumer, 1979:xxvi). Thomas (at the SSRC conference on the study) responded strongly to Blumer's Critique:

> Blumer here, and others elsewhere, have criticized the 'human document' as incomplete and unreliable, and this is correct in the sense that all human testimony and communication tend to be reserved, biased, and directed toward the production of desired attitudes in others'... [But] 'even a highly subjective, delusional, or fabricated document has significance, since it represents attitudes which may pass into action... In *The Polish Peasant*, the main line of inquiry was concerned with the problem of immigration and the changing attitudes and values in the movement of hundreds of thousands of the members of one cultural group into another cultural group, viewed in terms of individual and group organization and disorganization. At the same time, we had in mind the bearing of the results of this specific investigation on social problems in general. (Thomas in Blumer, 1979:84-6)

Thomas added:

> I regret a little bit the use of the words 'perfect document,' but I think the narrative of experience by the individual, whether guided or unguided, is basic, the starting point, in the study of motivation. (Thomas in Blumer, 1979:133)

Theory

Blumer recognised the importance of the theoretical ideas and insights of the study – for example, the contribution to the ideas of attitudes and values but questioned how these were defined and related – as in the formation of 'laws of becoming'. The notion of the 'four wishes' was a little inconsistent and can be considered as an initial device to establish a more 'social' notion of adaptation to a social environment. As Martindale argues, the 'four wishes' may be seen 'as a transitional phase in modern social theory during a time when the instinct theory of conduct was being abandoned'.[73] For Thomas, they were perhaps a 'convenient classification' using it 'somewhat differently in different places' (Martindale, 1961: 348-9, footnote; see Znaniecki, 1948:767). The subsequent challenges to the simplicity of various notions, such as the 'four wishes' and 'personality types' or, even if given later attention, a charge of imprecision, as in use 'attitudes' and 'values' (or at least in their connection) may have led to the

---

[73] Thomas and Znaniecki's used the notion of 'wishes' as an attempt to 'socialise' the biological idea of individual adaptation (Martindale, 1961:348-9).

neglect of much of the detailed conceptualisation and the broader theoretical perspective of *The Polish Peasant*.[74]

Martindale argues that Thomas tended to abandon ideas, such as those on personality and the four wishes, when challenged, and 'even became very defensive about his use of the case history'. It seems 'little was left except the notion of 'definition of the situation'' (Martindale, 1961:353). Martindale states that had it not been for a defensiveness following the loss of his job due to personal problems it seems Thomas would have pursued the comparative and general theoretical approach – with its 'applied' intent – heralded in *The Polish Peasant* and begun in Old World Traits Transplanted (1975, 1921). His 'fullest synthesis of symbolic interactionism remains the theoretical sections of *The Polish Peasant*'. The study shows in its 'practical' orientation and theoretical approach to action that at 'every critical point Thomas' affinities are with the pragmatists and symbolic interactionists' (Martindale, 1961:349).

Status of *The Polish Peasant*

The Polish Peasant in Europe and America was the first important research study undertaken in the Department of Sociology at Chicago (Bulmer, 1983: 470; 1984). It still has a prominent status in the development of sociological research:

> *The Polish Peasant* has a lasting significance as one of the most important methodological contributions to the establishment of the social as a distinct and legitimate area of enquiry. It rejected entirely any element of biological reductionism and sought to explain ethnic social behaviour in terms of sociological and social psychological categories. (Bulmer, 1983:474)

For Redfield, the study was a 'turning point', similarly, Coser describes *The Polish Peasant* a 'great landmark' in the early history of American sociology (Allport, 1942:vii; Coser, 1977:518):

> It was the peculiar genius of Thomas and Znaniecki to balance their emphasis on attitudes, subjectively defined meanings, and shared experience, by an equally strong emphasis on the objective characteristics of cultural values and their embodiment in specific institutions. (Coser, 1977:515)

While the contribution to sociological research of *The Polish Peasant* has been traditionally widely acknowledged, possibly reference to it has been renewed in

---

[74] Coser compares 'Personality types' in *The Polish Peasant* with Weber's ideal types, they are not real' individuals. He says the idea had some later influence on David Riesman and others (Coser, 1977:516-7).

recent years, in part due to the very extensive growth in life story or biographical research, and qualitative methods generally (see Plummer, 2001; Roberts, 2002). But, perhaps there still has been not enough consideration of how life stories and other personal documents can used, as in *The Polish Peasant*, as part of a mix of methods and related substantive concerns, and informed by a theoretical orientation that interlinks individual personality and culture. Finally, as Smith says:

> *The Polish Peasant* was staggeringly ambitious and remains impressive. Within a single intellectual framework were contained a comparison between processes of change in late nineteenth-century and early twentieth-century Poland and America. (Smith, 1988:103)

Old World Traits Transplanted (1921) – 'the 6th volume'

W. I. Thomas's *Old World Traits Transplanted* (1975) was concerned with a range of immigrant groups and the work of various agencies. It was produced as part of a series of volumes funded by the Carnegie Corporation on 'Methods of Americanization' or 'The acculturation of immigrant groups into American Society'. The study (as stated earlier) was originally attributed to Robert E. Park and Herbert A. Miller; it was not until 1951 that Thomas was credited as the main author (see Young, 1975:vii-viii; Janowitz, 1966; Smith, 1988:108-9)). The investigation could be considered a 'sixth volume' of *The Polish Peasant* following Thomas and Znaniecki's call for a comparative approach to immigrant groups. In the new volume, alongside the Polish community – Italians, Chinese, Japanese, Mexicans, Jews, Bohemians and Scandinavians were now examined. There are strong connections between the studies, for instance, Angell (in 1945) queried whether there had been access material from the earlier study due to the large number of Polish documents and the footnotes to *The Polish Peasant*. Also, a great deal of theory appeared to originate from Thomas and Znaniecki's study. Angell concluded:

> One might perhaps with fairness say that Old World Traits Transplanted is largely an attempt to discover to what degree the findings of *The Polish Peasant* regarding the acculturation of Poles to American life can be generalized for all immigrant groups. (Angell, 1945:204)

Old World Traits Transplanted is concerned with questions of 'immigrant heritages' - particularly 'antagonisms' and 'assimilation'. Immigrant heritages are said to relate to the 'regulation' of the 'four fundamental wishes' and the 'adjustment to individualistic society'. 'Immigrant experiences' are also described, including 'demoralization', 'immigrant types'; 'immigrant institutions'; 'immigrant communities'; and 'types of community influence'. Finally, the 'reconciliation' of heritages is discussed in relation to democracy, similarities in heritages, the psychology of assimilation, tolerance versus suppression, immigrant organization, and a concluding argument concerning the 'perpetuation' of groups.

Angell neatly summarises Thomas's theoretical argument in Old World Traits Transplanted, as follows:

> Immigrant heritages contain different systems of values and attitudes. Personal wishes are worked out in terms of the type of social organization in which people find themselves, and it is in this process that cultural values and attitudes are formed. Most immigrants come from a primary group type of situation which has characteristic attitudes and values. When an immigrant comes to this country he finds himself in a different type of society, one based on modern communication. Reorganization is greatly aided by immigrant institutions, which interpret American ways to the new arrivals, and by residence in an immigrant community here. (Angell, 1945:204)

For Thomas (1975) an immigrant enters America with a particular set of wishes, which shape behaviour. It may be that in a specific case a certain wish, such as desire for security, is strongest but, generally, it is the organisation of wishes that forms the character. The latter is partly shaped by temperamental elements (as 'Swedes' or some other group) which may be associated with 'original, inborn, temperamental dispositions'. However, he argues that an individual's or group's character is mainly formed by the social process or the 'definition of the situation' – 'by the whole of the experiences and social influences which modify, qualify, and organize the wishes' (Thomas, 1975: 81). Coser notes that the 'situational' analysis found in the investigation was used in his other work (as it had in *The Polish Peasant*) across a series of subjects:

> In all of them, Thomas clung to his view that society and individuals should always be conceived of as being involved in reciprocal interaction… He was much more aware than Cooley of the crises and dislocations that are bound at times to disrupt the harmonious interplay between them. (Coser, 1977:522; see Thomas and Thomas, 1928).

Thomas notes that representatives of different immigrant groups claim a 'similar social value' - that due to their 'racial peculiarities' and 'past experiences' they have developed 'individualized functions as groups'. So, they argue, that by 'permanently organizing along the lines of their aptitudes they will not only express their peculiar genius, but contribute unique values to America' (Thomas, 1975:299-300). Thomas argues against this position since it would only apply if immigrant groups were 'specialized by heredity' to take part in artistic, occupational or other practices. Instead, not even the 'most distinct races' can be separated in this manner and points to anthropologists (e.g. Boas) who argue that 'if such differences exist they are not very great' (Thomas, 1975:301-2). Thomas does not object to immigrant groups attempting to remain separate just as he would be against compelling such affiliation. However, the 'peculiarities' of such groups is not due to 'inborn or ineradicable traits' but to a 'long train of common experiences'. It would seem that there are only three ways to remain culturally separate – new generations being formed without losing traditional memories, by developing and sustaining superior values to those in America, and an 'ineradicable prejudice on one or both sides' (Thomas, 1975:303-4). Thomas adds that 'individuals and groups cling to their memories only so long as they are practically or sentimentally useful', while there are many cases of a 'superior culture' maintaining a long separation from a 'culturally inferior group'. In America, he observes, any immigrant group which is separate 'voluntarily' or by 'geographical isolation' will be culturally 'pauperized'. Thomas concludes that the 'question of prejudice and discrimination may be put aside as not serious enough in America to affect the persistence of immigrant groups' (Thomas, 1975:304-6).

Thomas put forward that it is possible to identify some broad immigrant types from different heritages. Even so, while there may be a great deal of homogeneity within certain groups, the difference between, for example, the 'intellectual Pole' and a Polish peasant is 'as profound as possible'. In all groups, specific individuals will be more similar to individuals in some other groups The types he identifies are usually 'not pure' and meant to represent types of attitudes brought to America by immigration rather than attempting to reflect immigrant groups in their 'totality' (Thomas, 1975:82-3). The discussion of types of immigrant experience introduced in *The Polish Peasant* (i.e. Bohemian, Philistine, and Creative Individual) is extended in the new account – including 'The Settler', 'The colonist', 'The Political Idealist', 'The Allrightnik', 'The Cafone', and 'The Intellectual':

> Each of these types, he suggested, reacted to the immigrant experience in a distinctive and characteristic manner. Typological distinctions, he felt, were most useful in breaking down global categories such as 'immigrants' into subcategories, displaying distinctive behaviors in their interaction with the host community. (Coser, 1977:522-3)

Thomas argues that immigrant organizations currently appear to enhance separateness but, in fact, exist to 'overcome' division. They are 'signs, not of the perpetuation of immigrant groups... but of their assimilation'. Such organisations are only of interest to the immigrant in so far they 'understand and supply' the needs of the immigrant (Thomas, 1975:306-7). However, here there is criticism of some Polish organisations – which in resisting Americanization have 'abandoned their unfit and misadapted' individuals to other welfare organisations, legal aid and the juvenile courts (Thomas,

1975:229).[75] Thus, in the Polish community there is a dearth of organizations that help members in 'adjusting' to 'complex American life'. Where Polish organisations try to meet all the needs of the individual immigrant, participation in 'American life and institutions' is restricted - a situation that 'contributes heavily through crime and poverty' and so to governmental costs (Thomas, 1975:232-4). For Thomas (as Angell observes), immigrant organisations are of central importance:

> From the practical standpoint... democracy requires that immigrants become a working part of a unified system. If they are to participate in public affairs they must live and think in the same social world as the natives or complete chaos will result. The problem is, therefore, to reconcile the heritages... this actually takes place by immigrants discovering those elements in our culture that 'click' with the apperception mass derived from their own culture. Once this point of connection is established, the process of acculturation ramifies rapidly. It therefore becomes of practical importance to help them make these connections as early and as intensively as possible. The value of immigrant organizations is great at this point. (Angell, 1945:204)

Thomas, echoing themes in a vital debate today, concluded that the 'assimilation' of immigrant groups was both inevitable and desirable:

> Through point after point of contact, as they find situations in America intelligible to them in the light of old knowledge and experience, they identify themselves with us. We can delay or hasten this development. We cannot stop it. If we give the immigrants a favorable milieu, if we tolerate their strangeness during their period of adjustment, if we give them freedom to make their own connections between old and new experiences, if we help them to find points of contact, then we hasten their assimilation. This is a process of growth as against the 'ordering and forbidding' policy and the demand that the assimilation of the immigrant shall be 'sudden, complete, and bitter'. And this is the completely democratic process, for we cannot have a political democracy unless we have a social democracy also. (Thomas, 1975:308)

---

[75] In at least part of *The Polish Peasant*, the emphasis is on the evolution of a Polish-American society, especially among the second generation who are taking on American attitudes. The new immigrant must adapt to this Polish-American society made from 'fragments' of both its origins (see, Thomas and Znaniecki, 1958, II: 1468-70).

The 'Migrations' of W. I. Thomas and F. Znaniecki

Migration was not only recognised as a major social and political issue for Thomas and Znaniecki, it also had a very personal referent – their own 'migrations'. Personal reflection, academic interests, the authors' own movements and the social context of migration were intertwined. An important feature of *The Polish Peasant* study is its 'transnational' character. It is not only a study of Poles in Chicago but also the process of transition from Poland to America (often from rural backgrounds to the cities in Poland, and then to work in Germany and the U.S) – and of social change in Poland itself. Both authors recounted their own journeys and experiences and could be considered 'transnational' individuals: for instance, both had travelled and studied widely in Europe before the embarking on *The Polish Peasant*, and Znaniecki, of course, was a Polish migrant to the U.S. Thomas and Znaniecki were not only aware of how the collection of life histories could be used to analyse the lives of others, they also considered their own lives and 'transformations' in autobiographical accounts.[76] As Blumer comments, on the use of life histories to understand personal change in regard to *The Polish Peasant*:

> Anyone who has taken the time to read *The Polish Peasant* must remain impressed by the way in which life histories provide telling data for the analysis of group and individual transformation (Blumer, 1979:xxvi-xxvii)

W. I. Thomas (1863-1947)

W.I. Thomas graduated in 1884 from the University of Tennessee. He studied in Germany (Berlin and Gottingen) during 1888-89 where he was influenced by the folk psychology of Lazarus and Steinthal (Martindale, 1961:347).[77] Not only

---

[76] This article does not attempt to be a comprehensive review of the various autobiographical writings on Thomas and Znaniecki and Park (or biographical commentaries).

[77] An instructive comparison here can be made with the life and work of Thomas's and Robert E. Park (1864-1944). Park also considered the effects of migration on individual outlook as in 'Human Migration and Marginal Man' (Park, 1928; see Smith, 1988:123-7). Park (like Znaniecki) was invited to Chicago by Thomas, and had similar concerns with immigration and its personal and social effects and was another advocate of the life history. Park studied in Germany (as did Thomas), had been a city newspaper reporter and secretary to Booker T. Washington with whom he wrote The Man Farthest Down (1984, 1911) on peasant labour (and emigration and return), in Poland and other parts of Europe following a tour in 1910. Interestingly, for both Thomas (in 1909) and Park (in 1910) it was their visits to Europe to study peasant backgrounds and issues of migration that gave their intellectual development a focus (Thomas and Park, in Baker, 1973: 249,258-9). Park later became involved in Thomas's Old World Traits Transplanted (1975). Both pursued the linkages between culture and personality in their work. Park's notion of the marginal man as an 'emancipated individual' (Park, 1928:888; see also Park, 1925) seems similar to the 'creative individual' in *The Polish Peasant* (Thomas and Znaniecki, 1958, II:1853-9), and Thomas's 'intellectual' immigrant (Thomas, 1975:104-117).

did Thomas move from rural origins to urban life in Chicago – he also travelled to Europe with an interest in European nationalities. He reports in a published 'life history', that following his doctorate in 1896 he travelled in Europe as far as the Volga and had an idea for comparative research on European nationalities but lacked experience and means of support for such a study (Thomas in Baker, 1973: 248-9). He wrote that prior to around 1909 he did not remember being 'thoughtful' in outlook but was 'exploratory', having a 'wanderlust'. However, he began to change and went to Europe again with the idea of a study of European 'peasant backgrounds' related to the problem of immigration (Thomas in Baker, 1973:249).

Thomas relates that his past seemed very 'remote' due to the recent changes in modern society that divided him and others 'profoundly' from early life. He adds that in his case this 'separation' seemed particularly wide:

> I was born in an isolated region of old Virginia, 20 miles from the railroad, in a social environment resembling that of the 18th century, and I consequently feel that I have lived in three centuries, migrating gradually toward the higher cultural areas. (Thomas, in Baker 1973:246)

His migration, therefore, had been across 'time' and 'space' – from rural to urban America, to a more 'complex' intellectual arena – also involving trips to study and explore groups and migration in parts of Europe.

Interestingly, Thomas says he was around forty years old before he had a critical orientation towards books and opinions. He describes his main interest in his 'sociological history' as being in the 'new experience of concrete types'; he even portrays himself as an 'extrovert leading an introvert life'. This description of his own personality is of interest because of his analysis (with Znaniecki) of Wladek and the formation of bohemian, philistine and creative types in migration (Thomas in Baker, 1973:250; Roberts, 2002; Smith, 1988:107-8). Given the circumstances of Thomas's departure from Chicago it seems that some did not merely consider him a 'creative individual' but a rather an unacceptable 'bohemian' (Smith, 1988:108-9).

Florian Znaniecki (1882-1958)

Florian Znaniecki studied at the University of Warsaw but was expelled by the Russian authorities for political activities (Martindale, 1961:418). In 1905, he extended his education at the University of Geneva, and then at the Sorbonne and the University of Cracow. In 1913, while working at the Society for Protection of Emigrants, an organisation in Warsaw which was founded to advise and help emigrants, he was visited by W.I. Thomas. The latter was looking to 'obtain concrete, factual material about the sociocultural background of various immigrant groups in the Unites States' from Eastern Europe (Znaniecki, 1948:765). Thomas invited Znaniecki to Chicago to 'translate and edit his material, perhaps collect some more material from the Poles in this country'. Znaniecki arrived in the U.S. in 1914 and after about a year and a half as Thomas's assistant was offered 'partnership in the whole work' (Znaniecki, 1948: 766). Znaniecki returned to (an independent) Poland in 1920 as a professor at the University of Poznan. He founded the Polish Review of Sociology and the Polish Institute for Sociology and became President of the Polish Sociological Society. Due to WWII he returned to America to join Columbia University, before moving to the University of Illinois and retiring in 1950. He was made President of the American Sociological Society in 1955 (Martindale, 1961:418).

A short (five page) anonymous 'autobiography' (included under the heading 'The Intellectual') attributed to Znaniecki was published in Old World Traits Transplanted as part of a number of other types of immigrant (Thomas, 1975:107-112). An editorial introduction maintains that it is the 'educated' immigrant (unless a chemist, engineer, etc.) rather than the worker who is more likely to be 'misadapted' and be less well received by American society. The intellectual may have been a 'failure' at home and may judge that America does not 'appreciate him'; but, due to 'superior and systematic training', the intellectual can 'contribute particular values to the culture of any nationality'. The writer of the autobiography is said to be a 'really superior man' whose account contains both a criticism of America and shows the 'psychology of the Polish intellectual' (Thomas, 1975:107).

The autobiographical statement begins with a positive assessment of America, including its 'democratic idea', 'social idealism', and welfare of others. But in other respects he felt a separation from American life and 'Americanization', for two reasons: First, this was due to a realization of the 'divergences' between the dominant 'aspirations' in America and his own 'ideals' informed by a 'cosmopolitan training', he has 'learned to revere as the best part of the general human civilization, independent of national differences. Secondly, and 'more particularly – the attitude of American society toward foreigners and foreign values…' (Thomas, 1975:107-8).

While criticising the 'lack of social freedom… particularly as it extends to the intellectual domain', the author expresses an interest in the future of America, the 'progress' of intellectual life and in making a contribution to 'really important cultural values". Unfortunately, America seemed to have a 'self-complacency' and is in 'general perfectly satisfied with itself' to need the "forcigner's" co-operation' (Thomas, 1975:108-9). In Europe, in countries familiar to the author, there is an 'intellectual hospitality', a willingness to learn and apply the values that the foreign intellectual brings. For the author, even allowing for any 'role which Polish national ideals' have played, his own 'psychology seems… less specifically national' than anyone else (American or European) he had met, even having 'actively participated', adapting and 'mixing intimately' in intellectual life in France, Switzerland and America. The author's 'bias' was a 'professional' one – a commitment to the 'scientific profession' and what it can benefit society, one independent of individual differences and membership of religion, class and race (Thomas, 1975:111-2). In this autobiographical account of a 'Polish intellectual' by Znaniecki, there is a keen awareness and feeling of the intellectual's situation in America when compared with the position in Europe – a critique of American cultural life is tempered by an appreciation of its ideals.

Legacies and Lessons

The Polish Peasant in Europe and America pioneered a number of theoretical concepts and methodological techniques. Only more recently have some of these methodological techniques been strongly developed and widely valued. What is extraordinary about the study, and its main 'lesson', is its conception - the use of a range of techniques to explore particular (but related) substantive concerns while being theoretically wide and sophisticated in its attempt to connect, by a range of intermediary concepts, personality and society. Its central, historically informed, theme is an exploration of contemporary social transition – an examination of social change in two societies and migration between them, with individual and group relationships still with society of origin.

A Translocal and Transnational Study

The Polish Peasant can be understood as a study of both local context and transnational connections – of migration within and between countries (Poland, Germany, US). The study investigates 'local-to-international' movements as experienced by individuals and groups within an unfolding, complex development. Today, as prefigured in *The Polish Peasant*, migration is broadly conceived as a life-long process and as involving the reformation of ethnic or other identities, and vital issues, including social cohesion, social participation and discrimination. The plea of Thomas and Znaniecki for the comparative study of immigrant groups and their 'adaptation' to a new society (as attempted in Old World Traits Transplanted (Thomas, 1975) remains an important injunction today – as well as the awareness complexities involved. Questions surrounding identity in relation to migration, ethnicity and minority-majority relations have become very important contemporary issues. As Thomson (1999) argues, it is important to understand the intricate interrelations between migration and the creation and development of migrant communities and ethnic identities, in theory and research. The outlook or identifications of different groups need not be confined to their origins; a specific group may view their immediate concerns as more important or try to distance themselves from contemporary stereotypes and adverse reactions of the 'immigrant', 'refugee' or 'asylum seeker' (Roberts, 2006: see Thomson 1999).

Thomas and Znaniecki studied migration not merely at point of arrival but as a complex process of transition. In recent anthropological and other work, transnationalism and transmigration (as a more than origin-to-destination but rather as new social spaces with forms of consciousness within or connecting locations) have been linked to contemporary global shifts. The interest has been in more than how social ties are maintained, in the recognition of new social and cultural relations – a new mixed or hybrid phenomenon with attendant multiple identities and biographical experience formed from elements of both original place and destination. These are new transnational constructions which are formed from family and communal associations across national locations. Much of this orientation could be said to be prefigured in *The Polish Peasant* – as in the use of personal (and other) materials not merely to study the changes in personality or family structure and values, etc. due to migration but to see the individual migrant and national group as part of the transition and interconnection between societies which are being transformed (see, for example, Benmayor and Skotnes, eds., 1994).

For some years there has been a challenge to the notion of an over-arching 'globalisation' process seen as eroding the 'communal' or 'local' bases of social life. The importance of 'micro' situations has been stressed but not to place the local or communal above more general processes but to attempt to understand interconnections between levels and how some 'local' sphere of action and distinctiveness (as source of resistance and new identities). For example, Smith (2001) describes 'transnational urbanism' within a social constructionist view of 'networks of power' from the local to the global – place, community and culture are not sealed but formed as 'circuits of communication'. He argues that local struggles and resistances, and new discourses, are 'played out' in the locality, while transnational migrants, entrepreneurs and activists form 'translocalities' and 'translocal relations'. In this approach, for Smith, research conceives transnational connections as localised, and localities as transnationally connected across social practices. Other writers have used terms such as 'glocalization', again to encompass local, national, regional and global situations as 'intercultural communicative processes' and also to demonstrate the commonness of 'cultural hybridity' (Kraidy 2002; see Roberts, 2006:136-7).

While using very different conceptualisation to these discussions, *The Polish Peasant* study methodologically (i.e. in its use of source materials to study processes within and between countries) and theoretically (i.e. by examining disorganisation and reorganisation at individual, family, communal levels) opened the exploration of local-to-global connections. Current transnational migration, due to its scale, can seem to be a new phenomenon, but, it is worth remembering past levels of population movement, for example, in 1906 alone 1m immigrants entered the U.S. to join a population of 80 million. *The Polish Peasant* study's main intention was to explore large-scale transmigration and communication of peoples and between continents and localities, and the associated social consequences.

Multi-sited Research

In the mid-1990s, in a well known and influential article, Marcus (1995) observed a change in traditional ethnography as based on a single 'conventional single-site location'. There was an 'emerging practice' of 'multi-sites of observation and participation' which breached 'old dichotomies' of local/global and 'life-world/system'. The new research practice recognised the 'circulation of cultural meanings, objects and identities' and the 'diffusion of time-space'. *The Polish Peasant* may be considered a sophisticated forerunner of such 'multi-sited' study, drawing on a very wide range of observation, materials and interpretation, to trace individuals, families and communities in their transition to another society. Again, at the same time, it closely examined the changes in social institutions and cultural patterns in the society of origin, Poland, and the experienced circumstances and institutions of the new society, the U.S. It is a complex, multi-sited account of origin, destination and of social transition at individual, familial, communal and societal levels across national contexts. In fact, it employed a number of the 'tracking strategies' that Marcus (1995) identified in the 'emerging practice' of more recent studies, to follow groups, institutional shifts, and individual biography.

Multi-Research Materials/Techniques

As noted earlier, *The Polish Peasant* used of a wide range of methods, e.g. letters, various kinds of organisational documents, and other information to explore and connect different substantive areas. Some of the materials and techniques involved have only more recently become commonly accepted in sociological research, with the growth of qualitative research and the broadening of research approaches to include multi-research materials or techniques (and even 'mixed methods' combining quantitative and qualitative methodologies). For example, the use of letters (and various kinds of 'personal documents'), a traditional source of materials for historians and others but generally overlooked by sociologists, is beginning to attract some renewed consideration within sociology (see Stanley, 2004; Plummer, 2001:52-55; Denzin, 1970:232). *The Polish Peasant* study can also be said to have been innovative in combining 'subjective', 'organisational' and other materials to investigate related substantive themes.

The Life Record

While the use of the 'life record' or 'life history' figured in later Chicagoan work (c.f. see Shaw, 1930, 1931, Shaw and McKay, 1938; Plummer, 2001: ch.5) it is only more recently with the growth of biographical research (e.g. oral history, narrative analysis) that life history materials have become widely developed – within the broader establishment of qualitative methods (see, Roberts, 2002). They have been used extensively in the past ten years or so in the study of migration and other areas. It has been recognised that written and oral testimonies can provide the 'unrecorded, ill-documented and hidden histories of migration', particularly of those oppressed or marginalised, rather than the traditional portrait from 'outside' (Thomson, 1999:26). Those studying migration have become aware that individual accounts allow the experience of the life to be given – the living out of the intricacies of social processes, involving social conflict, policies and practices as affecting individual and group lives and relations. Thus, for Thomson, they can deliver both 'empirical knowledge and aid theoretical understanding' (Thomson, 1999:28). Thomas and Znaniecki established a strong case for such 'subjective' materials in sociology. Thomson could be echoing something of the stance in *The Polish Peasant*, when describing the increasing study of migration by using oral accounts:

> 'Moving stories' is a crude but useful pun about the oral history of migration. These oral histories centre on the physical experience of movement between places. They are often redolent with the emotionality of disjuncture, and are deeply moving for the narrator and for his or her audience. And the stories are themselves constantly evolving and moving, presenting living histories in every sense of the term and a unique resource and opportunity for social and historical understanding. (Thomson, 1999:36)

As Benmayor and Skotnes (1994) argue, the problems of migration and the 'resulting reconfigurations of social identity' are fundamental issues. They say that in the 1990s the use of oral history in particular social settings contributed to an understanding of migration by providing 'glimpses' into the inner life of migration experiences. Oral history was able to show the processes involved in the formation and reformation of identity, while also demonstrating the connection between oral testimony and global experiences (Benmayor and Skotnes, 1994). Within sociology, the study of migration, including communal or ethnic identity formation, has also become a major area of methodological and theoretical study (Roberts, 2006:137-8). The lesson of *The Polish Peasant* is that migration research should include an attempt to apply or formulate an array of concepts concerning the individual and community – which attempt to interconnect the changes in the individual life record its wider contexts and thereby link personality and culture. What is also of interest, particularly in the light of recent attention to the researcher's own position in research (e.g. by auto/ethnography or relating emotional aspects of research practice, see Roberts, 2007) is the way in which *The Polish Peasant* study was not merely concerned with the social and political issue of migration but how it was intimately related to the personal experiences and reflections on their own lives by Thomas and Znaniecki.

Conclusion

Thomas and Znaniecki's *The Polish Peasant* in Europe and America (1918-20) was a major achievement in the study of migration and social transition in individual, communal, institutional and national levels terms. It pioneered multi-sited research not merely by studying a small context in one society - the destination of a communal group from another society, but was an ambitious attempt to understand social change at a number of levels within two societies and what occurs during communal transition. Such an ambition – including detailed commentary on extensive substantive materials and sophisticated theoretical analysis – is worthy of revisit now when discussions of globalisation, transmigration, transnationalism and their effects are so current. The study also brought attention to research materials such as the life history and letters, which have unfortunately either been overlooked or relegated to something of a minor tradition, at least until recently, in subsequent research. Here, we should also not forget the extensive and broad range of documentary secondary materials the authors employed. In theoretical terms, while there are doubts on the exact relationship between the concepts (and their definition) used and the materials gathered, the study had an ambition which remains inspiring - to theorise the processes involved in the 'adaptation' of personalities, the changes in attitudes and values, and social disorganisation and reorganisation – while describing the broad societal shifts taking place. Finally, it is clear that the major concerns regarding migration and its effects were not merely 'abstract' questions for Thomas and Znaniecki, but related to pressing both practical, social issues - and were intimately associated with their own experiences both in Chicago and Europe – their own intellectual life and personal migrations.

References

Allport, G.W. (1942) *The Use of Personal Documents in Psychological Science*. New York: Social Science Research Council.
Angell, R. (1945) 'A Critical Review of the Development of the Personal Document Method in Sociology', in Gottschalk, L, Kluckhohn, C. and Angell, R. (1945) *The Use of Personal Documents in History, Anthropology and Sociology*. New York: Social Science Research Council.
Baker, P.J. (1973) 'The Life Histories of W.I. Thomas and Robert E. Park', *American Journal of Sociology*, 79 (2):243-60.
Benmayor, R. and Skotnes, A. (1994) 'Some Reflections on Migration and Identity', in Benmayor, R. and Skotnes, A. (eds.). (1994) *Migration and Identity, International Yearbook of Oral History and Life Stories*. Vol. III, Oxford: Oxford University Press.
-----.(eds.) (1994) *Migration and Identity, International Yearbook of Oral History and Life Stories*. Vol. III, Oxford: Oxford University Press.
Blumer, H. (1939) *Critiques of Research in the Social Sciences: An Appraisal of Thomas and Znaniecki's The Polish Peasant in Europe and America*. New York: Social Science Research Council.
-----.(1979) *Critiques of Research in the Social Sciences: An Appraisal of Thomas and Znaniecki's The Polish Peasant in Europe and America*, (with a new Introduction by Herbert Blumer), New Brunswick, New Jersey: Transaction Books.
Bulmer, M. (1983) "The Polish Peasant in Europe and America': A

Neglected Classic'. *New Community*, Vol. x, (3), Spring:470-6.
-----.(1984) *The Chicago School of Sociology*. Chicago: The University of Chicago Press.
Burgess, Ernest W. (1928) 'What Social Case Records Should Contain to be Useful for Sociological Interpretation', *Social Forces*, VI:526-532.
Coser, L. (1977) *Masters of Sociological Thought: Ideas in Historical and Social Context*. 2nd edn, New York: Harcourt, Brace, Jovanovich.
Denzin, N.K. (1970) *The Research Act in Sociology: The Theoretical Introduction to Sociological Methods*. London: Butterworths.
Dollard, J. (1935) *Criteria for the Life History: With Analyses of Six Notable Documents*. New Haven: Yale University Press.
Gottschalk, L., Kluckhohn, C. and Angell, R. (1945) *The Use of Personal Documents in History, Anthropology and Sociology*. New York: Social Science Research Council.
Janowitz, M. (1966) 'Introduction' to *W.I. Thomas on Social Organization and Social Personality*. Chicago: The University of Chicago Press.
Kraidy, M.M. (2002) 'The Global, the Local, and the Hybrid: A Native Ethnography of Glocalisation', in Taylor, S. (ed.). *Ethnographic Research: A Reader*, London: Sage.
Marcus, G. (1995) 'Ethnography In/Of the World System: the Emergence of Multi-Sited Ethnography', *Annual Review of Anthropology*, 24:95-117
Martindale, Don (1961) *The Nature and Types of Sociological Theory*. London: Routledge and Kegan Paul:347-353.
Madge, J. (1963) *The Origins of Scientific Sociology*. London, Tavistock.
Mills, C. Wright (1964) *Sociology and Pragmatism*. Oxford: Oxford University Press
-----.(1970a) *The Sociological Imagination*. Harmondsworth: Penguin.
-----.(1970b) 'Social Psychology: Model for Liberals', in Stone, G. P. and Farberman, H. A. (eds.). *Social Psychology Through Symbolic Interaction*. Waltham, MA: Xerox College Publishing.
Park, R.E. (1925) 'The Concept of Position in Sociology'. Presidential Address, Proceedings of the Twentieth Annual Meeting, *American Sociological Society*.
-----.(1928) 'Human Migration and the Marginal Man', *The American Journal of Sociology*, Vol. XXXIII, May 1928, (6):881-893.
Plummer, K. (2001) *Documents of Life 2: an invitation to a critical humanism*. London: Sage.
Brian R. (2002) *Biographical Research*. Buckingham: OU.
-----.(2006) *Micro Social Theory*. Basingstoke: Palgrave.
-----.(2007) *Getting the Most Out of the Research Experience*. London: Sage.
Shaw, C.R. (1930) *The Jack-Roller: A Delinquent Boy's Own Story*. Chicago: The University of Chicago Press (1967, reprinted with an Introduction by Howard S. Becker).
-----.(1931) *The Natural History of a Delinquent Career*. Chicago: The

University of Chicago Press.
Shaw, C.R. and Henry D. McKay (1938) *Brothers in Crime*. Chicago: The University of Chicago Press.
Smith, D. (1988) *The Chicago School: A Liberal Critique of Capitalism*. Basingstoke: Macmillan.
Smith, M.P. (2001) *Transnational Urbanism: Locating Globalization*. Oxford: Blackwell.
Stanley, L. (2004) 'The Epistolarium: on Theorizing Letters and Correspondences'. *Auto/Biography*, 12: (3):183-200.
Thomas, W.I. and Znaniecki, Florian (1918-20) *The Polish Peasant in Europe and America*. (5 volumes – first 2 by The University of Chicago Press, subsequently all 5 by Richard Badger, Boston. In 1927 Alfred Knopf published a 2 volumes edition, which was republished by Dover, Boston/New York in 1958 – references in this article are to this edition).
Thomas, W.I. (1975[1921]) *Old Word Traits Transplanted*. Montclair, New Jersey: Patterson Smith. (Together with Robert E. Park and Herbert A. Miller).
Thomas, W.I. and Thomas, D.S. (1928) *The Child in America*. New York: Alfred A. Knopf.
Thomson, A. (1999) 'Moving Stories: Oral History and Migration Studies', *Oral History*, 27 (1):24-37.
-----.(1999) 'Moving Stories: Oral History and Migration Studies'. *Oral History*, Spring:24-37
Washington, B.T. and Park, R.E. (1984) *The Man Farthest Down*. With a new Introduction by St. Clair Drake, Transaction Books: New Brunswick (USA) and London (UK) [original editions 1911 The Outlook Company, 1912 Doubleday, Page and Company].
Young, D.R. (1975) 'Introduction' to the Republished Edition, W. I. Thomas (1975) *Old World Traits Transplanted*. Montclair, New Jersey: Patterson Smith.
Znaniecki, F. (1948) 'William I. Thomas as a Collaborator'. *Sociology and Social Research*, 32:765-7.

CHAPTER 4

Human Ecology and the Emergence of Global Society: The Theoretical Insights of Roderick D. McKenzie

Dennis W. MacDonald
Saint Anselm College, Manchester, USA

Introduction

Central to the intellectual legacy of Roderick D. McKenzie is his pivotal role in the development of human ecology. Although Park and Burgess (1921:103) are often credited with the Chicago School's ecology idea, McKenzie was the main theoretician and proponent of human ecology.[78] His doctoral dissertation contains many elements that subsequently were identified as "ecological" (McKenzie, 1923). Eubank in his obituary of McKenzie clearly implies that the ecology idea was mainly McKenzie's.[79] Somewhere along the line, as he was working with Dr. Robert E. Park in conducting his widely known community study of Columbus, Ohio, the conviction gradually grew within his mind that there was an aspect of human relations of which sociology had not up to that time been aware (Eubank, 1940:71).

Hawley stated in his introductory essay to a collection of McKenzie's writings, that because

---

[78] Park and Burgess are often cited, erroneously, as having been the first to use the term "human ecology." In fact, the origins of human ecology pre-date Park, Burgess, and McKenzie. As Matthias Gross points out, earlier Chicago sociologists (Small, Vincent and Hayes) and Chicago geographers had earlier explored the idea. Gross, Matthias, (2004), "Human Geography and Ecological Sociology." *Social Science History* 28:575-805.

[79] Furthermore, Amos Hawley pointed out that McKenzie and Park had a falling out over Park's alleged use of materials that McKenzie had given him. Furthermore, the first edition in 1915 of Park's, "The City: Suggestions for the Investigation of Human Behavior in the City Environment," makes no reference to ecology. The 1925 edition that appears in Park, Burgess, and McKenzie's book, *The City*, makes extensive reference to ecology. One wonders whether that is what McKenzie was upset about. The reference to human ecology in Park & Burgess, *Introduction to the Science of Sociology* is exceedingly brief and in reference only to the principle of competitive cooperation (1969 [1921 edition]:558).

the highly imaginative and restless mind of Park was impatient with details and with the rigors of closely reasoned argument" and Burgess was "drawn irresistibly to specific empirical problems," it "fell to McKenzie ... to write the first definitive statements of human ecology. (Hawley, 1968:xi).

There are difficulties involved in an assessment of McKenzie's work, particularly from a theoretical point of view. His writings, with few exceptions, are not explicitly theoretical. There is much theory woven into his work and he is evidently aware of important theoretical dilemmas, but there is little sustained, explicit, and deliberate discussion of the theoretical issues involved in the ecological view apart from a couple of early essays. His thinking seems to undergo significant transformation over time. Unfortunately, his most explicitly theoretical statements come early in his career and represent a "tentative" attempt to define human ecology "in the absence of any precedence" (McKenzie, 1924:288). Statements made in the early 1920's do not appear completely consistent with his later views of the ecological. And, most importantly, he left his work undone. McKenzie's major treatise on human ecology which likely would have provided a more definitive theoretical statement remained unfinished at the time of his death in 1940 at the age of 55 from a debilitating illness which severely curtailed his ability to work in his last couple years. Whatever of it had been written and the notes for the book were forever lost in a fire in 1950 at the University of Michigan that destroyed the building housing Amos Hawley's office (Hawley, 1975). Nonetheless, McKenzie's relative short academic career (from entering Chicago in 1913 to his death in 1940) was remarkably productive. A careful reading of his works yields a number of significant theoretical insights.[80]

McKenzie's major insights fall into two main categories. The first, the major point of his ecology, can be stated as follows: Human social life, both in terms of human action and human relationships, transpire within and through a larger system of relations, an essential aspect of which is physical or material. The second which emerges out of his careful observation of the physical world is his assertion that the growth in integration - particularly physical integration - characterizes the development of modern society. This he discusses in terms of institutionalization, regionalism, and globalization.

McKenzie's "Ecology" Idea

It is clear from his doctoral dissertation, The Neighborhood: A Study of Local Life in Columbus, Ohio, (1971 [1921, 1922]) that McKenzie was impressed with

---

[80] McKenzie's legacy extends far beyond the few aspects of his work discussed in this paper. In particular, his work on race, ethnicity and immigration (see his *Oriental Exclusion*, for example) should be noted. McKenzie, Roderick D. (1927), *Oriental Exclusion*. New York: Institute of Pacific Relations.

the significance of the outward physical structure of social life in that community – the rivers, roads, buildings, etc. It was out of this study that "human ecology" emerged.

By far, the dominant element of the work of Roderick D. McKenzie is the idea of physical or material relations of human beings and the worlds of nature and culture. In his human ecology, McKenzie attempts to find a way to incorporate into his study of society what Eubank referred to as "an aspect of human relations of which sociology had not up to that time been aware" (Eubank, 1940:71). That aspect was the relation of human beings and human communities to the material world - rivers, mines, hills, roads, factories, gardens, churches, etc. Social life has a material structure and cannot be understood solely in terms of individuals or groups of individuals.

Human ecology was defined by McKenzie "as the study of the spatial and temporal relations of human beings as affected by the selective, distributive, and accommodative forces of the environment" (1924:288). But his idea of human society as an ecological phenomenon included far more than is evident in this brief and formal "tentative" definition. Human social life consists of myriad relations beyond those abstracted by sociology in its conception of the social in terms of the "group," that is relational systems made up exclusively of human beings.

The component elements which constitute the human community are bound together not merely by common traditions, habits, beliefs, and rules of conduct which have become formally expressed in legislative enactments and enforced by governmental machinery, but also by the vital linkages represented in the division of labor and adjustment to the physical habitat (McKenzie, 1968 [1936]:103).

Several aspects of what McKenzie calls the "physical basis of social relations" are discussed extensively in his writings (1924:288). First is the obvious importance of the world of nature. McKenzie focuses on, among other things, the "sustenance relations" of human beings, competition for resources in the natural environment, and nature as a source of nutriment. He discusses the biological nature of the human animal, the fact that "he cannot live alone; he is relatively weak and needs not only the company of other human beings but shelter and protection from the elements as well" (McKenzie, 1924:289). Citing Jean Brunhes' Human Geography, he suggests that among the prerequisites of human social life are "the house, the road, and water" (McKenzie, 1924:289).

In conjunction with cultural developments, the location of the community and its character are shaped by the objects of nature.
(W)hen trade and commerce develop, larger communities arise at points of breaks in conveyance, that is, at the mouths of rivers, junctions of streams, at waterfalls, and shallows where streams are forded (McKenzie, 1924:289).

The food supply itself is, in McKenzie's view, the primary determinant of the size and stability of communities. Natural elements, then, are significant factors in determining the location, structure, size and stability of communities, cities, towns and villages (McKenzie, 1924).

Culture and the "Human" in McKenzie's Ecology

Human ecology has been criticized for its focus on nature and the neglect of "cultural factors."[81] It is a point well taken for much ecological theory, in so far as there is at least some equivocation on this point. Even aspects of McKenzie's work, the role of nature in shaping communities and his ecological processes, for example, can lead to the conclusion that there is a sort of natural determinism involved in the ecological approach.[82] However, Park, Burgess, McKenzie and Hawley, all make extensive reference to cultural and other exclusively human elements. McKenzie, far from neglecting the cultural, emphasizes its centrality. Cultural objects constitute a significant part of the environment, the body, of the human community. Most of the structure, the physical basis of social life, that he discusses, is the result of human cultural activity. By far, the most important of these are institutions which will be discussed below. But other specific examples are numerous in McKenzie's writings. Technological developments in particular are emphasized by McKenzie.

> The coming of the motor vehicle and electric energy in the early part of the present century, together with the rapid development of communications—the newspaper, telephone, and later the radio introduced another revolutionary change in the institutional structure of society and one which in its composite effect on the texture of social relations has perhaps been

---

[81] Hollingshead stated that "the 'classical' ecologists by definition ruled the cultural factor from their theoretical purview." Ecological analysis, he argued, must face the fact that "human activities are organized within a sociocultural framework." Hollingshead, A. B. (1961). 'A Re-examination of Ecological Theory', in *Studies in Human Ecology*, edited by G. Theodorson. New York: Harper & Row:108-114.

[82] Park, for example, stated that "Human ecology, in so far as it is concerned with a social order that is based on competition rather than consensus, is identical, in principle at least, with plant and animal ecology." But, he adds, "Human ecology has, however, to reckon with the fact that in human society competition is limited by custom and culture." Park, Robert E. (1936), "Human Ecology." *American Journal of Sociology* 42:1-15. Amos Hawley in his *Human Ecology* sees it as a "specialization" within the broader field of ecology and is only comprehensible in light of its "parent discipline." He discusses culture, but in a way which seems to reduce human cultural activity to biology. "The elements of human culture are ... identical in principle with the appetency of the bee for honey, and the nest building activities of birds, and the hunting habits of carnivores." Hawley, Amos. (1950), *Human Ecology: A Theory of Community Structure*. New York: Ronald Press.

even more significant than that occasioned by the introduction of steam transportation (McKenzie, 1968 [1936]:106-107).

Clearly, for McKenzie, such objects have tremendous significance for social life and must be seen along with human beings as constituent elements of society. Just as there is no society or community apart from persons, so also there is no society or community apart from the objects of nature and culture.

The emphasis on the physical aspects of social relations – whether seen as natural or cultural - has also been the subject of some criticism. Martindale wrote that ecological theory "started analysis off on the wrong track by orienting it to the geo-physical aspects of the city rather than to its social life." He continues,

> Social life is a structure of interaction, not a structure of stone, steel, cement, asphalt, etc. It is, to be sure, not altogether inappropriate to suggest that one can understand much about the activities of a household by a careful analysis of what passes through its sewerage system and what ends up in its garbage can – but this is true only if these are taken as by-products of activity and as evidence on which to establish inferences (Martindale, 1958:29).

Along the same lines, Martindale asserts that the ecological theory "omitted precisely those concepts most traditionally sociological – groups, institutions, social structure"(Martindale, 1958:30).

The early formulations of ecological theory by McKenzie notwithstanding, he is unequivocal about the distinctive nature of human as opposed to plant and animal ecology. And, in the process, he makes it quite clear that he sees human activity, based in human consciousness and thinking, as essential to understanding the organization of the social (including ecological) world. Much of human ecology is about the so-called ecological processes and forces which often are discussed in such a way as to suggest that they are the determinants of human social organization. Is society or the community organized as it is due to ecological laws of invasion, succession, segregation, dominance, etc.? Is the community the product of the operation of invariable laws of ecology? McKenzie did not address this issue head on, but suggested in several contexts that there is a major difference between the workings of these ecological processes in the biological versus the human spheres. Humans shape their "habitat." Conscious control is involved in various ways. "Cultural forces" are as much responsible for social organization as are environmental forces. McKenzie emphasizes in several places that when human beings are brought into the ecological picture, the situation is quite different from that involving a focus on plants and non-human animals. He writes that plant and animal ecology "is not sufficiently comprehensive to include all the elements that logically fall within the range of human ecology" (McKenzie, 1924:287-288). Among these "elements," the most significant is the capacity of human beings to shape their own environment. McKenzie writes that "the human animal has the ability to contrive and adapt the environment to his needs." In a word, the human community differs from the plant community in the two dominant characteristics of mobility and purpose, that is in the power to select a habitat and in the ability to control or modify the conditions of the habitat (McKenzie, 1924:288-289).

In a similar vein, in his "Demography, Human Geography and Human Ecology," McKenzie refers to man as a "cultural animal," emphasizing the distinctive capacities of human beings.

> The basic difference between human ecology and the ecologies of the lower organisms lies in the fact that man is capable of a higher level of behavior in his adaptation process. As a cultural animal man creates, within limitations, his own habitat. Symbiotic relations in human society represent adjustments to a cultural as well as to a biogeographic setting (McKenzie, 1968[1934]-a:41).

Unlike plant and animal ecology, the human ecologist sees the community as an organic unit, "a functional association of human activities; in other words, a community" (McKenzie, 1968 [1934]-a:33). The implication is that human action is basic (and, therefore, presumably, human thought and direction). That human beings, at least collectively, exercise some degree of control is also made clear by McKenzie. Although he discusses "how competition, division of labor, commensalism, parasitism, etc., operate to give form and cohesion to human settlement," he goes on to say, "The forms in which these fundamental relations express themselves in human society, unlike their natural prototypes in plant and animal communities, are largely determined by the culture and collective controls of the human group concerned" (McKenzie, 1968 [1936]:103). The forces responsible for the kinds of spatial and sustenance relations in the human community are "a complex of environmental and cultural forces" (McKenzie, 1968 [1926]-b:19).

McKenzie further argues that the ecological organization of people and their activities results from "the interplay of forces which effect a more or less conscious, or at any rate dynamic and vital, relationship among the units comprising the aggregation" (McKenzie, 1968 [1926]-b:20). Finally, in "The Ecology of Institutions," his last published word on the subject, McKenzie writes,

> The main reason for considering human ecology a separate discipline is that man has so gained in dominance over the lower organisms that his relationships with them have, to a large extent, become consciously regulated and controlled. On the other hand, the most significant and least understood aspects of man's symbiotic relations are those which he effects with his fellow men. It is within this latter sphere of activity that the major problems of human ecology present themselves (McKenzie, 1968[1936]:102-103).

Modern Society and the "Thickening of the Web of Relationships"

McKenzie's detailed observations of the physical aspects of communities and human social life lead him to the further significant insight that a predominant characteristic of modern society was a trend toward ever increasing integration. This growth in integration is of two main types. The first is the increasing institutionalization of human activity. The other is the expansion of the scope of human relations from local to regional and ultimately global. In both, but particularly the latter, this thickening of relations has a very significant physical or material dimension.

The Ecology of Institutions

In "The Ecology of Institutions," he states, "It is with the growing importance of institutions that I am particularly concerned at present" (McKenzie, 1968 [1936]:105). The institution, he claims, "has become the fundamental unit in modern society and... the trend is away from individual enterprise in almost every line of endeavor" (McKenzie, 1968 [1936]:115). The nature of institution, as suggested by McKenzie, is consistent with the objective conception of social relations discussed previously. Institutions are not merely "constellations of statuses and roles," as often conceptualized by sociologists. They are, rather, concrete things. While students of sociology are frequently warned against the danger of thinking of institutions in terms of "bricks and mortar," McKenzie seems to see them exactly in those terms, or, rather, as including "bricks and mortar." Among the many examples of institutions mentioned in his writings are the grocery store, barber shop, bank, church, school, and university. An institution,

> ...represents on the one hand a closely integrated aggregate of individuals performing a specialized social function, and on the other hand an accumulation of cultural artifacts assembled and organized to facilitate the performance of that function. The growth of material culture at once has necessitated and facilitated the rise of social institutions. The machines, mechanical energy, and other technical achievements of civilization have required spatially established centers for their accumulation and use. Thus the institution has acquired a physical structure and a definite locus in space. It likewise has a continuum in time which is not identical with that of its operative personnel. It is less mobile than the individual and less stable than the community, and it has come to constitute the fundamental unit in the ecological organization of modern society (McKenzie, 1968[1936]:105).

An institution is not merely people in relation, nor is it merely a mode of behavior in McKenzie's view. It is, in fact, an actor, a sort of person or an extension of the person's capacities, one constituted by relations of people and things. As "the most dynamic units in our modern social order,", institutions shape the modern community, not only spatially, in terms of population distribution, etc., but also shape the "life and character of the local community"(McKenzie, 1968 [1936]:113, 110).

Institutions are also unique to human society, providing to human beings extraordinary capacities to change the world. As such, they are instrumental to the progressive development or evolution of society. The emergence and development of civilization, in McKenzie's view, is largely seen as the growth in institutional structure.

> The advance of civilization has been accompanied by the multiplication and differentiation of social institutions. Indeed, it is through the development of institutions that man has risen above the level of lower animal life. It is by institutions, likewise, that the successive steps in cultural evolution have been attained (1968[1936]:105).

The evolution of society is characterized by a movement from few and simple institutions in primitive societies to a multiplicity of complex institutions as civilization advances. Elsewhere, McKenzie described the development of the local community in terms of institutional development, "from the simple to the complex, from the general to the specialized" institutions (1924:296). In small towns and villages, a few simple institutions (general store, church, school, and home) meet the basic needs. A sequence of development typically involves: "first the grocery store, sometimes carrying a few of the more staple dry goods, then the restaurant, poolroom, barber shop, drug store, dry-goods store, and later bank, haberdashery, millinery, and other specialized lines of service (McKenzie, 1924:296).

But just as McKenzie sees their great power as tied to social progress, with the Great Depression slowly subsiding, McKenzie was also aware of the negative aspects of the rise of great institutions. As society and communities become more organized institutionally, the competition among institutions forces them to consider their own institutional interests and survival, above that of the people who accomplish their ends and maintain themselves through these institutions. The result is often "unemployment and complete destitution" (McKenzie, 1968 [1936]:114). As competition ensues, the number of institutions that "make it" decreases, while the size of those that do increases. While McKenzie seems to have believed that competition has made for greater efficiency, quality, availability of goods, etc., he notes:

> But this process has reduced the masses of the population to the status of wage-earners and salaried employees and has created a social order in which a relatively small number of powerful individuals direct the economic activities of their fellow citizens (1968 [1936]:115).

In the final analysis, the fundamental problem of modern society is the control of the massive institutions toward the ends of its members, that is, in the public interest, or for the social good. How can these large corporate entities be controlled without stifling their natural tendencies, and their freedom to plan and act? The dilemma is one to which McKenzie claims no solution. In any case, if the solution eluded McKenzie, he seems to have framed the issue correctly in placing problems and progress squarely in the institutional context.

Regionalism and Global Society: The "Organic Cohesiveness of the World"

In "The Rise of the Metropolitan Community," published in the Report of the President's Commission on Recent Social Trends, McKenzie argued that the community which previously consisted of the village, neighborhood, town, or city, had come to encompass a much larger area, the "metropolitan region" (1933b:445). In ecological terms, the "communal organism" had grown in size and complexity.

Recent developments in means of communication have so enlarged the scope of local life that the ordinary individual, in the pursuit of his daily activities of work and leisure, is no longer confined to a single village, town, or even city. The modern community usually embraces a number of centers of different size, each more or less specialized in its institutions and its services (McKenzie, 1933b:445). In McKenzie's view, the coming of the motor vehicle was instrumental in this development (McKenzie, 1933a:6).

Linked very closely to his discussions of the growing significance of regional relations is some of his most insightful work on the emergence of global society. In "The Basis of Interregional Unity," McKenzie notes that the more regions became internally integrated, the more they relate to other regions. The interrelations of regions seemed to him so extensive as to justify discussion in terms of the "organic cohesiveness of the modern world"(McKenzie, 1934:360). The growth in physical integration thus goes far beyond the city and the region.

In "Movement and the Ability to Live," McKenzie noted that the recent emergence of the world market had occasioned regional specialization which brought various regions of the world into competition on the one hand and greater interdependence on the other.

> The world is becoming territorially divided into wheat belts, corn belts, sugar, coffee, rubber, and tobacco areas. Canada competes with Argentina and Australia in the production of wheat; Egypt, with Georgia and our other Southern States in the production of cotton; Brazil with Ceylon in coffee; Cuba with Hawaii in sugar; British Malaya with Java in rubber... Manchester competes with Bombay and Osaka in the manufacture of textiles; Pittsburg and Gary with Birmingham and Essen in the manufacture of steel and iron products; Glasgow with Amsterdam in the construction of ships (McKenzie, 1968[1926]-a:136-137).

More than three-quarters of a century ago, McKenzie wrote extensively of what we now commonly refer to as "globalization."[83] Though he used different terminology – world society, world organization, the great society, etc. -- his discussions touch on many aspects of today's raging debate on globalization. Is globalization real? Does it promote or detract from human development? What is its impact on cultural diversity? Does it result in tremendous progress for some at the expense of others? Does it advance civilization, or does it simply advance the power and wealth of the West or of corporate interests?

Although his comments on a number of these issues are interesting and useful, his detailed description of the fact of globalization, or the emergence of global society, is perhaps his most valuable contribution. McKenzie's exploration of "world organization" dates to his year of foreign travel as a Kahn Foundation fellow.[84] His first and most detailed account is his book length report to the Albert Kahn Foundation which had awarded him a fellowship for around the world travel during 1925 and 1926. The emphasis in the report, as the title, "The Evolving World Economy" indicates, is on economic globalization[85] (McKenzie, 1926). Nonetheless, the economic is always examined in its connections to the social, political, and cultural.

The global division of labor is extensively described by McKenzie. "The world is a great integrated unity in which each region, according to its natural resources, contributes its quota to the common table of humanity" (McKenzie, 1926:24). As McKenzie and his wife traveled around the world, they "saw as in a moving picture the regional bases of a vast variety of articles that enter into our daily consumption" (1926:24). Numerous examples, both agricultural and industrial, are cited. There is specialization in logging in Puget Sound, sugar and pineapples in Hawaii, mulberry trees and rice in Japan, maize and wheat in China, rubber in Malay, tea in Ceylon, olives in Palestine, grapes in Italy, and

---

[83] As Giddens stated in his BBC Reith lecture on Globalization several years ago, the term has become commonplace around the world in recent years. The phenomenon, however, is neither new, nor newly discovered. McKenzie wrote on it extensively. It was a central idea in the sociology of his student, Erich Ahrens, and Ahrens' students (History Professor David Wrone at the University of Wisconsin at Stevens Point and Sociology Professor Melvin Bobick at the University of New Hampshire) in whose classes I sat in the late 1960s and 1970s, listening to lectures on the global nature of modern society. Needless to say, I borrowed heavily from McKenzie, Ahrens, Wrone and Bobick in my own Sociology lectures.

[84] Although McKenzie's ideas about global society are clearly developed in his report to the Kahn Foundation and reflect their development through his world travel, it is quite likely that these ideas occurred to him in some form at an earlier time. That Ahrens, a graduate student of McKenzie's at the University of Washington from 1924-26, incorporates a distinctly global view of human ecology in his own work suggests that McKenzie was lecturing on these themes prior to his travels.

[85] A longer version is published in French under the title, *L'Évolution Économique du Monde*. McKenzie, Roderick D. (1928b), *L'évolution économique du monde (The evolving world economy)*: [Boulogne-sur-Seine, Imprimerie d'Études sociales & politiques.

continuous wheat fields in Canada. The same holds for industrial specialization, with various areas specializing in textiles, others in machine and metal manufacturing. That these areas are part of a world, not a local, economy is apparent in many ways.

> One cannot travel through these immense industrial belts without realizing that they are world rather than local or national producing centers. This fact becomes doubly apparent when one learns that the great hordes of idle men and women who line the streets and cluster around the taverns, have lost their jobs because India and China have ceased to purchase, in previous quantities, the products of their labor (McKenzie, 1926:26-27).

The Global Division of Labor is Constantly Increasing, Bringing More of the World into the "Great Society."

Such in brief is the present world order. It is a rapidly evolving economic unity composed of a large number of geographically differentiated economic belts and centers competing with or supplementing one another in the production of goods for a world market. The web of regional interdependence is constantly increasing in scope and complexity. Every year new regions come within the sphere of dominance of the Great Society pattern. As communications break down physical barriers and human wants become more varied new sections of the globe are drawn within the scope of the world market (McKenzie, 1926:27).

In subsequent writings, McKenzie elaborates on this theme. In "Industrial Expansion and the Interrelations of Peoples," the purpose of which was "to indicate in broad outline the development of the present ecological organization of world society," McKenzie (1968[1934]-b:124) argues that the general trend throughout the world "has been toward a constant thickening of the web of relationships, the development of a more clearly outlined settlement structure, a contraction of space as measured in time and cost, an extension of territorial limits, the inclusion of an ever-increasing number and variety of peoples and a general leveling of cultural differences" (1968[1934]-b:123). Different regions and peoples of the world have been brought "within a common economic order and a common cultural milieu" (McKenzie, 1968[1934]-b:123). In McKenzie's view, "the human population of the globe may be conceived as an aggregate of peoples, geographically and politically set apart but economically and culturally bound together" (1968[1934]-b:132). McKenzie was greatly impressed with the world-wide division of labor implied in the manufacture of modern devices. "Even in so simple a mechanical device as a modern telephone, 14 different minerals are used, and these are collected from almost as many different countries" (McKenzie 1934:360). Elsewhere, McKenzie noted that "The Tamils of Malaya cooperate with the workers of Akron in the production of rubber tires" (1968[1926]-a:139).

Explanation of Globalization

As for the reasons behind the growth in world organization, McKenzie credited it largely to the modern methods of transportation and communications which shrunk drastically the "size" of the world in terms of time, cost, and effort. For example,

The completion of the Suez Canal in 1869 and of a trans-American railway line in the same year opened a new transportation route around the world. By cutting in half the time required to encircle the globe, the completion of this thoroughfare reduced the distance between East and West (McKenzie, 1968[1934]-b:127).

These developments in transportation and communications were in turn made possible by major developments in energy, specifically the shift from human to mechanical power. Writing during the 150th anniversary of the founding of the United States, McKenzie begins his Report to the Kahn Foundation with an interesting discussion contrasting the transportation and communications facilities of 1926 and 1776. The changes are staggering (How surprised would McKenzie be were he to see the developments of the following 75 years!) He notes that it took a week for George Washington to learn of his election as president, and ten days for the news of his death to reach Boston. In contrast, "During our say in Europe Lord Cecil and M. Poincaré...gave addresses to which all Europe listened... The great steamer which bore us across the Pacific was in much closer touch with the world at large than was London or New York" 150 years ago. And "each and every city that we visited in our tour of the globe seemed to be a veritable center of the world; in constant touch with happenings everywhere" (McKenzie, 1926:10-11). According to McKenzie, "Transportation has knit the new order together into a single complex of vital interdependence" (1926:11). Elsewhere, McKenzie wrote, "The point I wish to emphasize is that modern communication by transcending all our old local and political boundaries is bringing the world into single economic unity" (McKenzie, 1968[1926]-a:137).

Developments in energy use, specifically the development of mechanical sources to replace human energy, seem particularly significant in global ecological organization in McKenzie's view. A chapter of his report to the Kahn Foundation is taken up with the topic, and it enters into discussion in other chapters as well. The world is largely divided into regions of mechanical power and regions of human power, with the type of power having profound effects on social life and position in the world economy.

One is impressed in passing through the densely populated rice areas of Japan and China by the absence of travel on paths or trails. The people seem to carry on their daily existence within a very small compass" (McKenzie, 1926:13).

The dominant form of energy use, particularly in relation to transportation, is closely related to the spatial patterns of social and political institutions. Human powered communities are characterized by "narrow, winding, tunnel-like paths" versus mechanically powered communities with "wider and straighter" streets, for example. The canal has had considerable importance in the spatial pattern and civilization structure of the Orient, but has lost its importance in Europe with "coming of mechanical energy in the form of steam and electric power" (McKenzie, 1926:15).

McKenzie likewise accounts for global inequality and unequal participation in the global economy partly in terms of energy development. China's social organization, for example, is a function of human or animal energy.

> Work in gangs replaces the division of labor of the West... The family is the fundamental economic unit both for production and mutual aid. Kinship is associated with fixity of place; it is a vertical rather than horizontal pattern of organization (McKenzie, 1926:15).

The spread of mechanical energy is itself a global phenomenon. "Mechanical energy is gradually spreading over the globe; the world of the future will be one in which mechanical energy dominates the structure" (McKenzie, 1926:17). Regional differences will gradually disappear. Vast changes will occur in the civilization structure of China, for example, "as mechanical energy becomes more generally utilized." Changes in population distribution will occur regionally and within local communal units. "Changes in spatial distribution will inevitably be followed by profound changes in the social and economic organization of the nation" (McKenzie, 1926:16-17).

McKenzie does not specifically address the question of what is responsible for these major changes in energy, transportation, and communications which result in global integration. However, in his more general discussions of human ecology, for example in his article, "The Scope of Human Ecology," his explanation is in terms of ecological processes. The ecological organization of society changes "in response to the operation of a complex of environmental and cultural forces" (McKenzie, 1968 [1926]-b:19). Here and elsewhere, McKenzie seems to suggest that natural laws are ultimately responsible for and govern the process of globalization. The role of human intelligence in societal evolution is neglected. Though, as we have seen, McKenzie is somewhat inconsistent on this point.[86]

---

[86] Ahrens' discussion of global society takes place in the context of a large treatise on the evolution of society, most of which is beyond the scope of this paper. With respect to identifying the growing physical integration of social life as a defining feature of modern society, Ahrens does not deviate from McKenzie's view. But Ahrens offers a radically different explanation as to how this came about. Ahrens argues that these changes, though accidental in many respects, are the by-product of human action. In attempting to create objects, humans have pushed beyond the limitations imposed by the natural environment. In other words, work as creative human activity reshaping the world is central to Ahrens' view of societal evolution. In each succeeding epoch, from village to city to region to nation to world, humans further developed their capacity to act by expanding the corporate structures through which action is possible. Ahrens, Erich. (2000 [1950]) *Order and Disorder in Society*. Unpublished manuscript.

While recognizing problematic aspects of globalization, McKenzie argues ultimately that it represents an expansion of the capacity for human activity. He writes, "The social order may not be better than it was before but each individual now lives in a wider world with the possibility of possessing more of its advantages" (1926:11-12). He also sees globalization as a force unifying the human community.

> Great changes are taking place the world over as a result of the new methods of transportation and communication. Everywhere the changing speed of movement is of profound significance. Time and space are two great factors in human existence. The physical world is spatial. Human beings and human institutions are distributed in space. Contact is a function of time. Modern communications, by shortening distance, are bringing humanity into one community and thus leveling local and regional differences (McKenzie, 1926:63).

A source of global unity is seen in the uneven distribution of resources around the world.

> I wish to call attention to the integrating significance of the new forms of power resulting from; first, the distribution of the prime sources of mechanical energy and second, from the methods of distribution for use... In fact, some of the most culturally backward nations possess the most important sources of petroleum and water power while many of the leading nations are practically without either of these two great sources of energy. This misdistribution on the part of nature is an important reason why the peoples of the world must act together as a unified whole. If the resources of the earth are to be effectively utilized for the betterment of mankind it is essential that many of our primitive ideas of sovereignty be discarded and that a system of international organization and control be substituted. Moreover the use of electrical energy involves regional integration of a new kind. The super-power systems that are now being developed throughout America, Europe and parts of the Orient are binding regions together in new and vital ways (McKenzie, 1926:23).

Even competition in a world market could provide a new basis for "community life" in that producers of the same product in a region previously in competition with each other join forces to compete in the world market against producers from other regions. "This change of relationship furnishes a new basis for community life serving to unite rather than disintegrate the local group. Its significance is especially noticeable when the local community is composed of different racial elements" (McKenzie, 1926:30).

Each of these succeeding epochs [river age, canal age, railroad age, auto and airplane age] has enhanced the flexibility of the spatial structure by bringing into accessibility regions previously isolated... A similar trend toward flexibility has taken place with respect to communication... These early avenues of communication, the telegraph, cable and telephone, were relatively rigid in structural pattern, but the advent of wireless communication has broken down this initial rigidity and has suddenly brought within the zone of common contact countless centers that were previously isolated (McKenzie, 1926:62-63).

Problems of Globalization Acknowledged

McKenzie recognized that there are problems in the modern world, and some of these are linked to economic globalization. McKenzie writes, for example, that "people are washed hither and thither over the world in obedience to the dictates of capital," and that the West treats the East "as though it were a subordinate outpost" (1968 [1934]-a:140). There is a problem with maintaining equilibrium in "the new world order, that is under capitalism and machine production," where mobile-equilibrium is said to replace biological-equilibrium. (McKenzie 1926:49) Particularly where "increasing use of mechanical energy and the general improvements in technical efficiency are causing disequilibrium everywhere, but especially in those parts that were densely populated in accordance with the conditions of a human energy rural economy" (McKenzie, 1926:60). But even in Europe, McKenzie recognizes, machinery is creating large groups of unemployed. There are numerous barriers to human migration, including cultural differences, racial factors, and political boundaries. Migration when possible often results in abnormal population patterns (disproportionately adult males) (McKenzie, 1926:54-56). McKenzie sees this as an issue that requires a global solution.

> The subject of human increase and dispersion has become an international question of the first magnitude. Nations can no longer live as separate biological entities any more than as individual economic entities (McKenzie 1926:58).

The unequal nature of development is a further problem highlighted by McKenzie. In the Introduction to his Report to the Kahn Foundation, after having described the state of transportation and communications of the 18th century, he says,

> Such was the world of a hundred and fifty years ago, and such is the world today for a vast number of the inhabitants of the globe. But how different is the new order of the West, the order that is now rapidly spreading over the world and breaking down all the physical barriers to human association. (1926:9)

And a few pages later, he writes,

> But the world is not uniformly modernized in the sense that the fruits of science are the common possession of peoples everywhere. Large regions are still as backward, if not more so, than were the Europe or America of the eighteenth century. Backward, I mean, in the sense that they do not share in the advantages of world unity (McKenzie, 1926:12).

Other than attributing this unequal development to lack of energy, transportation and communications developments, there is little recognition of reasons for the unevenness. McKenzie, as noted above, did see problems in the relations of East and West, but there is little to indicate that he appreciated the exploitative nature of colonialism.[87]

The Lack of Appropriate Global Political and Social Structure

A fundamental problem of global society for McKenzie is that lack of appropriate global political or governmental institutions to control the global economy. When McKenzie completed his travel around the world, he said that during that trip he was struck by the disharmony between the nationalism of the political order and the internationalism of the economic order of Europe. In his report to the Kahn trustees, he stated,

> My general impression of Europe, if it is permissible to have a general impression of such a complexity, is that there is at present a striking disharmony between the political and economic order. The industrial order, which requires raw materials and markets, is hampered at every point by the political order, which is the inheritance from a time of comparatively local economic interests (New York Times, 1926:16).

The problem is also manifested in the barriers represented by political boundaries. "The most potent barriers to movement in the present world order are political frontiers" (McKenzie 1926:65). McKenzie suggests that the shrinking of the world with modern transportation and communications has made global democratic government possible, perhaps desirable.

---

[87] McKenzie's tendency to be blind to problems is illustrated by the following quotation:

"New systems of communications, however, have made it possible for such parts of the world to serve as vital units in the great economy. A good example of this is furnished by the sudden development of the Caribbean region. Mr. Victor M. Cutter, President of the United Fruit Company, relates in a recent article, how the radio and motor car have made possible the enormous development of the sugar and banana plantations of the West Indies" (1926:70).

Aristotle's conditions regarding the maximum area in which democratic government is feasible, namely the zone in which the voice of a herald may be heard, are now met for the world as a whole as the sound of the human voice can be relayed around the globe in a few seconds' time (1926:11).

Further, the nature of economic competition in the global economy would seem to require some kind of global control. Current political boundaries are "artificial." At present the economic changes resulting from the larger market have developed more rapidly than the machinery of control. Much trouble arises from the fact that the existing political organization of the world bears no relation to the new interregional economy. Political boundaries frequently intersect natural regions and divide supplementary ones. Competing regions may lie in different countries as is the case of the cotton, sugar, silk and grain belts of the world. Inasmuch as the products are sold on the world market the producers in different regions have problems in common and are united by common economic ties. The cotton growers of Egypt are in many respects more vitally related to the cotton producers of America than either group is to other occupational groups within its own country... Regional organization which is limited to the national unit cannot effectively deal with a problem that is international in scope. Everywhere the clash between the natural region and the artificial political organization is manifest (McKenzie, 1926:35).

In McKenzie's view, the national systems of politics also promote war and conflict, which further stunts the development of global relations. "The feeling of insecurity is the most potent barrier to efficient regional specialization at the present time. So long as individual nations must prepare for war there can be little genuine regional cooperation" (McKenzie, 1926:35).

The Cultural Diversity Issue

In his discussion of standardization, McKenzie foresaw some of the current debate on the tendency of globalization to decrease cultural diversity in favor of a global monoculture (see Norberg-Hodge, 1996). "Recent trends in international trade are speeding up the movement toward standardization and cultural homogeneity throughout the world" (McKenzie, 1926:42). He acknowledges the criticism that standardization receives for

> making automatons of human beings and reducing civilization to a canned and card-indexed condition." Yet, he argues, it is nonetheless "advancing with increasing rapidity and to the great gain of humanity.... Standardization of material culture is an achievement of the new world order. It is the outgrowth of machine production and rapid communications (McKenzie, 1926:36-37).

It is

> ...an essential phase of the great economy... The more standardized material culture becomes the more fluid is life and the more extended the zone of common participation. In an interregional exchange economy in which commodities pass from one district to another standards of measurement, quality and price are essential. The fact that perishable fruits may now be bought by grade and shipped thousands of miles is an achievement made possible by standardization. Such standardization requires cooperation and organization, also confidence in the integrity of the system (McKenzie, 1926:40-41).

At times, McKenzie seems merciless on the topic. Local cultures, it seems, must give way or civilization will be stunted.

> In a word the basic elements of the new world civilization do not permit of local adaptations such as were possible under the old and less vital regime of foreign commerce. The new world order is developing on the basis of science, and science knows no local preferences. Wave lengths and electric currents have no concern with local traditions (McKenzie, 1926:43).

For global integration,

> ...it will be necessary for the nations to surrender much of what they now consider to be their sovereign rights. Not merely is it necessary that there be standardization in units of measure, currency, grades, and systems of credit but also in language, laws, political machinery and ethical codes. International intercourse everywhere is hampered by unnecessary cultural diversity. The area of common life can extend only as the universe of common discourse extends... There is need of international 'rationalization' for the world as well as for Europe (McKenzie, 1926:45).

But McKenzie recognizes that there are areas where such standardization is necessary, and others where it is neither necessary nor desirable.

> Physical differences, geographical and racial, necessitate certain regional cultural diversities... Moreover, standardization in certain aspects of culture does not imply monotonous uniformity. Cities everywhere may have similar systems of plumbing, lighting, sanitation, water supply, hospitalization, policing, statistics and transportation, although their inhabitants do not all play the same games, worship the same deities, wear the same clothes, or appreciate the same forms of art and music. While efficient communal life demands certain external uniformities still each individual is unique and the

search for variety in individual expression is just as natural as the search for uniformity in communal action (McKenzie, 1926:46).[88]

Conclusion

In the Chicago tradition, Roderick D. McKenzie was an astute observer of the world around him. In his careful examinations of the details of everyday life in modern society, from the neighborhoods of Columbus, Ohio to slums of Calcutta, McKenzie perceived fundamental features of modern society not widely examined or understood by sociologists. His focus on the material aspects of society suggests that society is more than the interrelationships of people. A more realistic conception of the "social" includes its essential material aspects. Society can be best understood in the totality of relations that constitute it, relations of human beings as well as relations to natural and cultural objects.

The details of the material or physical relations in the modern world provide ample evidence of a fundamental aspect of modern society, that is, the increasing complexity, intensity and intimacy of these relations. The modern world is characterized, in McKenzie's view, by an ever growing integration. From one perspective, this growth in relations is represented by institutions assuming ever greater importance in society, replacing individuals as the basic units of social life. From another perspective, the "Great Society" as McKenzie calls it, or "Global Society" in today's terms, emerges mainly in response to tremendous developments in transportation and communications. These developments have shrunk the world, establishing relations, for example, between the "Tamils of Malaya" and the "workers of Akron" (McKenzie, 1968 [1926]-a:139). On these and other issues, McKenzie's long neglected writings have much to offer those trying to make sense out of modern society.

References

Ahrens, E. (2000[1950]). *Order and Disorder in Society*. Unpublished manuscript.
Eubank, E. (1940) 'Roderick Duncan McKenzie: Sociologist', *Sociology and Social Research*, 25:70-73.
Gross, M. (2004) 'Human Geography and Ecological Sociology', *Social Science*

---

[88] Ahrens suggests an approach for maintaining diversity while creating a global society and global culture. He argues along with McKenzie, as noted above, that the nation-state is not compatible with global social organization. However, this "does not mean that cultural differences should be wiped out in favor of a universal culture. Nothing is achieved by force, nor does the basic difficulty lie in regional cultural differences. It would be quite possible to have diversity of culture and still build a universal culture above and across it. The difficulty, we hold, lies in the way cultural variations have been exploited to the ends of business domination and political process." Ahrens, Erich. (2000 [1950]) *Order and Disorder in Society*. Unpublished manuscript.

History, 28:575-805.

Hawley, A. (1950) *Human Ecology: A Theory of Community Structure*. New York: Ronald Press.

-----.(1975) 'Letter.' edited by Dennis W. MacDonald.

-----.(1968) 'Introduction.' in *Roderick D. McKenzie on Human Ecology*, (ed.). Hawley, A.H. Chicago: University of Chicago Press.

Hollingshead, A.B. (1961) 'A Re-examination of Ecological Theory', in *Studies in Human Ecology*, (ed.). Theodorson, G. New York: Harper & Row:108-114

Martindale, D. (1958) 'Prefatory Remarks: The Theory of the City', in *The City*, Max Weber. Glencoe, Ill.: Free Press.

McKenzie, R. D. (1923) *The Neighborhood: A Study of Local Life in the City of Columbus, Ohio*. Chicago: University of Chicago Press.

-----.(1924) 'The Ecological Approach to the Study of the Human Community', *The American Journal of Sociology*, 30:287-301.

-----.(1926) 'Finds Europe Hurt by Trade Ambitions', in *New York Times*. New York: New York Times:16.

-----.(1926) 'The Evolving World Economy', in *Albert Kahn Foundation for the Foreign Travel of American Teachers: Reports*. New York: Trustees of the Albert Kahn Foundation:9-71

-----.(1927) *Oriental Exclusion*. New York: Institute of Pacific Relations.

-----.(1928a) *L' Évolution Économique du Monde*. Boulogne-sur-Seine: Imprimerie d'Études Sociales & Politiques.

-----.(1928b) *L'évolution économique du monde* (The evolving world economy): [Boulogne-sur-Seine, Imprimerie d'Études sociales & politiques.

-----.(1933a) The Metropolitan Community. New York: McGraw-Hill.

-----.(1933b) 'The Rise of the Metropolitan Community', in *Recent Social Trends*, (ed.). by President's Research Committee on Social Trends. New York: McGraw-Hill:443-496

-----.(1934) 'The Basis of Interregional Unity', in *Readings in Human Ecology*, (ed.). by McKenzie, R.D. Ann Arbor, MI: George Wahr:360-364

-----.(1968 [1926]-a) 'Movement and the Ability to Live', in *Roderick D. McKenzie on Human Ecology*, (ed.). Hawley, A.H. Chicago: University of Chicago Press:134-140

-----.(1968 [1926]b) "The Scope of Human Ecology." in *Roderick D. McKenzie on Human Ecology*, (ed.). Hawley, A.H. Chicago: University of Chicago Press. Chicago: University of Chicago Press:19-32

-----.(1968 [1934]a) 'Demography, Human Geography and Human Ecology', in *Roderick D. McKenzie on Human Ecology*, (ed.). Hawley, A.H. Chicago: University of Chicago Press. Chicago: University of Chicago Press:33-48

-----.(1968 [1934]b) 'Industrial Expansion and the Interrelations of Peoples', in *Roderick D. McKenzie on Human Ecology*, (ed.). Hawley, A.H. Chicago: University of Chicago Press:121-133

-----.(1968 [1936]) 'The Ecology of Institutions', in *Roderick D. McKenzie on*

Human Ecology, (ed.). Hawley, A.H. Chicago: University of Chicago Press:102-117

-----.(1971 [1921/1922]) *The Neighborhood: A study of Local Life in the City of Columbus, Ohio*. New York: Arno Press.

Norberg-Hodge, H. (1996) 'Break Up the Monoculture', in *The Nation*.

Park, R.E. (1936) 'Human Ecology', *American Journal of Sociology*, 42:1-15.

Park, R.E. and Burgess, E.W. (1921) *Introduction to the Science of Sociology*. Chicago: University of Chicago Press.

CHAPTER 5

Mind, Self and Society: The Overlooked Potential of G.H. Mead's legacy

Julie Kirby
Faculty of Health, Edge Hill University,
Lancashire, England

> Mind can never transcend the environment in which it operates.
> (G.H. Mead, 1932:118)

Introduction

In 1894 at the invitation of John Dewey, North American Pragmatist philosopher G.H Mead (1863-1931), joined the Department of Philosophy and Psychology at the newly founded University of Chicago, he remained there until shortly before his death age 68 years. He died a relative unknown, but was esteemed by some colleagues and students as an extraordinary thinker: Mead was an empiricist and a profound theorist (Joas, 1980). He developed an important framework for conceptualising mind/body, self/society, subjective/objective, structure/agency that placed situated embodiment at the centre of existence and lived experience. Baldwin (1986:9) suggests that Mead's ideas have the potential to build a unifying theory for sociology that brings together diverse schools of thought such as economics, conflict theory, social change, systems theory, cognitive theories, structuralism, symbolic interactionism, biosocial, historical and ecological sociology. In this approach there is no absolute separation between nature and culture, body and mind, materiality and knowledge, they are all interconnected dimensions of social experience (Burkitt 1998a). The far-reaching potential of Mead's approach as a unifying approach for sociology remains largely unrealised. It has even been suggested that since Berger and Luckmann's (1975) attempt to link up the macro level of society with the micro level of individual experience, work dichotomising the macro/micro interface threatens to undermine advances previously made by Mead (Burkitt, 2000). In Mead's thought there is no dichotomy between society (macro) and the individual (micro), they are interdependent and reflexively in process.

Mead argued that the natural environment – situated embodiment – took precedence over the transcendental in terms of solving the problems arising within everyday lived experience. He drew upon pragmatism to pursue his central themes and concepts:

> Striving to root 'mind' or 'spirit' in the organism (body).
> Attempt to elaborate a theory of intersubjectivity that conceived of the self as socially originated.
> Confidence in the emancipatory prospects of the scientific method.
> A social approach to the development of the inner mental processes (psychological apparatus) of mind and self rooted in action and intersubjectivity within a general concept of situated sociality. (Joas, 1980)

Mead presents us with an overlooked but important ontologically rooted bio-psycho-social approach to overcoming dualisms operating within Cartesian approaches to the mind/body, self/society and agency/structure debates:

> Mead's genius lay in seeing the self as inseparable from society [....] the self emerges from social experience [....] is not part of the body, and does not exist at birth. Mead rejected the position that personality is guided by biological drives (as asserted by Freud) or biological maturation (as Piaget claimed). For Mead the self develops only through social experience. (Marcionis and Plummer, 1998:138).

Through developing a situated, embodied, reflexive ontology (see Figure 1), Mead insisted that humans are simultaneously natural and social becomings. Their interaction within the collectivity of a pre-existing society as they become members of that society is largely non-conscious in the absence of socially encountered 'problematics'. Encountering problems within everyday life promotes the reflexive problem-solving cognitive act of thinking. Within this problem-solving process, the application of the 'scientific method' is something all humans do, not just professional scientists (Joas, 1980, Baldwin, 1986):

> Mind, as constructive or reflective or problem-solving thinking, is the socially acquired means or mechanism or apparatus whereby the human individual solves the various problems of environmental adjustment which arise to confront him in the course of his experience, and which prevent his conduct from proceeding harmoniously on its way, until they have been dealt with (Mead, 1967:308 sic, my italics).

Mead treated the word 'intelligent' as a verb – an action/doing word (Strauss, 1977). Contemplation gives way to empiricism as humans hypothesise and 'test' ideas for their utility to solve problems. All ideas can thus be evaluated for the consequences that arise from them (Baldwin, 1986). For Mead, the everyday application of the 'scientific method' is the engine of social evolution and social change:

> One must take the attitude of the others in a group in order to belong to a community; he has to employ that outer social world taken within himself in order to carry on thought. It is through his relationship to others in that community, because of the rational social relations that obtain in that community, that he has being as a citizen. On the other hand, the individual is constantly reacting to the social attitudes, and changing in this co-operative process the very community to which he belongs. Those changes may be humble and trivial ones' (Mead, 1967:200, sic).

Mead's social theory thus sought to unify all facets of society and social experience; the mind/body dualism and the schism between the micro and macro level of social analysis were rejected (Baldwin, 1986). In Mind, Self and Society, Mead set out a conceptual framework within which human beings are simultaneously biological and social. The bodily/physiological variations/potentialities of the 'natural' organism (body) is the situating foundation for the social development of mind and self; the process through which humans become members of a community/society. Self is thus structured from the outside to the inside; inner experiences being the culmination of the integration of physical and mental activity (Baldwin, 1986). Ontologically, the situated body pre-dates the later development of the inner psychological apparatus of mind and self:

> It cannot be said that the individuals come first and the community later, for the individuals arise in the very process itself, just as the human body or any multi-cellular form is one in which differentiated cells arise. There has to be a life-process going on in order to have the differentiated cells; in the same way there has to be a social process going on in order that there may be individuals. It is just as true in society as it is in the physiological situation that there could not be the individual if there was not the process of which he is part (Mead 1967:189 sic).

Mead's interest in the inner mental processes of mind and self was thus not orientated towards recording a person's unique experience: he viewed mind and self as the key to understanding the relationship between an individual and society (Layder, 1994). The social processes that permeate the environment of the situated mind and self 'individualise' individuals into his/her subject positions within the collective of a given community/society. Baldwin (1986) summarises that in Mead's approach socialisation processes structure each individuals' mind and self in two complementary ways:

Common traits that are shared with others,
Unique personal traits make a person a distinct individual.

Social processes frame and shape both commonality and differences among and between individuals. Therefore, each individual develops a sense of belonging to a given community/society, as well as a sense of being different to others:

> Every individual self has its own peculiar individuality, its own unique pattern [which reflects the whole, but] does so from its own particular and unique standpoint within that process… (Mead, 1934 cited in Baldwin, 1986: 113)

Mead insisted that collective social processes and emergence of the individual are indivisible. In ontological terms the 'natural organism' - body - comes first and situates the later development of mind and self within a social collectivity. Mead termed this collectivity the 'generalized other' (discussed further below). The transformation of the biologic individual to the minded organism takes place under the controlling influence of the 'generalized other' that gives shape and meaning to the lived physiological capacities of the individual organism. Sociality and intersubjectivity are thus central to how individuals adapt to, and simultaneously organise their natural and social environment within extant collective norms rules and values of a pre-existing community/society:

> The appearance of the retinal elements has given the world color; the development of the organs in the ear has given the world sound. We pick out an organised environment in relationship to our response, so that these attitudes, as such, not only represent our organised responses but they also represent what exists for us in the world. (Mead, 1967: 128)

Mead thus draws attention to how the body functions not only as the means to experience the world in a sensory sense; it also situates an individual's cognitive development within his/her social environment. A situated body must exist before a mind and self can develop. The biological/physiological variations/potentialities of an individual's body (organism) acquire biographical meaning (sense of self) for the individual within the collective social meanings of time and place. In the widest sense, Mead developed a theoretical and methodological framework that brought together genetic factors - 'natural' bodily/physiological variations/potentialities of the organism - and the social environment - collective norms, rules and values of the 'generalized other',

> …the organism (biological body) gets expression in the relation of the community and its environment. [….] the individual organism determines in some sense its own environment by its sensitivity. The only environment to which the organism can react is one that its sensitivity reveals. (Mead, 1967: 245).

The later development of mind and self are situated and reflexive. Embodiment, sociality and cognition are central tenets to the self-consciousness that underpins this approach. Bodily differences/physiological potentialities and variations such as those linked to anatomical sex differences and 'racial' variations – such as skin colour and body shapes - situate a human being's 'sensitivity' to its environment and the collective community into which it - the organism (body) - has been born and socialised':

> Through self-consciousness the individual organism enters in some sense into its own environmental field; its own body becomes part of the set of environmental stimuli to which it responds or reacts. (Mead 1967:172)."

For Mead, humans are in a perpetual state of becoming, the self does not remain static, it remains in flux and in process within ongoing social activity (Mead, 1934/1967). Mead thus rejects the individualistic principle taken to the actions and behaviours of human beings. Whilst appearing to follow Descartes by declaring that we can distinguish between our self and our body, Mead retains the connection between mind and body through the cognitive (social) act of thinking. In the process of becoming members of society, individuals draw on shared symbols that attach meaning and social significance to objects or actions. From this starting point Mead sought to undo the subjectification of meaning in the monadic sense:

> It is absurd to look at the mind simply from the standpoint of the individual human organism; for although it has its focus there, it is essentially a social phenomenon; even its biological functions are primarily social…. We must regard mind, then, as arising and developing within the social process, within the empirical matrix of social interactions. (Mead, 1967:133)."

Sociality thus permeates the adaptive individualisation process as an individual's situated organism (body) sensitizes the individual organism to its environment. Mead thus rejects introspection in favour of reflexivity, an action rooted in sociality and ntersubjectivity (Joas, 1980, Gronow, 2008). Sociality has both concrete (bodily/material) and abstract (ideas/discourse) dimensions that incorporates hermeneutical acknowledgement that individual realities/lived experiences are shaped by collective social processes (see Figure 1).

This chapter presents an application of Mead's framework to a recently completed qualitative study exploring the phenomenon of voice-hearing from the perspective of those who experience it. The starting point of the study was that for some voice-hearers the phenomenon can be experienced as distressing, whilst for others it can be enriching and life enhancing (Romme and Escher,

Figure 1: *Situated, embodied, reflexive ontology*

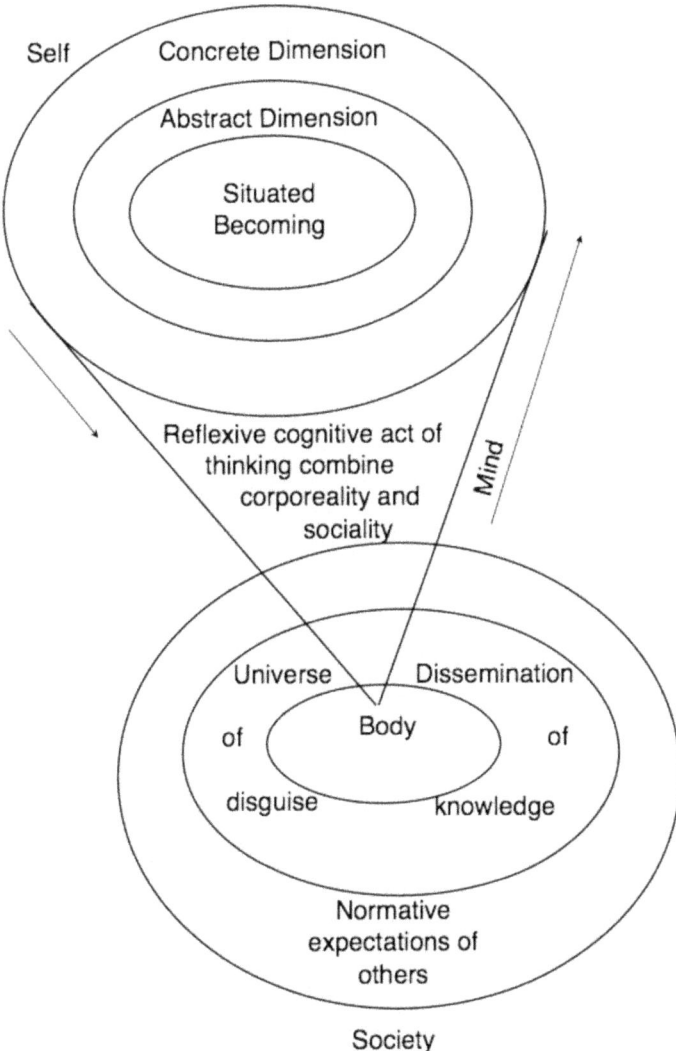

1993). The purpose of the study was to explore the phenomenon in a way that might help to illuminate possibilities around why voice-hearing is highly distressing for some voice-hearers, and a life-enhancing experience for others.

A grounded theory approach was taken; the theoretical framework was developed as the study progressed. The exploration began with fieldwork with voice-hearers as a way of developing basic principles around what is important about the phenomenon of voice-hearing from the perspective voice-hearers. Voice-hearers articulated:

Feeling 'different' to 'normal' or 'ordinary' people
The need for an explanation
Personal experiences of the phenomenon reflected aspects of the voice-hearer's social circumstances; distressing social circumstances were reflected in the content of the voices

Mead's approach to the individual/society emerged as a good foundational framework for the study. Data generation tools were developed with voice-hearers.

Sixty-two voice-hearers self-selected to participate in the study. Ethical approval was secured through the researcher's HEI base. The sample was recruited purposively (Miles and Huberman 1994, Silverman 2000) through national (England and Wales, UK) advertisements placed in the newsletter of the National Hearing Voices Network (NHVN), and the 'Big Issue' sold in aid of the homeless, TVS Arts Magazine, Daily Mirror and Leeds and Yorkshire Times. The recruitment advertisement sought participants with the following question "hearing voices?". A total number of 95 potential participants responded to the advertisement, 62 went on to generate data. The participants were comprised of three groups; mental health care service users (n=37), ex-users (n=15) and non-users (n=10).

The 'Problematic' Phenomenon of Voice-hearing:
A Universe of Competing Discourses

> *"I have spent my whole life since I've heard that voice in my head genuinely and I went through loads of suggestions, what it could be, was it a ghost, was it my granddad, was it an angel, was it Jesus, was it God and I've been through loads of different scenarios of what it could be"* (Paul, 43 years, non service user).

All research participant names are pseudonyms.

Written accounts of voice-hearing date back at least to 400BC, with many prominent figures such as Socrates, Joan of Arc, Joanna Southcott, Carl Jung, Mahatma Ghandi, William Blake, Martin Luther King Jr., Elizabeth Kubler-Ross and classical composer Robert Schumann amongst those who claim to have heard voices (Balleine, 1956; Leudar and Thomas, 2000; Watkins, 1998). However, social acceptability of voice-hearing as being 'normal' for some people remains elusive (Grierson 1993, Pearson 1998). The phenomenon is associated with forms of individual pathology that can include biological dysfunction, biochemical imbalance, psychopathology, breakdown in the reality discrimination process, delusional thinking, irrational beliefs and in particular to the highly debated diagnostic category of 'schizophrenia' (Gelder, et al 1994;

Romme, et al 1992; Bentall, 1997, Boyle, 1990). voice-hearing has become associated with 'madness', 'imaginings' and 'hallucinations' that have been subjected to mechanisms of social control that has oscillated between the Church and medicine (Sarbin and Juhasz, 1967; Screech, 1985). Leudar and Thomas, (2000) estimate that less than 5% of the general population hear voices regularly. Other studies suggest that up to one in ten of the general public will hear voices at some time in their lives (British Psychological Society 2000), whilst Slade and Bentall (1988) suggest that this figure is nearer 25% of the population. However, given the cultural dominance in the West of the association between voice-hearing and mental health disorder and in particular with 'schizophrenia' (Slade and Bentall, 1988; Boyle, 1990, Thomas, 1997; Watkins, 1998), there is a general reluctance to report experience of the phenomenon (Kirby, 2006).

Voice-hearing is a cross-cultural phenomenon in terms of both time and geography, cutting across social variables such as race, class and gender (Kirby, 2006). The phenomenon has remained an enduring enigma thousands of years of recorded human history, and has been described within religious, psychological, fictional and mythical frames of reference (Heery, 1989). In Mead's terms, the very fact that voice-hearing continues to be a topic of debate, suggests that it is a 'problem'. The phenomenon of voice-hearing is a 'problem' for all voice-hearers in the sense that it 'others' them from 'normal' or 'ordinary' people (Kirby, 2006):

"It feels like it is taking my peace away because I can't just be normal because it makes me not normal, whereas other people would be like whatever and not have to think about these things and where I can just be like normal and get along with day to day activities and be able to think proper, normal things, but instead I've got all these things on me head which are in the way." (Shelly, 25 years, ex-service user)

Experiencing the 'otherness' of feeling 'not normal' promoted feelings of lack of 'fit' or 'belonging'. Re-establishing some sense of fit and belonging became the driving force behind problem-solving. Socially disseminated ideas - 'universes of discourse' (Mead, 1972) – were necessarily drawn upon by voice-hearers to 'explain' their otherness. Explanatory frameworks, whatever their epistemological/paradigmatic foundations from the biomedical to the supernatural, presented voice-hearers with emancipatory power in the sense that they offered voice-hearers a route out of 'otherness' be it as a mental health care user or a psychic/medium (Kirby, 2006). Each voice-hearer hypothesised and 'tested' an explanatory framework before adopting it as a 'best fit'. This 'best fit' remained in flux and open to challenges from other explanatory frameworks and was fraught with the contingencies framing the complex everyday lives of each voice-hearer. This process is necessarily ontologically rooted as each voice-hearers cannot transcend the concrete and abstract dimensions of his/her environment as s/he draws upon his/her own particular material existence, experiences and knowledge of the world. These environments frame both the commonality between voice-hearers as voice-hearers and the differences between voice-hearers in terms of how they act upon the phenomenon.

The voice-hearer's faith in his/her 'best fit' understanding can be influenced, challenged as well as undermined through social relations, which may lead to the voice-hearer revising his/her 'best fit' in order to take account of the challenges. In this respect Mead's approach to time is illuminating. In Mead's view the present is a 'knife edge' present, a shifting boundary between the extended domains of the past and future within a perpetually ongoing social process (Joas 1980). Voice-hearers drew upon ideas and past experiences to understand voice-hearing experiences in their present and possible actions/consequences in the future. Voice-hearers who had experienced abuse of some form drew upon this experience to construct a 'best fit' as an understandable response to that abuse and sought out mental health care intervention. Other voice-hearers drew upon ideas around/experience of supernatural or paranormal activity and constructed a 'best fit' as having psychic powers or having had a religious conversion experience (Kirby, 2006). There is no consensus of opinion around the 'cause' of the phenomenon instead there is a plethora of competing ideas which promoted varying degrees of 'chaos' among voice-hearers:

> *I have read extensively on schizophrenia, including R.D. Laing and Susan Greenfield. I find all theories useful but have found most comfort in more general theories about life experiences such as Buddhism and existentialism. I have heard of Romme and Escher and I think their ideas are really cool! But I still don't know what causes the experience."*
> (Natasha, 23 years, service user)

Experiencing a phenomenon that problematised the bodily ear as the 'normal' way a body deals with sound occupied 'Enid's' thoughts as she sought to make sense of it:

> *"I find it very puzzling that disembodied voices (sounds or noises) can form sentences, talk about watching or seeing me in all aspects of my life, criticise or condemn every move I make. I try to figure out where they are coming from"* (Enid, 74 years, ex-service user)

Voice-hearers articulated 'internal chaos' as they sought to understand what was happening. 'Internal chaos' is used frequently to describe confused states within mental health care theory and practice. However, its usage remains within an individualistic model, when it may be more fruitfully understood by conceptualising the person as a member of society, with their 'internal chaos' being a consequence of collective rather than individual processes (Kirby, 2006). Despite its long history with written accounts dating back to at least 400BC (Leudar and Thomas, 2000), voice-hearing remains a poorly understood phenomenon (Grierson, 1993, Watkins, 1998). However it is fair to say that there has been a copious amount written about the possible 'causes' and 'meaning' of voice-hearing ranging from the scientific to the supernatural. From the 'universes of discourse' (Mead, 1967/1934, Mead, 1972) that has taken shape around the phenomenon, voice-hearers have formulated an impressively wide range of explanatory frameworks as they attempt to understand it, some of which appear weird and wonderful (Grierson, 1993), whilst others have gained professional acclaim for their efforts (for example Jung, 1967, 1969):

> Inner voices, invisible companions, the voice of conscience, locutions, inner guides, angels, demons, ghosts, muses, thoughts-out-aloud, radio waves of divinity, the voice of God, language magic, the Other Order, cold castigation language, persecutors, court-of-law punishment language, self-talk, inner helpers, splinter psyches, sub-personalities. (Watkins, 1998:1)

Watkins' list is not exhaustive, a cursory glance at the literature will reveal a multitude of other 'explanations' that include higher or extra-sensory perception, spirit guides, aliens, the unconscious, telepathy, projection, possession, mental radio, mind control, white noise, other realms, clairaudience, mediumship, channelling, someone watching over me, voices of abusers, chemical imbalances or faulty wiring in the brain, innermost thoughts, repressed thoughts, post traumatic stress disorder, tuning into the conscience collective of society, voices of homophobia and racism....the possibilities continue to grow and proliferate. Explanations are intimately bound up with the evolution of ideas and knowledge production within wider society at specific historical times and places, be they spiritual, religious, scientific, technological, science fiction or mental health related (see Kirby, 2006).

Voice-hearing as a Symptom of Mental Illness

Voice-hearing is termed medically as 'auditory/aural/verbal' hallucination and associated with forms of mental illness, it is necessary to consider the approach taken to the phenomenon and the individual within professional mental health literature. This literature is informed by a fragmenting, transcendent dualistic Cartesian approach that presupposes the separateness of mind and body, which in turn leads to a separation between concrete and abstract dimensions of social experience. This has led to biological approaches to voice-hearing that ignore the psychological and social aspects of personal experience, as well as psychosocial approaches that ignore the biological (material) aspects of the lived experience of the person (Blackman, 2001). The exception to this separating of mind and body is found within Freud's psychoanalytical theory wherein the mind (mental processes) is considered to be intrinsically connected in some way with the body (bodily processes). Psychoanalytical theory thus ties in psychology to physiology and biology (Freud, 1953), however, it neglects the social context thinking and behaviour arises. This neglect in turn appears to be linked to the downplaying as well as the overall neglect of consciousness within psychoanalytical theory (Rycroft, 1995). The tendency of psychoanalysis to regard consciousness as being of secondary importance to unconscious forces has led to the development of much existential criticism of Freudian psychoanalysis (Rycroft, 1995).

In Mead's approach there is no conceptual room for the unconscious 'repression' of unacceptable impulses as anxiety rooted defence mechanism. Mead's argument is thus, if I am aware of something I am conscious, if I am not aware of it, it cannot affect my thoughts (Joas, 1980). For Mead, when an impulse is deemed by an individual to be 'unacceptable' and anxiety-provoking, it begs the question as to how it became positioned as such. Freud explained this in terms of a psychological 'censor', which in turn is the conceptual ancestor of the super-ego. Mead observed:

> Freud's conception of the psychological "censor" represents a partial recognition of the operation of social control in terms of self-criticism, a recognition, namely with reference to sexual experience and conduct. But this same sort of censorship or criticism of himself by the individual is reflected also in all other aspects of his social experience, behaviour, and relations – a fact which follows naturally and inevitably from our social theory of the self. (Mead, 1967:255, sic)

Mead is critical of Freud's neglect of the social context of individuals. For Mead, self criticism and the psychological 'censor' of Freudian theory is social in origin. Unacceptable impulses are reflexively self-consciously identified as such by individuals within the controlling influence of the 'generalized other'. Also, unlike Freud, Mead's interest in the impact of social control over individuals thought and behaviour extended beyond sexuality. In Mead's analysis unacceptable impulses permeate all aspects of natural (concrete/bodily) and abstract social experience and are consciously defined as such by an individual through their internalisation of the collective attitude ('generalized other'). In this sense the mind cannot transcend the interlinked concrete and abstract dimensions of the environment within which it operates. Therefore, central to Mead's (1967) approach is the influence of collective power embedded within the 'generalized other' permeating the social contexts that frame the psychological development of individuals. Therefore, human thought and action cannot be understood outside of the intersubjective social systems in which human beings are involved (Crossley, 1996).

Asocial psychological approaches to the person individualise the mind by situating pathology within the person, effectively setting them apart from the impact of wider social relations within which they developed. Therefore, the responses of voice-hearers to the phenomenon of voice-hearing arrived at through reflective cognitive processes seeking to understand as well as explain their experiences, have tended to be considered to be symptomatic of 'delusional thinking' within professional mental health care practice. Psychiatry in particular has traditionally assumed these beliefs or 'secondary delusions' to be 'empty speech acts, whose informational content refers neither to world or social being' (Berrios, 1991:12). This view has been challenged by the work of social psychiatrist Marius Romme (Romme and Escher, 1989, 1993) who found that both the content of the voices and the diversity of explanatory frameworks developed around the experience, are meaningful within the lived reality of the voice-hearer. However, Romme and Escher's work does not signal a paradigm shift toward recognition of the ontological import of a non-transcendent socially situated mind and its immersion in the lived experiences of the individual. Romme and Escher continue to draw upon Freud's ideas around 'healthy' and 'unhealthy' minds wherein coping strategies are developed in response to anxiety-provoking situations. Romme and Escher thus compared the coping strategies of mental health users and never been users developed in response to their experience of voice-hearing. They concluded that voice-hearing in itself is not necessarily indicative of mental illness, rather it is the individual response to the phenomenon that is the problem. Romme and Escher (1993) explored the coping strategies of non-distressed voice-hearers for their potential therapeutic value in developing effective coping strategies for distressed voice-hearers. They concluded that voice-hearing per se does not necessarily indicate mental illness, rather it is the voice-hearers response to the phenomenon. They suggest that voice-hearing becomes 'problematic' to the voice-hearer only when they lose control and become unable to 'cope' with the experience. It is at this point, they argue, that voice hearers may come to the attention of the mental health care services:

> [....] the crucial advantage enjoyed by those who succeed in coping well is their greater strength with regard both to their voices and to their environment, and in their more favourable experience of that environment as supportive rather than threatening. We may therefore view the hearing of voices not solely as a discrete individual pathological experience, but as an interactional phenomenon reflecting the nature of the individual's relationship to his or her own environment, and indeed vice versa. (Romme and Escher, 1993:16)

They highlight the social complexity of how voice-hearing is experienced and responded to, however, the far reaching implication of this insight is not fully carried through in their recommendations. They suggest that voice-hearers who had not come to the attention of mental health care services were better able to 'cope' with their experiences than mental health care users and thus presumably had potentially useful advice to give to 'non-copers'. The corollary of this is that those who 'cope' have greater natural resolve and possess 'greater inner strength' than those who do not. This in turns reinforces an individualising therapeutic approach to voice-hearing that places the onus of responsibility on individual voice-hearers to learn to cope better with their experiences, neglecting the social contexts that create differences in the experience of the phenomenon that may not only undermine this endeavour, but also contributed to the original distress.

Romme and Escher's work appears to have re-ignited interest within clinical psychology around the therapeutic value of cognitive behavioural approaches for voice-hearing and other forms of 'psychosis' in those who are experiencing distress (see Chadwick, et al, 2000a, 2000b; Birchwood and Tarrier, 1992; Fowler, Garety and Kuipers, 1995; Haddock and Slade, 1996; Kingdon and Turkington, 1994; Nelson, 1997, and Perris and McGorry, 1998). Cognitive models propose that dysfunctional assumptions and their resulting biases in other systems lead to, as well as maintain mental disorder (Haw, 2000). Within the cognitive-behavioural approach, 'delusional thinking' is understood in terms of normal psychological principles wherein normal problem-solving thought processes are utilised to understand an anomalous experience (Delahunty, 2001). However, the transcendent individualising approach taken towards the individual adopted by this form of intervention prevents its full therapeutic realisation and potential, as well as its political power in terms of drawing attention to problematic social environments rather than problematic individuals. This is because the Freudian approach to mind is retained within cognitive interventions in that individual 'coping strategy enhancement' is the aim of therapy (see Tarrier, 1987), with the voices considered to be 'symptoms' of individual 'psychosis' rooted in some form of 'breakdown in the reality discrimination process' (Grierson, 1993). Mead provides an alternative to both psychoanalysis and cognitive therapeutic interventions that take a transcendent asocial approach to the individual and their 'illness'. Within Mead's framework body and mind are linked through the cognitive (social) act of thinking as the biological and social aspects of experience come together simultaneously within conscious reflective thought. Attempts to change the way(s) in which an individual thinks about and 'copes' with their experiences without due consideration to the social context framing their experiences and ideas, runs the risk of being harmful at worst (Rose, 2005) and ineffective over the long term at best (Delahunty, 2001).

Some Findings: Situated Embodiment and Inter-subjective Social Processes

It has been suggested that biological factors might pre-dispose some individuals to experience the phenomenon of 'hearing voices' (Bleuler, 1950; Wing, 1987, Gelder, et al 1994). However, whilst biology situates a person's body as the foundation for his/her social life, biology alone in a physiological sense cannot provide an adequate explanation around the actual 'content' of the voices (White, 1995). Mead's insight into the non-transcendent mind as being situated within concrete and abstract social processes is crucial here. The ways in which the phenomenon of voice-hearing is experienced has clear links with each voice-hearer's interlinked 'natural' (biological) and abstract (discourse/ideas) social environment both in terms of their commonality and their differences. The commonality' centred on 'hearing' of 'feeling' a voice that has no obvious material origin that problematised the bodily ear as the 'normal' way a body deals with sound. In this sense, the participants were not 'born' voice-hearers; rather they became voice-hearers when they became reflexively consciously aware of experiencing a problematic phenomenon (see Figure 2).

Sociality, Cognition and the Power of the Collective

> "[....] *the chatter can dominate [....] It is exhausting and it is excruciatingly painful, that is a word that describes it very well, absolute panic [....] nearly every interaction and even when I'm on my own, it is replaying. There is very rarely a time when I'm not feeling a little stressed out, or very stressed out because I'm constantly alert to people's body language, to everything. I am on alert a hell of a lot of time. I find it very difficult to be casual or carefree, because there are all these little antennae up there and they are all blethering on and picking up on that and picking up on what she has just done and how she has moved that chair. It is constant commentary on anything and everything that is happening, be it something that has really got nothing to do with any sodding thing, or it is important. [....] I'm working beside someone and there is all this going through the air waves and I'm wound up to the hilt because it is so noisy [....] people I don't even speak to at all, people who just look at me. They are saying things to me, so they have to be answered. They haven't actually spoken at all, it has just been a glance exchanged. One busy girl you are speaking to.*" (Emma, 37 years, ex-service user)

Emma's account brings sharply into focus the highly complex intersubjective processes that impact upon her experience of voice-hearing. She details the minutiae of social influences framing and shaping her everyday interactions that in turn is reflected in her experience of voice-hearing. Emma complained of bombardment and a lack of privacy even in her own 'private' thoughts. In Goffman's (1969) terms, this could be understood as a lack of a 'backstage' within which to retreat and recuperate from the everyday socially induced stresses. However, for Mead there is no 'backstage' (Burkitt, 1998) given that society is always 'inside' individuals. Shelly elaborates on these complex intersubjective processes by articulating how sounds in the form of 'noises' and the 'babblings' of people encountered socially become meaningful to her in that they appear to speak her exact thoughts, some of which are embarrassing because they discuss her 'bad habits' and past misdemeanours:

> "*Noises seemed to come together at such time to interpret my thoughts, my past anything. I felt my hearing them made other people hear them. I know to this day I was stared at. [....] I have had toddlers 3 years 'in their babblings' speak my exact thoughts... I am embarrassed and humiliated*" (Shelly, 25 years, ex-service user)

The impact of intersubjectivity on how voice-hearers experience something meaningful out of background noise by 'hearing' what they expect to hear has clear links with their reflexive engagement with the 'generalized other'. Particular social relations frame the cognitive intersection between the 'I' and the 'me' where the socially framed existence, experience and accumulated knowledge of a person meet, giving 'unique' shape and meaning to 'personal' experiences. This in turn clearly impacts upon how the phenomenon of voice-hearing is personally experienced:

> A basic though obvious premise of the (interactionist) perspective is that individuals are never considered in isolation from interactive partners – actual or ideal, real or imaginary. In contrast to all individualistic theories, interactionists suggest that it is not possible to understand the distinctly human aspects of social life unless one constantly questions the part played by others in influencing an individual's action. (Plummer, 1975:17)

Through the development of a self an individual voice-hearer is never alone. Experiences of voice-hearing are fundamentally linked to the social life of the voice-hearer, both in terms of the content of the voices and in the identification of its 'problematic' form.

The 'generalized other' is one of Mead's most important, as well as misunderstood concepts. It is a similar in meaning to the Freudian concept of 'superego', but with one key difference – social control is central to Mead's 'generalized other'. The 'generalized other' provides the essential component for intelligent thought among its individual members (Mead, 1964). It is important here to emphasise that Mead used the term 'intelligent' as a verb, an action/doing word. An approach to power reminiscent of Foucault permeates Mead's 'generalized other' in the sense that the effectivity on subjectivity of othering social processes inherent within the 'generalized other' is dependent upon shared meanings and mutually meaningful interactions between individuals at an intersubjective level. The 'taken-for-granteds' operating within the collective attitude of everyday life can be maintained as well as problematised (Stewart, 2003). In the absence of 'problematics' the 'taken-for-granteds' remain largely non-conscious and thus maintained in that they are not routinely consciously reflected upon and questioned. However, when problems are encountered, habitual action ceases as the individual reflexively thinks and problem-solves. Problematic social encounters/experiences bring collective norms, rules and values (taken-for-granteds) of the 'generalized other' into the conscious experience of the individual. Within this inherently social activity, the individual becomes an object to him/herself within the inherent 'othering' power relations of the 'generalized other' as s/he 'sees' the collective view of him/herself as s/he problem-solves and considers courses of action;

> It is by means of reflexivity – the turning-back of the experience of the individual upon himself – that the whole social process is thus brought into the experience of the individual involved in it; it is by such means, which enable the individual to take the attitude of the other toward himself, that the individual is able consciously to adjust himself (sic) to that process, and to modify the resultant of that process in any given social act in terms of his

adjustment to it. Reflexiveness, then, is the essential condition, within the social process, for the development of mind. (Mead, 1967:134, sic)

Mead developed the "I/me" conversation as a way of explicating the reflexive process. Mead's basic insight is that through the conversation between the 'I' and the 'me' of the unified self, a human being is capable of becoming an object to him/herself through reflexive interaction with the internalised generalized other (Plummer 1975). The 'me' is the social structure formed through the interaction with the 'generalized other' during the social process of becoming a member of society. The 'I' refers to the creative impulses for social action that holds within it the potential to change the 'me'.

> The 'I' is the response of the organism to the attitudes of others; the 'me' is the organised set of attitudes of others which one himself (sic) assumes. The attitudes of others constitute the organised 'me' and then one reacts towards that as an 'I' [....] The 'I' both calls out to the 'me' and responds to it. Taken together they constitute a personality as it appears in social experience. (Mead, 1967:175-178).

The 'me' thus refers to an individual's knowledge of collective norms, rules and values. This knowledge remains non-conscious (as distinct from unconscious) and action is habitual in the absence of 'problematics' encountered socially. When 'problematics' are encountered an individual becomes reflexively self-conscious as previously non-conscious actions become reflected upon by the 'I' as the self becomes an object to itself. The reflexivity within the 'I'/'me' dynamic that links up the lived concrete experiences of the organism (body) with abstract social meanings (mind) prevents Mead's conceptualisation of the self becoming nothing beyond a mere reflection of the social structure. Whilst avoiding dualism, Mead's approach to mind/body and self/society creates a conceptual space within which to explore the relationship between the concretely situated biologic individual ('I') and the abstract development of a collectively organised social individual ('me'): '…both aspects of the 'I' and 'me' are essential to the self in its full expression"(Mead, 1967:308 sic).

The collective object 'me' and the situated biologic subject 'I' together make socially originated reflexivity and thinking possible. Conceptualising the 'I' as the biologic subject with all its bodily / physiological potentialities / differences / variations is especially useful when conceptualising the 'me' as the meaning-making depository of lived bodily experiences. For Mead, in the absence of problematics it is possible to be conscious of bodily sensations without being self-conscious. However, problematic social encounters/experiences promote reflexive self-conscious thought and action as individual thinks and problem-solves. In effect the conversation between the 'I' and the 'me' reflects the temporal concerns of the subject under the collective influence of, the 'generalized other' internalised as the 'me'. Social control over the creative impulses of the 'I' is thus exerted by the 'me'. In the case of voice-hearers, the socially controlling influence of the 'me' over the creative potential of the organism ('I') can be evidenced as a voice-hearers becomes an object to him/herself on account of 'hearing; or 'feeling' a voice of no obvious material origin, leading to the response what is wrong with 'me', what is happening? (see Kirby, 2006). 'Why me?' was a subtext running throughout the accounts. 'Deviance' from the 'generalised other' without explanation appeared not to be an option. Voice-hearers began to problem-solve within their own specific social contexts. Stuart articulates his concern around 'what people would think' as he describes how he became consciously aware of experiencing a 'problematic' phenomenon:

> *"When I started (hearing voices), I didn't know anyone who had had those problems and so it was just like something really abnormal and weird and freaky and I was worried that people would be hostile if they knew [....] so I was quite worried that (a) what would happen to me and (b) what people would think."* (Stuart, 29 years, ex-service user)

This is embodied reflexivity in action, both concrete and abstract dimensions coming together in action. Firstly, Stuart draws attention to 'othering' inter-subjective relations of power within his everyday life as he became aware of the 'problem'. Secondly, he already 'knew' what people would think; his internalised knowledge of the 'generalized other' gave Stuart the self-conscious means to both predict the possible responses of others to his experience as 'abnormal', 'weird' and 'freaky'. The corollary of this is that voice-hearers may continue to live 'normally' or at least 'unproblematically' within society unless they become consciously aware of their 'othered' status as 'different'. Relativity thus operates within the generalized other':

> *"I myself did not know that I heard voices [....] whereas I thought it was normal and it was happening to everyone and then I realised that it wasn't actually happening to everyone [....] I thought it was happening to everyone, until I read a magazine article [...] That article was a revelation to me!"* (Emma, 37 years, ex-service user)

Emma's 'generalised other' had clearly been a voice-hearer, until she learned differently. This reflexively promoted an 'I'/'me' conversation around an experience that had previously been 'unproblematic' in the sense that she previously non-consciously assumed everyone heard voices. From Mead's non-dualistic approach to sociality and cognition, abstract collective attitudes towards voice-hearing as 'not normal' are shaped through inter-subjective relations of power. There is thus an inherent socially located relativity involved in the constitution of 'generalized other' that can be reflexively re-constituted.

The differences between the voice-hearers centred on the content of the voices, which again reflected the unique social circumstances of each voice-hearer. In general terms, relatively unproblematic voice content was linked to relatively unproblematic lives. Those who experienced distressing voice content also experienced distressing social circumstances. The way(s) in which voice-hearers experience/act upon the phenomenon is in essence a reflection of their situated environment; a product of a voice-hearer's interconnected 'natural' and social worlds. The content of Sheila's 'voices' did not trouble her because she loved and trusted the parents with whom she linked the voices. Sheila has never experienced the need to seek out mental health care intervention for her voices, and would be sad if they stopped. However, when asked whether she would like the voices to go away if they became nasty or negative she answered:

> "I don't know, I've often thought about that and I think so, yes. [...] I think I would maybe have to wonder why they were being nasty, maybe it was something that was happening that wasn't right for me." (Sheila, 53 years, non service user)

If her voices became 'nasty', Sheila would seek to understand why her voices changed. In particular she would consider the possibility that a change in her the content of her voices may reflect a change in her life circumstances. Sheila thus got to the crux of why the experience of voice-hearing differs from voice-hearer to voice-hearer. Not all voice-hearers experience Sheila's 'good relationship' with their voices, a difficult and distressing material existence impacts on the experience of voice-hearing because it is reflected in the content of the voices. Distressed voice-hearers felt 'opened up' to the scrutiny and thoughts of others that included pejorative and prejudicial content, and wanted it to stop, as well as the voices of people who have abused them or treated them badly.

Carrie's account is highly complex in terms of the biological and social factors impacting on the content of the voices she hears. Her conscious awareness of problematics linked to her 'race' (Chinese origin) and sexuality contain clear reference to foundational biological and social factors that frame and shape her self-conscious lived experience, which in turn impacts on the content of the voices she hears. In terms of race, biological factors linked to physical variation from the 'white' norm are illuminated through Carrie's reference to the physical appearance of her body:

> "Boys are threatening and bullies and men are the same and both racists. I fear males, I feel inferior they tell me I'm ugly so I must be. I look yuck! Disgusting. They call me yellow. Even paki. I'm not Pakistani, not that there's anything wrong with them or other race people. I hear males in the street shouting, it scares me, I feel in danger or too exposed and may be attacked. I hate males laughing, it causes paranoia. I hate pubs, clubs or groups of males more than one man alone. I can't look at them, I can't make friends with them, except in mental health safe services whom seem after a while and change to get use to same ones. If females are present in same building though I'd approach females for help more. I can't cope with physical or too close for comfort contact. Also I'm asexual. Not a tomboy, not queer people have me thought. But male voices reflect the fear within. As males don't accept me the voices that are male are the nasty self hatred. The songs sung to me stick in the voices in my head 'We are Siamese if you don't please', and 'Hong Kong phooey' and 'I think I'm turning Japanese'. [...] it is like

mocking the race really because I am an oriental person, so I look a bit different to the people in this country that come from this country and of course some of them don't know what country I come from so they will just make up songs that sound Japanese or some wild guess you know." (Carrie, 36 years, service user)

Lived experience of racism clearly impacts upon Carrie's experience of voice-hearing. Bodily/physiological differences/variations of the 'natural' organism and social factors such as those linked to gender and 'race' become implicated in how a particular individual perceives, organises and thus adapts to their environment. Human beings learn about the significance/meanings attached to the organism in a social context. This process underpins and maintains (or not) a unified sense of self and belonging that can also promote feelings of lack of fit and belonging. Fanon (1984/1952) in *Black Faces, White Masks* analysed the construction of blackness and colonialism in relation to a white 'generalized other' that reflected his black bodily being back to him in a highly oppressive way. Carrie's account highlights how she becomes aware of, and experiences as 'problematic' the racialised meanings attached to her body. Leder (1990) argues that the body remains a latent (Mead would say non-conscious) part of our 'corporeal background' and only appears during problematic experiences be they of a physical or social theme. For Mead, the social and physical are interlinked. Leder introduces the concept of 'dys-appearance' to refer to the body 'reappearing' as a thematic and sensory focus of our experience but in a pathological or socially deviant form. Carrie's account draws attention to the 'dys-appearance' of her body as 'raced' and 'sexed'. This is illuminated not only through her self-definition as 'other' on account of being a voice-hearer, but also through her perception of racism linked to bodily 'differences' as an ethnic minority in a 'white' society. Carrie has clearly internalised a 'white' non voice-hearer generalized other as the norm. The content of the voices reflect details of the linkage between Carrie's body and mind as her 'individualised' subjectivity reflects her lived experience.

In terms of sexuality, biological factors linked to the anatomical sex of her body are illuminated through Carrie's reference to the socially constructed meaning framing the sexual identity of her body in terms of gendered expectations. Social factors linked to gender are illuminated through her gendered discussion around sexuality and how she feels others perceive her based on her internalised knowledge of the 'generalized other' in relation to taken-for-granted assumptions around acceptable forms of sexuality for female persons. In this sense, socially acquired meaning around sexuality is embedded within Carrie's account, and again highlights the linkage between her mind and body during the 'individualised' 'othering' development of her 'subjectivity'. It lends support to the argument that contrary to the individualising Freudian notion that sexuality determines our social being; social meanings given to it in social situations determine and affect our sexuality (Plummer, 1975). Garfinkel's (1967) ethnomethodological study of 'Agnes', a transsexual seeking male to female sex reassignment, provided an in-depth description of the gendered challenges/problems Agnes encountered as she sought social legitimation as a 'natural' woman whilst having the anatomy of a 'natural' man. Mead's conceptualisation of humans as simultaneously biological and social becomings is insightful here. In the Second Sex, existential feminist Simone De Beauvoir (1997/1949) summed this up neatly by observing that one is not born a woman, one becomes one. Generally speaking, for feminist and gender theorists, the 'generalized other' will reflect gendered relations of collective social power. For race theorists, the 'generalized other' will reflect white ethnocentric relations of social power. Human beings learn about the significance/meanings attached to the concrete environment of the organism (body) in an intersubjective social context infused with power relations permeating the abstract environment. This process underpins and maintains (or not) a unified sense of self and belonging.

The taken for granted 'naturalness' of expected gendered behaviour that underpins socially 'acceptable' sexuality becomes consciously experienced only when it becomes 'problematic' in some way. Carrie had identified herself as being 'asexual', whilst gay male voice-hearers in the sample consciously reflected upon their sexual 'otherness' to the heterosexual norm:

> *"Well I have never felt very happy about it (my sexuality) until recently. It is only in the last 2 years that I've accepted it. A lot of the voices that I've had have been in connection with my homosexuality which have been negative because a lot of people's reactions to it are negative, but the last year or two I've not become so religious and when I've been to churches and told them that I was gay I've had terrible reactions and people have been aggressive and I've had very negative responses and I've had the bible preached at me."*
> (Tim, 49 years, service user)

Tim's sexuality as a gay man was not unconsciously repressed in a Freudian sense; rather he consciously attempted to suppress under the controlling influence of societal expectations (generalized other) around socially acceptable sexuality. In his youth, Tim tried to be 'straight' by dating girls and women, and heard voices he described as 'female' mocking, abusive and homophobic. The content of the voices heard by Tim are framed within a morality discourse around the 'wrongness' of homosexuality. Voice-hearers who perceive themselves to have 'failed' in some way experience a feeling of 'exposure' or 'social insecurity' in public spaces, when every 'look' or gesture from others is meaningful in terms of the other 'knowing' about the 'failures' and/or 'secrets' of the voice-hearer. This has been described by some voice-hearers in terms of telepathically 'tuning into' the thoughts and feelings of others, which are then expressed as voices framed within a morality discourse. The 'accuracy' of the content of the voices in terms of relevance to the voice-hearer's material world leads many to explore the possibility of telepathy:

> *"I feel I'm in some sort of perverse game. Long before mobile phones were common I believe (and I'm still not sure) that people communicated with one another and I'm able to*

read what they're thinking (Telepathy). I sometimes think I know what they're thinking and they know some of what I'm thinking. Weird or what?" (John, 46 years, service user)

'Tuning in' to the thoughts and feelings of strangers either on the streets or in social gatherings have culminated in feelings of persecution in some voice-hearers; and has clear links to an internalised 'generalized other'. The secrets, regrets, mistakes, perceived faults, shortcomings and 'bad' behaviour are perceived by the voice-hearer to be public knowledge, inasmuch as the voice-hearer fears that people around him/her can pick up on them telepathically, telepathy being a two-way process. Some voice-hearers even take action to try and prevent their private thoughts and privacy being made public and 'opened up' to other people:

"I heard everyone making comments about me, I got scared, I tried to disconnect my brain from them by wearing a hat so my thoughts would not be heard. I was very paranoid, I thought everyone was calling me a cheat and wife beater." (Jonathan, 37 years, service user)

Jonathan feels ashamed of his bad behaviour in the past – he believes he has treated girlfriends badly. He now considers himself a reformed character; however, the voices are continually 'raking up the past'. By wearing a hat, Jonathan hoped that other people would not hear the words in his head detailing his 'shameful past behaviour' – which in turn would elicit a response from them. Mead argues that with our internalised knowledge of the 'generalized other', we are able to interact with ourselves and others. By drawing on his internalised knowledge of the 'generalized other', Jonathan 'knows' that the response of other people to his past misdemeanours will mirror his own. Indeed from Mead's perspective, we come to know our own minds when we know the minds of others (Gronow, 2008). The content of the voices heard by Carrie, Tim, and Jonathan can be fruitfully understood as a form of self-talk in relation to the 'generalized other'. Lived experience of racism and sexism are clearly shaping the content of this 'self-talk'. Bodily/physiological differences/variations of the 'natural' organism (concrete) and social factors (abstract) such as those linked to gender and 'race' become implicated in how a particular individual perceives and organises their environment. In this dynamic, materialist and reflexive approach, sexism and racism would only be 'problematic' to organisms that encounter it in lived experience.

Discussion and Conclusion: Mead's Overlooked Legacy

Mead's framework facilitated an exploration of the phenomenon of voice-hearing that yielded a fresh perspective on the phenomenon. The self-conscious

SOCIAL PROCESS OF VOICE-HEARING

Antecendent Conditions
Refelexively becoming consciously aware of socially 'problematic' experiences

∨

Phenomenon: 'othered' social status as 'different
Promotoing lack of 'fit' and 'beonging' at an ontological level

∨

Contextual conditions: Person as a member of pre-existing
Society Body as vessel of mortal constraint is foundation for social life and cognition as reflexive thought links mind and body

∨

Intervening conditions: Interactional social relations.
Particular interactional social relations framing and shaping the cognitive intersection between existence, experience and knowledge linking mind and body at an ontological socially situated level

∨

Existence
Time and place

∨

Experience → **Cognition** ← **Knowledge**
Everyday material relations   Access to socially disseminated ideas

∨

Consequences: Phenomenon shaped differently in terms of content and possible interpretation

∨

Action strategy: Past, present and future come together within reflective action to re-establish a fit and belonging through socially authenticable explanation for 'difference'

∨

Consequences: 'best fit' – existence, experience and knowledge cognitively intersect within reflective intelligent action (thinking)

∨

'best fit' remains in flux
Range from biomedical to supernatural and remain open to challenge from other competing 'best fits' encountered during ongoing interactional social relations

Figure 2: *Social process of voice-hearing*

reflexive identification of voice-hearing as a 'problem', arises through interlinked concrete and abstract dimensions of social experience. In this sense, whilst some individuals might be biologically predisposed to the phenomenon, voice-hearers are not born 'voice-hearers', they become voice-hearers through othering social processes within communities/societies within which voice-hearing is not the norm. The problematisation of the bodily ear as the 'normal' way a body deals with sound was the commonality shared by the voice-hearers in the study and was the pre-condition to becoming a 'voice-hearer. The general concept of sociality and intersubjectivity within Mead's non-dualistic approach offers a non-transcendent understanding of differences between voice-hearers in terms of how they experience the phenomenon. For some voice-hearers, the content is distressing and for others it is enriching, even life-enhancing. The voice content and even identity of the voice is frequently attributed to people (alive or dead) known of (for example famous people/personalities/religious figures/entities) or personally to the voice-hearer. The voice-hearers frequently identify a voice by what it says in the sense that the content is typical of what s/he would expect a particular person to say or do. Interestingly, the voice content can expand/change as voice-hearer's encounter new people. This draws attention to the non-static quality of voice content, it, like the 'best fit' remains 'in flux' and in process immersed within the lived experience of the voice-hearers. This highlights the fundamental importance of the social contexts of voice-hearers in terms of how the phenomenon is 'problem-solved' (responded to/acted upon) as well as in shaping the content of the voices. The findings from this research suggest that relatively unproblematic lives are reflected in relatively unproblematic voice content. This in turn problematises individualised interventions informed by dualistic asocial transcendent approaches/interventions to/for mental distress. Attempting to change how individuals cope with distressing experiences without full consideration given to the problems in the environment that gave rise to those experiences in the first place is clearly problematic.

Given Mead's innovative non-dualistic, non-transcendent, non-Cartesian approach to understanding sociality, consciousness, cognition within embodied lived experience, his ideas are perhaps of especial importance since the 'corporeal turn' in sociology (Williams and Bendelow, 1998). However, Mead's illuminating theoretical insights – and in particular his approach to the non-transcendental embodied mind and concept of the 'generalized other' - remain largely overlooked. Yet, his approach has wide application in terms of providing the 'missing link' between macro and micro debates in sociology, and the 'crisis' in social psychology – linking individual and collective social processes (see Augoustinos and Walker, 1999) - and, linked to this, Mead's counter argument to the individualistic approach dominating the evolutionary psychology perspective. Mead's ideas also have resonance with post-structural thought in the sense that he recognised the importance of language and the discursive in constructing social life and fluidity in meaning making, but crucially, Mead's framework retains the concrete, lived materiality of the body by situating it as an active agent within these meaning-making processes (Burkitt, 1998b). Mead thus avoids the criticism levelled at overly discursive accounts found in the likes of Judith Butler (Burkitt, 1998b). In addition to his yet to be fully acknowledged contribution as a classical sociological thinker, Mead's ideas have a lot to offer used in conjunction with the work of philosophers Martin Heidegger (hermeneutical challenge - situated being-in-the-world), Michel Foucault (power as lived), Jean-Paul Sartre (reflected and non-reflected consciousness), and theorists such as Pierre Bourdieu (habitus and the collective), Norbert Elias ('civilising' processes), Mauriice Merleau-Ponty (social life mediated through the body), Jurgen Habermas (communicative action) and Anthony Giddens (reflexive project of the self). Indeed, Mead's work would enrich any attempt to explore in a non-transcendent, non-dualistic way the macro-micro interface.

The recent corporeal turn in sociology by bringing the body 'back in' has led to the emergence of literature seeking to draw upon, and re-configure existing theory that would enable the body to be understood in a non-reductionist, non-essentialist way, an approach that takes account of concreteness and social processes in how bodies are constructed and experienced (see for example Shilling, 1993; Williams and Bendelow, 1998; Shilling, 2003; Crossley, 2006; Shilling, 2007). However, whilst Mead offers a conceptualisation of the body that avoids the limitations of both essentialism and constructionism, he remains largely overlooked in this literature. Mead's conceptualisation of humans and simultaneously biological and social becomings, their minds and selves as non-transcendental and situated, has unrealised potential to unify the theoretical disciplines of biology, psychology and sociology (Baldwin, 1986) without losing sight of the organising influence of cultural/political power operating within the concomitant evolution of ideas – 'universes of discourse'. Mead thus has much to offer across the human sciences from the biological to the existential. There are signs that Mead's ideas are beginning to be been utilised to explore embodiment and sociality (Jackson and Scott, 2007). It is hoped that the application of Mead's conceptual framework to the data presented in this chapter exploring the impact of interlinked concrete and abstract dimensions of social experience on individual experiences of the problematic phenomenon of voice-hearing, will lead to further work exploring the as yet overlooked potential of Mead's legacy.

References

Augoustinous, M. and Walker I. (1999) *Social Cognition: An Integrated Introduction*. London, New Delhi: Sage Publications.
Baldwin, J.D. (1986) *George Herbert Mead: A Unifying Theory for Sociology*. California: Sage Publications.
Bentall, R.P. (ed.). (1998) *Reconstructing Schizophrenia*. London: Routledge.
Balliene, G.R. (1956) *Past Finding Out*. London: S.P.C.K.

Berger, P.L. and Luckmann T. (1975[1966]) *The Social Construction of Reality: A Treatise in the Sociology of Knowledge*. Harmondsworth: Penguin.

Berrios, G.E. (1991) 'Delusions as "wrong beliefs": A conceptual history', *British Journal of Psychiatry*, 159 (14):6-13.

Birchwood, M. and Tarrier, N. (1992) *Innovations in the Psychological Management of Schizophrenia: Assessment, Treatment and Services*. Chichester: John Wiley & Sons.

Blackman, L. (2001) *Hearing Voices: Embodiment and Experience*. London and New York: Free Association Books.

Bleuler, E. (1950) *Dementia Praecox or the Group of Schizophrenias*. New York: International Universities Press.

Boyle, M. (1990) *Schizophrenia: A Scientific Delusion?* London: Routledge.

British Psychological Society (BPS) (2000) 'Recent advances in understanding mental illness and psychotic experiences'. A report of The British Psychological Society Division of Clinical Psychology, St. Andrews House, 48 Princess Road East, Leicester, LE1 7DR, UK.

Burkitt, I. (1998a) 'Sexuality and Gender Identity: From a Discursive to a Relational Analysis'. *The Sociological Review*:483-504.

-----.(1998b) 'Bodies of Knowledge: Beyond Cartesian Views of Persons, Selves and Mind'. *Journal for the Theory of Social behaviour*, 28:1:63-82.

-----.(2000) *Social Selves: Theories of the Social Formation of Personality*. London: Sage Publications.

Chadwick, P.D.J., Birchwood, M.J. and Trower, P. (2000a) *Cognitive Therapy for Delusions, Voices and Paranoia*. Chichester: Wiley.

Chadwick, P.D.J., Sambrooke, S., Rasch, S. and Davis, E. (2000b) 'Challenging the Omnipotence of Voices: Group Cognitive Behaviour Therapy for Voices', *Behaviour Research & Therapy*, 38:993-1003.

Crossley, N. (1994) *Politics of Subjectivity*. Aldershot: Avebury.

-----.(1996) *Intersubjectivity*. London: Sage Publications.

-----.(2006) *Reflexive Embodiment in Contemporary Societies*. Buckingham: Open University Press.

De Beauvoir, S. (1997[1949]) *The Second Sex*. London: Random House.

Delahunty, T. (2001) 'Hearing Voices: An exploration of beliefs, coping strategies and emotional well being of those who find the experience distressing'. Unpublished Doctorate in Clinical Psychology, Edinburgh University

Fowler, D., Garety P. and Kuipers E. (1995) *Cognitive Behaviour Therapy for Psychosis: Theory and Practice*. Chichester: Wiley.

Freud, S. (1953) *A General Introduction to Psychoanalysis*. New York: Liveright/Pocket books.

Garfinkel, H. (1967) *Studies in Ethnomethodology*. Englewood Cliffs NJ: Prentice Hall.

Gelder, M., Gath, D. and Mayou, R. (1994) *Oxford Textbook of Psychiatry*. 2nd edn. Oxford, New York, Melbourne: Oxford University Press.

Goffman, E. (1969) *The Presentation of Self in Everyday Life*. London: Allen Lane.

Grierson, M.G. (1993) 'Hearing voices: a sociological study'. Unpublished PhD

Thesis, University of Manchester.
Gronow, A. (2008) 'The Over- or the Undersocialized Concpetion of Man?' *Practice Theory and the Problem of Intersubjectivity Sociology*, 42(2):243-259.
Haddock, G. and Slade, P.D. (eds.).(1996) *Cognitive-behavioural Interventions with Psychotic Disorders*. London: Routledge.
Haw, C. (2000) 'Psychological Perspectives on Women's Vulnerability to Mental Illness', in Kohen D. (ed.). *Women and Mental Health*. London and Philadelphia: Routledge
Heery, M. (1989) 'Inner Voice Experience: An Exploratory Study of Thirty Cases', *Journal of Transpersonal Psychology*, Vol.21, (1):73-82.
Jackson, S. and Scott, S. (2007) 'Faking Like a Woman? Towards an Interpretive Theorization of Sexual Pleasure.' *Body and Society*, Vol. 13(2):95-116.
Joas, H. (1980) *G.H. Mead: A Contemporary Re-examination of his Thought*. Translated by Raymond Meyer. New York: Polity Press in association with Basil Blackwell, Oxford.
Jung, C. (1967) *Memories, Dreams, Reflections*. London: Montana
-----.(1969) *On the Nature of the Psyche*. Princeton: Princeton University Press.
Kingdon, D. and Turkington, D. (1994) *Cognitive-Behavioural Therapy for Schizophrenia*. , Hove: Lawrence Erlbaum.
Kirby, J. (2006) 'Voice-hearing and Gender: An exploration of the 'problematic' experience of voice-hearing'. Unpublished PhD Thesis, awarded 2006 by University of Lancaster.
Layder, D. (1994) *Understanding Social Theory*. London: Sage Publications.
Leder, D. (1990) *The Absent Body*. Chicago and London: The University of Chicago Press.
Leudar I. and Thomas, P. (2000) *Voices of Reason, Voices of Insanity: Studies of Verbal Hallucinations*. London and Philadelphia: Routledge.
McGorry P., Chanen A., McCarthy, E., Van Riel, R., McKenzie, J. and Singh, B. (1991) 'Posttraumatic Stress Disorder Following recent Onset Psychosis', *Journal of Nervous and Mental Disease*, 179(5):253-258.
Mead, G.H. (1967[1934]) *Mind, Self & Society*. Chicago and London: The University of Chicago Press.
-----.(1932) *The Philosophy of The Present*. Chicago: Open Court Publishing Company.
-----.(1977) *On Social Psychology: Selected Papers*. Edited and introduced by Anselm Strauss. Chicago and London: The University of Chicago Press Originally published in 1934.
-----.(1972[1938]) *The Philosophy of the Act Edited*. 'Introduction' by Charles W. Morris. Chicago and London: The University of Chicago Press.
Miles, M.B. and Huberman, A.M. (1994) *Qualitative Data Analysis: An Expanded Sourcebook*. 2nd edn. London, New Delhi: Sage publications.
Nelson, H. (1997) *Cognitive Behavioural Therapy with Schizophrenia – A Practice Manual*. Chettenham: Nelson Thornes.
Pearson, D. (1998) 'The Social Acceptability of Children Hearing Voices'. Unpublished Doctorate in Clinical Psychology, University of Leicester.

Perris, C. and McGorry, P.D. (1998) *Cognitive Psychotherapy of Psychotic and Personality Disorders: Handbook of Theory and Practice*. Chichester: John Wiley & Sons Ltd.

Plummer, K. (1975) *Sexual Stigma: An Interactionist Account*. London: Routledge & Kegan Paul.

Romme, M.A.J. (1998) *Understanding Voices: Coping with Auditory Hallucinations and Confusing Realities*. Handsell Publishing.

Romme, M.A.J. and Escher, A. (1989) 'Hearing Voices'. *Schizophrenia Bulletin*, 15:209-16.

-----.(eds.).(1993) *Accepting Voices*. London: Mind Publications.

Romme, M.A.J., Honig, A., Noorthoorn, E.O. and Escher, A. (1992) 'Coping with Hearing Voices: An Emancipatory Approach', *British Journal of Psychiatry*, 161, 99-103.

Rose N. (2005) *Power in Therapy: Techne and Ethos*. http//www.academyanalyticarts.org/rose2.htm

Rycroft, C. (1995) *A Critical Dictionary of Psychoanalysis*. 2nd edn. Harmondsworth: Penguin Books.

Sarbin, T. and Juhasz, J. (1967) 'The Historical background of the Concept of Hallucination'. *Journal of the History of the Behavioural Sciences*, Vol.3, pt.4:339-58.

Screech, M.A. (1985) 'Good madness in Christendom'. In Bynum, W.F., Porter, R. and Shepherd, M. *The Anatomy of Madness: Essays in the History of Psychiatry*. Volume 1: People and Ideas. London and New York: Tavistock Publications.

Shilling, C. (1993) *The Body and Social Theory*. London: Sage publications.

-----.(2003) *The Body and Social Theory*. 2nd end. Thousand Oaks: London, New Delhi: Sage publications

-----.(2007) *Embodying Sociology: Retrospect, Progress and Prospects*. Malden, Mass: Blackwell.

Slade, P.D., Bentall R.P. (1988) *Sensory Deception: A Scientific Analysis of Hallucination*. London: Croom Helm.

Tarrier, N. (1987) 'An Investigation of Residual Psychotic Symptoms in Discharged Schizophrenic Patients'. *British Journal of Clinical Psychology*, 26:141-143.

Thomas, P. (1997) *The Dialectics of Schizophrenia*. New York: Free Association Books.

Watkins, J. (1998) *Hearing Voices: A Common Human Experience*. Melbourne: Hill of Content Publishing.

White, M. (1995) *Re-Authoring Lives: Interviews and Essays*. Adelaide, Dulwich Centre.

Williams, S. and Bendelow, G. (1998) *The Lived Body: Sociological Themes, Embodied Issues*. London: Routledge.

Wing, J.K. (1987) 'Epidemiology of Schizophrenia'. *Journal of the Royal Society of Medicine*, 80:134-135.

CHAPTER 6

Blumer's Dilemma Revisited: Is Social Science Possible?

Martyn Hammersley
The Open University, England

> 'At least knowing where the difficulty lies, we should be prevented from engaging in the practice of the ostrich or in expecting some form of magic to make the problem vanish.'
>
> Herbert Blumer

Introduction

My main focus in this chapter is on the methodological ideas of Herbert Blumer, who was an important figure in the development of what has come to be labelled the Chicago School of Sociology, particularly as regards methodology.[89] He has usually been viewed as a critic of positivism - of the growing dominance of quantitative method, and specifically of operationism and variable analysis - within US sociology from the 1930s to the 60s; and as advocating naturalistic case study. While this is true, it does not capture the complexity and acknowledged uncertainty of his position. Furthermore, it obscures the extent to which he was committed to ideas that would be dismissed by many qualitative researchers today as positivistic. These include, not just the insistence that we must investigate real social phenomena whose characteristics exist independently of our accounts of them, but also his commitment, at least at the start of his career, to a model of social science that is concerned with developing universal laws that identify causal relations.

---

[89] There are other important aspects of his work too: see Lyman and Vidich, (1988), Maines, (1988), Maines and Morrione, (1990).

My interest in Blumer's work here is not just historiographical, even though I believe it is important for us to have a clear sense of how our methodological and sociological ideas developed in the past (Hammersley, 2004). It also arises from serious concern about dominant trends within qualitative methodology today; in particular, the influence of various sorts of epistemological radicalism that dismiss social scientific inquiry as impossible, undesirable, or both.[90] In my view, there is still a great deal to be learned from Blumer's work; even though, as we shall see, he did not solve the problems he raised.

I will start by examining a dilemma facing social science that Blumer identified in his early work. After that I will examine his methodological recommendations in his book *Symbolic Interactionism*, published in 1969. In the final section, I want to assess his arguments in the context of social science today.

The Dilemma

Early on in his career, Blumer was preoccupied with a fundamental difficulty that he saw facing social research. In his commentary on Thomas and Znaniecki's (1918/20) *The Polish Peasant in Europe and America*, prepared for a conference on that book which took place in the late 1930s, he writes the following:

> My own feeling is that this work of Thomas and Znaniecki presents a dilemma as far as social research goes [...] in the following form: on the one hand, an inescapable need of including the subjective element of human experience, but, on the other hand, an enormous, and so far, unsurmounted, difficulty in securing devices that will catch this element of human experience *in the way that is customary for usable data in ordinary scientific procedure in other fields*.
> (Blumer, 1939:111, emphasis added)

Blumer had identified, though not specifically labelled, this dilemma in his doctoral dissertation, completed in 1928. There, focusing in particular on social psychology, he outlined what is involved in adopting a scientific approach to studying the social world. But he recognised that social scientists had not been very successful in applying this approach, and that some had employed, and sought to justify, a rather different and less-than-fully-scientific strategy, relying upon 'sympathetic introspection' and the study of cases in their uniqueness rather than as exemplars of types. At the same time, he insists that this approach

---

[90] These trends are exemplified in many of the chapters in recent editions of the *Handbook of Qualitative Research* (Denzin and Lincoln, 2005). For an analysis of some key aspects of these developments see Hammersley (2008).

had produced genuine knowledge, a judgment repeated in his appraisal of the *Polish Peasant* (Blumer, 1939).[91] Against this background, he raises the possibility that sociologists' difficulties in adopting a scientific approach stem from the peculiar nature of the social world, by comparison with other fields of scientific enquiry; in other words from what, in the quotation above, he refers to as 'the subjective element'. At the same time, he also mentions the possibility that the problem could arise from the fact that social scientists have not yet found adequate ways to conceptualise the phenomena they study.

The word 'dilemma' refers to 'a position of doubt or perplexity' in which there is a tension between two conflicting commitments. But it is not necessarily implied that both commitments are felt equally strongly. And what was fixed, above all, for Blumer was his view of the nature of human social life.[92] So, the problem was how, and indeed whether, a scientific approach could be developed in this field. In practical terms, the nub of the dilemma was whether sociologists should try to implement a scientific approach or, instead, use those (less than fully scientific) means by which it nevertheless did seem possible to produce knowledge of the social world, as Thomas and Znaniecki had demonstrated.

In order better to understand Blumer's dilemma, we need to look in more detail at each side of it: at what Blumer takes to be a scientific approach, and at why he believes subjectivity generates problems for this.

The Nature of Science

In his doctoral dissertation, Blumer spelt out the nature of science at considerable length (Blumer, 1928). Moreover, he did this in generic terms, seeking to specify what is common to science of any kind. This is in line with the position taken by some other Chicago sociologists, notably Park, and with that of pragmatist philosophers like Dewey and Mead.[93] At the same time, Blumer adopts a sophisticated form of scientific monism, one that distinguishes between the generic function and logic of science, on the one hand, and the techniques that are appropriate to particular fields of scientific inquiry, on the other.[94] The function of science is implied to be achieving social control, an idea

---

[91] He argues that Thomas and Znaniecki failed to identify any universal laws but that despite the deficiencies of the work from the scientific point of view some of their interpretations are 'genuinely revealing'; that even if not true 'in the particular case' some 'would be generally true, and would be true in other particular cases' (Blumer, 1939:50).
[92] This was because he regarded it as confirmed by ordinary, everyday experience of the world. He writes: 'The premises of symbolic interactionism are simple. I think they can be readily tested and validated merely by observing what goes on in social life under one's nose' (Blumer, 1969:50).
[93] It is at odds with nineteenth-century historicism, hermeneutics and neo-Kantianism, which hade identified a different kind of scientific approach as being necessary for the historical and social sciences (see Hammersley, 1989a:ch1).
[94] For a more recent, even more sophisticated, monist approach, see Haack (2003).

which he probably took over from Thomas and Znaniecki (1918/20b), though it is also to be found in Dewey and elsewhere. As regards the logic of science, Blumer argues for example that, while laboratory experimentation is a crucial method in some natural sciences, it is not used in others, such as astronomy or geology. This means that it is a *technique*, rather than being part of the logic of science. However, he insists that the comparative method, on which experimentation relies, *is* essential to that logic.

Blumer's views here are very close to the position taken by Znaniecki, as presented for example in *The Method of Sociology*, and to that of other advocates of analytic induction, such as Alfred Lindesmith (Znaniecki, 1934; Lindesmith, 1937, 1968, and 1981). From this point of view, science involves the development and testing of explanatory hypotheses, designed to identify underlying causal laws which portray one set of factors as both invariably producing some type of effect and as the only cause of that type of effect. So, causal relations are treated as deterministic: if the relevant necessary and sufficient conditions are met, the cause will *always* produce the effect.[95] Indeed, this was a key basis for opposition on the part of some sociologists at Chicago, and elsewhere (notably MacIver at Columbia University), to the growing dominance of quantitative method: the latter was criticised as unscientific because it was concerned with probabilistic relations. Along these lines, Blumer writes: 'natural science gets its laws by starting from intensive studies of individual cases and building up a type; statistics is a means of working with a mass or aggregate – not a means of studying intensively a separate case' (Blumer, 1930:1103). For Blumer, then, the task of social science was to discover causal laws through intensive case study that employs the comparative method; but to do so in ways that are appropriate to the distinctive character of social phenomena.

In more specific terms, Blumer argues that scientific method involves, first of all, studying simple cases that clearly belong to the class of phenomena that is of interest. What he means by cases being 'simple' is that they are closed, or semi-closed, systems (Blumer, 1928:366). In other words, they:

Consist of a series of happenings that is indefinitely repeatable; and

Other factors are either excluded or their effects are kept stable within the system.

The reason why it is necessary to study closed systems is that in these cases not only can one examine variation in the factors one is treating as cause and effect but the influence of *other* potential causal factors is minimised. The model

---

[95] This view of causation was common in the nineteenth century, and earlier, and is to be found for example in the writings of Durkheim, see Schmaus, (1994:ch4).

here is, of course, the experiment, but the idea is that the comparative method can be applied outside the laboratory, 'in the wild' as it were. Like Znaniecki, Blumer argues that closed systems 'may prevail in the ordinary course of events without the necessity of the artificial simplifying conditions of the laboratory' (Blumer,1928:367), and he makes an implicit reference to the solar system as an example. However, unlike Znaniecki, he expresses some doubt about finding closed systems in the social realm. His initial conclusion is that if these are *not* to be found then 'social psychology must resign itself to the complexity of its subject-matter, to the impossibility of strictly natural scientific laws, and must continue to rely upon methods which give only a rough understanding and control of this complexity' (Blumer,1928:367-8). Here we have a hint of what he later labelled as a dilemma. However, immediately following this, Blumer offers an alternative conclusion:

> But perhaps a closed system, as applied to social behavior is not impossible; perhaps its failure or absence is merely due to an ignorance of what are the pertinent factors in human behavior. This suggests that perhaps the attainment of the simplified situation represented in the closed system depends on a new conceptual orientation. (Blumer, 1928:368)

So, while Blumer is committed, above all else, to the image of human social life presented by Mead and Cooley, there is also a strong attachment not only to the value of science as a means of understanding the social world, but also to a conception of science which treats its goal as the discovery of causal laws. He was not, therefore, in any sense anti-science, in the way that many qualitative researchers are today. Nor did he propose a different *kind* of science, in the manner of some nineteenth-century German philosophers. This can be seen from the fact that he presents the alternative that must be adopted if the requirements of science cannot be met as clearly inferior and problematic in scientific terms. For example, he writes:

> There is nothing in the discussion of 'sympathetic introspection' by its advocates which shows how this method can lead to the detection of the genuine and the spurious, nor that easily permits of the verification which marks scientific advance.
> (Blumer, 1928:341)

And that:

> It is an acknowledged principle of science that a theory to have value must admit of continual test by the facts or the kind of facts from which it arises. The individual element which enters into the use of sympathetic introspection, however, seems to make this impossible.
> (Blumer, 1928:342)

At the same time, as already noted, Blumer insists that the less-than-fully-scientific method adopted by Thomas and Znaniecki and others is capable of producing genuine knowledge. He perhaps saw this knowledge as analogous to the kind of practical wisdom developed by some lay people in the course of their activities. But, if so, we start to see a discrepancy between Blumer's position and that of Znaniecki, who emphasised the superiority of the abstract, theoretical knowledge produced by science as against pragmatic, commonsense knowledge (Thomas and Znaniecki, 1918/20b and Znaniecki, 1934).

The Nature of Human Social Life as a Barrier to Scientific Study

It is worth specifying in a bit more detail what Blumer means by the 'subjective element of human experience', and why it is a problem for scientific inquiry.

As we have seen, like nineteenth-century historicists and neo-Kantians, and like many of his Chicago colleagues, Blumer believed that human actions are constituted by meanings, rather than being caused by physical features of the environment in which they take place. In other words, human actions do not consist of behaviour triggered in fixed ways by physical stimuli. He identifies two respects in which this fact potentially conflicts with the requirements of science: the need to rely on socio-cultural understanding in making sense of people's behaviour; and the individually distinctive character of instances belonging to sociological categories.

1. *Socio-cultural understanding.* The argument here is that social phenomena can neither be *reduced to* what is observable nor be *specified in a fixed way by* observable indicators. Yet science requires that the application of concepts must not depend upon judgment or special expertise possessed by the observer: in other words, what is observed should be accessible to anyone.[96] While Blumer rejects positivist demands that concepts be operationalisable, in other words that they must be *defined* in terms of specific measurement operations, he nevertheless insists that it is necessary to pin down their meaning (Blumer, 1969:43) in ways that can be checkable by others. The core of the problem with sympathetic introspection is that it:

> depends on the judgment, the purpose, and the values of the investigator; it arises from the alignment of things within the nexus of the meanings which are peculiar to him and his time. The meaning of an instance is likely to vary with the interpreter. (Blumer, 1928:352)

---

[96] This requirement can be traced back at least to Francis Bacon, who explicitly denied that natural philosophy requires special expertise or personal judgment, in the way that Renaissance scholarship had done. However, meeting this requirement was recognised to be a difficult problem from the beginning: see Shapin (1994).

And Blumer made the same point much later in his career: 'the identification of the human experience or subjective factor, seemingly, is not made at present in ways which permit one to test crucially the interpretation. Identification and interpretation remain a matter of judgment' (Blumer, 1939:79-80). While he recognises that the observation of physical phenomena depends upon inference, he sees an important difference between this and what is involved in social observation. The difference lies in the fact that physical objects can be 'translated into a space-time framework or brought inside of what George Mead has called the touch-sight field' (Blumer, 1940:714). By contrast, the observation of many social phenomena requires:

> A judgment based on sensing the social relations of the situation in which the behavior occurs and on applying some social norm present in the experience of the observer; thus one observes an act as being respectful, for example, by sensing the social relation between the actor and others set by the situation, and by viewing the act from the standpoint of rights, obligations, and expectations involved in that situation. (Blumer, 1940:715).

He adds that in identifying social phenomena we also often rely on noticing gestures that are familiar to us from our own experience. Furthermore, we must 'take the role of the other' in order to be able to view the situation in the way that the participants do. But, because we need to use a social rather than a space-time framework in interpreting human behaviour, there are likely to be frequent disagreements, and this is an obstacle 'in bringing our concepts to effective empirical test' (Blumer, 1940:716).

2. *Individual distinctiveness of social phenomena.* Blumer also mentions another obstacle to applying a scientific approach, what he refers to as the individual distinctiveness of social phenomena. He argues that:

> The success of classification in the natural and biological sciences depends upon the presence of fixed characters in the objects or instances to be classified; characters which can be easily identified by interested observers. It is these characters, of course, which lay the basis for classification. If, however, in the case of historical instances, the 'characters' vary with the current values and meanings, and indeed from individual to individual..., the way to easy classification and comparison would seem to be blocked. (Blumer, 1928:353)

And, once again, he presents more or less the same argument in his later writings:

> I take it that that empirical world of our discipline is the natural social world of every-day experience. In this natural world every object of our consideration – whether a person, group, institution, practice, or what not – has a distinctive, particular or unique character and lies in a context of a similar distinctive character.

As a result of this, in studying the social world we cannot confine our investigation of phenomena of a particular type to:

> what is covered by the abstract reference of the concept. We do not cleave aside what gives each instance its peculiar character and restrict ourselves to what it has in common with the other instances in the class covered by the concept. To the contrary, we seem forced to reach what is common by accepting and using what is distinctive to the given empirical instance. In other words, what is common (i.e., what the concept refers to) is expressed in a distinctive manner in each empirical instance and can be got at only by accepting and working through the distinctive expression. (Blumer, 1954:7-8)

Blumer concludes from this that definitive concepts, of the kind characteristic of natural science, may not be achievable in sociology. Instead, sociological concepts seem to have a sensitising function. A sensitising concept lacks 'specification of attributes or bench marks and consequently it does not enable the user to move directly to the instance and its relevant content', but 'it gives the user a general sense of reference and guidance in approaching empirical instances' (Blumer, 1954:7).

So, Blumer presents the social scientist's reliance on sensitising concepts as arising from the individually distinct character of social phenomena:

> If our empirical world presents itself in the form of distinctive and unique happenings or situations and if we seek through the direct study of this world to establish classes of objects and relations between classes, we are, I think, forced to work with sensitizing concepts ... because of the varying nature of the concrete expression from instance to instance we have to rely, apparently, on general guides and not on fixed objective traits or modes of expression. To invert the matter, since what we infer does not express itself in the same fixed way, we are not able to rely on fixed objective expressions to make the inference (Blumer, 1954:8)

What is left unclear in these later discussions, however, is whether reliance upon sensitising concepts is compatible with a scientific orientation, or whether it indicates adoption of the less-than-scientific alternative that Blumer had identified in the work of Thomas and Znaniecki and others. In short, while he insists that sensitising concepts can be refined and developed, and thereby clarified, it is unclear whether, on his definition of 1928, this could ever meet scientific requirements.

Blumer on Naturalistic Case Study

In his published articles on methodology during the 1930s and 1940s, Blumer does not explicitly mention the dilemma, though as we have seen it is implicit in much of his discussion. He was primarily concerned with critical assessment of the kind of quantitative method that was gaining increasing influence within US sociology. Also, for the most part, he does not directly address the question of how social research *ought* to be pursued. This may be partly because he was writing against the background of an established tradition of case study research at Chicago. However, in 1969 he did address this issue, and in some depth. This occurred when he was persuaded to bring his earlier methodological articles together in a single volume, and to write an introductory chapter on 'The methodological implications of symbolic interactionism'.

This chapter begins with criticism of the failure of much contemporary sociology to respect what he calls 'the obdurate character of the empirical world under study' (Blumer, 1969:24): in other words, to recognise the complex character of human social life, and the role of meaning within this. Instead, he argues, the currently dominant model of sociological research gives priority to a notion of scientific method that legislates the use of a particular set of techniques. Here, of course, there is considerable continuity with arguments in his dissertation and in his later published articles. For example, Blumer insists that: 'the principles that comprise the methodology of an empirical science have to cover the act of scientific inquiry, not in some detached logical form of its own, but in the form that such scientific inquiry must take in grappling with a given kind of empirical world' (Blumer, 1969:27). In line with this, he rejects the importation of techniques from other areas without due attention to whether or not they are appropriate to the character of the phenomena being studied.

One of Blumer's targets here is the preoccupation with hypothesis testing in the dominant methodological approach (Blumer, 1969:29-30). He attacks this in two ways. First he argues that hypothesis-testing is frequently not carried out properly in currently influential quantitative research: that the hypothesis often does not 'genuinely epitomize the model or theory from which it is deduced', and that the testing that takes place does not involve 'scrupulous search for negative empirical cases'. But his central theme is the need for direct examination of the empirical world to which any theoretical interpretation is being applied. He argues that what is needed is 'meticulous examination of [this world, to find out] whether one's premises or root images of it, one's questions and problems posed for it, the data one chooses out of it, the concepts through which one sees and analyzes it, and the interpretations one applies to it are actually borne out' (Blumer, 1969:32). This task, he suggests, has been seriously neglected.

In part, what is presented here is an argument for participant observation, at least as the starting point for any sociological research (Blumer, 1969:35). Blumer identifies two aspects of this, what he refers to as exploration and inspection. He criticises the training of social scientists because: 'There is no demand on the research scholar to do a lot of free exploration in the area, getting close to the people involved in it, seeing it in a variety of situations they meet, noting their problems and observing how they handle them, being party to their conversations, and watching their life as it flows along' (Blumer, 1969:35). Yet this, he insists, is essential.

One reason for its importance is that human social life is very variegated, and that in order to understand what is going on in a particular situation one must have local knowledge. Here he highlights:

> the persistent tendency of human beings in their collective life to build up separate worlds, marked by an operating milieu of different life situations and by the possession of different beliefs and conceptions for handling these situations. One merely has to think of the different worlds in the case of a military elite, the clergy of a church, modern city prostitutes, a peasant revolutionary body, professional politicians, slum dwellers, the directing management of a large industrial corporation, a gambling syndicate, a university faculty, and so on endlessly. The modes of living of such groups, the parade of situations they must handle, their institutions and their organizations, the relations between their members, the views and images through which they see their worlds, the personal organizations formed by their members – all these and more reflect their different empirical worlds' (Blumer, 1969:38-9).

So, for Blumer, an essential starting point is 'exploratory investigation', and the purpose of this is to enable movement towards 'a clearer understanding of how one's [research] problem should be posed, to learn what are the appropriate data, to develop ideas of what are significant lines of relation, and to evolve one's conceptual tools in the light of what one is learning about the area of life' (Blumer, 1969:40).

He concludes that 'One of the interesting values of exploratory study is that the fuller descriptive account that it yields will frequently give an adequate explanation of what was problematic without the need of invoking any theory or proposing any analytical scheme'. However, he goes on to insist that exploration is not enough, that inspection is also required (Blumer, 1969:42). This involves 'analysis', by which he means inquiry aimed at casting the research problem 'in theoretical form, at unearthing generic relations, at sharpening the connotative reference of [the] concepts, and at formulating theoretical propositions' (Blumer, 1969:43).

In other words, 'scientific analysis requires two things: clear, discriminating analytical elements and the isolation of relations between these elements' (Blumer, 1969:43). And Blumer suggests this is best achieved through inspection: 'an intensive focused examination of the empirical content of whatever analytical elements are used for purposes of analysis, and this same kind of examination of the empirical nature of the relations between such elements' (Blumer, 1969:43).[97] What is demanded is that one 'goes to the empirical instances of the analytical element, views them in their different concrete settings, looks at them from different positions, asks questions of them with regard to their generic character, goes back and re-examines them, compares them with one another, and in this manner sifts out the nature of the analytical element that the empirical instances represent' (Blumer, 1969:44-5).

What is striking about Blumer's discussion in his 1969 chapter is that he clearly labels the kind of naturalistic investigation he recommends here as scientific. For example, he writes that the methodological stance of symbolic interactionism is:

> that of direct examination of the empirical social world [...] It recognizes that such direct examination permits the scholar to meet all of the basic requirements of an empirical science: to confront an empirical world that is available for observation and analysis; to raise abstract problems with regard to that world; to gather necessary data through careful and disciplined examination of that world; to unearth relations between categories of such data; to formulate propositions with regard to such relations; to weave such propositions into a theoretical scheme; and to test the problems, the data, the relations, the propositions, and the theory by renewed examination of the empirical world. (Blumer, 1969:47-8)

There is no suggestion here that this naturalistic approach faces the kind of dilemma Blumer had previously identified. Indeed, he seems specifically to rebut such a claim. At one point he writes:

> This methodological stance provides the answer to the frequent charge that symbolic interactionism does not lend itself to scientific research. This is an astonishing charge. It is evident that those who advance it are using the ideas of scientific inquiry in current methodology as the standard for judging symbolic interactionism. (Blumer, 1969:48)

What Blumer is challenging here, presumably, is any criticism to the effect that the naturalistic approach he is recommending is inferior to the kind of social science that, over the course of his career, had become dominant within US sociology. Indeed, he is arguing, and had consistently argued from the beginning, that this influential quantitative mode of inquiry, at least taken on its own, fails to live up to the demands of science. What is left unclear, however, is

---

[97] He explains that what he means by 'analytical elements' here are general, or theoretical, concepts like integration, social mobility, assimilation, and so on.

what the relation is between the sort of naturalistic inquiry that he advocates in *Symbolic Interactionism* and the account of science he had presented in his dissertation.

How are we to make sense of this? Clearly, Blumer has not changed his views about the nature of human social life, and the implications of this for how it must be investigated. It is also evident that he has not abandoned his commitment to science. And there is certainly no evidence that he saw the naturalistic form of investigation he recommends in *Symbolic Interactionism* as a second-best, or a less than fully scientific, approach.

One interpretation might be that in 1969 he believed that he had resolved the dilemma through re-conceptualising the nature of science as it applies in studying the social world. There is some evidence for this. In 1966, in a Foreword to Bruyn's *The Human Perspective in Sociology*, Blumer had rejected the idea that the task is to apply scientific method to the study of social phenomena, on the grounds that there is no consensus about what that method is. Instead, he argued, it is necessary to *find out* how to study the social world scientifically; and the cardinal requirement here is to respect the nature of that world, to make sure that the methods used do not involve assumptions that are at odds with that nature (Blumer, 1966). This seems to imply that he was now treating much of what, in his dissertation, he had included under the heading of the logic of science as a matter of technique that varies across the sciences. All that he seems to retain as a logical requirement is the insistence that the nature of the phenomena studied be respected.

While this interpretation has some plausibility, we should note that in neither his 1966 nor his 1969 discussion does Blumer explicitly claim to have resolved the dilemma. Furthermore, in 1979, when his appraisal of *The Polish Peasant* was republished, not only did he comment in the new introduction that 'the conference never succeeded in resolving the dilemma' but he added that 'it has not been resolved at all during the intervening time' (Blumer, 1979:xxxi).

An alternative way of interpreting the puzzle is to argue that, in 1969, Blumer put forward naturalistic case study as an essential preliminary in order to develop our conceptual understanding of social phenomena, and thereby lay the foundation for a scientific approach. In other words, he may have believed that it was only through applying this approach that we would ever reach a position to determine what a scientific approach to the study of social life entails, and whether it is possible.

Of course, the circumstances in which Blumer was writing in 1969 also need to be taken into account. Quantitative methods had been dominant in US sociology for several decades but had recently come under challenge from qualitative approaches. No doubt Blumer was keen to fuel this challenge, and the adoption of what he regarded as more promising approaches. Raising questions about the scientific status of the latter would not have been desirable in this context; indeed, an insistence on their scientific nature was probably essential if they were to gain influence.

Evaluating Blumer's Position

In this final section I will briefly assess Blumer's arguments. Social science has, of course, changed dramatically since his time in many respects. However, as will become clear, I do not believe that the dilemma he identified has been resolved, nor do I think it can be easily avoided.

Taken as a whole, Blumer's methodological writings involve reference to at least four actual or potential approaches to studying the social world, and it is worth distinguishing these and examining their complex relations with one another. First, there is the generic conception of science presented in his dissertation, modelled on the work of natural scientists but probably drawing primarily on nineteenth-century philosophical discussions of scientific method. Second, there is statistical method. While Blumer does not deny the value of numerical data, he does believe that statistical method cannot be the primary form of sociological investigation, on the grounds both that it fails to conform to the logic of science and that it does not respect the intrinsic character of the social world. Third, there is the less-than-scientific approach that, in his dissertation, Blumer identifies many social scientists as using in practice: relying upon sympathetic introspection, and attention to the unique features of particular cases. Finally, there is the sort of naturalistic case study that he outlines in the first chapter of *Symbolic Interactionism*.[98]

So, in summary, we can derive the following typology from Blumer's methodological writings:

Figure 1 *Typology of the approaches to social inquiry mentioned by Blumer*

	Produces genuine knowledge and facilitates control	*Does not produce genuine knowledge and therefore does not facilitate control*
Scientific investigation	Natural science Naturalistic case study?	
Non-scientific investigation	Case study method as actually practised in social science	Statistical method as used in social science

The question mark in Cell 2 indicates the uncertainty at the heart of Blumer's dilemma: about whether a scientific approach, of the kind outlined in his dissertation, could be applied in studying the social world, in such a way as to produce genuine knowledge. In the dissertation, and in his appraisal of *The Polish Peasant*, he expresses uncertainty about this but also suggests that a

---

[98] While these last two may be substantially the same, it is worth allowing for the possibility that Blumer saw them as distinct.

scientific approach may not be essential in meeting the functions of science. By contrast, his 1969 account portrays naturalistic case study as scientific, but as we have seen it does not appear to match the features of science that he had identified in his earlier work. For this reason, I have presented it as straggling the boundary between science and non-science.

In his dissertation, Blumer had identified two respects in which case study method is problematic from a scientific point of view:

> Whether, and how, it can produce data that are reliable, in the sense of being assessable by others.[99]

> Whether, and how, the comparative method can be applied so as to distinguish causal from accidental relations; that is, in Blumer's terms, to identify what is generic.

It is worth considering the force of his arguments in both areas.

Reliable Data

As regards the first, we can identify at least four, rather different but not incompatible, forms of understanding mentioned by Blumer on which case study can rely; all of which are problematic from the point of view of the scientific perspective he outlined in his dissertation:

> *Worldly wisdom.* This refers to broad and/or deep understanding of human nature and society, acquired over the course of life, through both experience and reflection upon it.[100] Blumer makes a reference to worldly understanding in his *Appraisal* when he writes that: 'I should expect a person like Mr Thomas, who has had much intimate contact with human beings, who has studied them extensively, who has a marked ability in human nature, on the whole to make a reasonable interpretation' (Blumer, 1939:146).

> *The capacity to engage in empathy, or to take the role of the other.* This is portrayed by Cooley and Mead as a universal human attribute, but it can also be seen as a capacity that varies in degree across human beings, and one that can be cultivated. Thus, it might be argued that social scientists need to develop a superior capability in this respect, which enables them to understand the people, actions, and institutions they are studying more soundly than others

---

[99] I am using the term 'reliability' here in its ordinary, everyday sense, not in the specialised (and in my view misleading) manner in which it is now routinely used in the methodological literature.
[100] Aristotle, of course, insisted that this is essential in political science or practical philosophy in a way that it is not in studying nature (Ackrill, 1987:364-6).

(see Blumer, 1928:338).

Learning the relevant culture. Especially in his 1969 chapter, Blumer emphasises that people live in different 'worlds', and that it is necessary to understand the particular 'world' someone lives in if we are to grasp *why* they do what they do. It is not hard to see this as analogous to the idea that if we are to study societies that are different from our own we need to learn their cultures; in other words, the distinctive ways of thinking and acting that characterise them. This has, of course, long been a central feature of ethnographic method.

Careful, flexible, first-hand observation. In 1969 Blumer seems to place particular emphasis on actual participant observation by the researcher in the locale and among the people being studied. And he emphasises that this is not just a matter of learning how people see themselves and their actions but of 'digging deeper' than this, presumably to discover aspects and causes of their behaviour of which they are unaware.

What is problematic about these four means of understanding others' behaviour, from the point of view of (some perspectives on) scientific method, is that they are thought to rule out the kind, or degree, of checking by fellow researchers that is needed to produce scientifically reliable knowledge. Thus, in the case of the first two, we are required to judge accounts on the basis of the 'qualifications' of the researcher. Much the same is true with the third, unless readers of the research report are themselves familiar with the relevant culture. The problem with the fourth form of understanding is that it may not be replicable: it is rarely possible to repeat the observational process in more or less the same way, precisely because of its flexible character and that fact that it takes place in 'natural' settings. Nor is it clear that there will be any reliable signs that a researcher has properly carried out this sort of observation.

However, in the light of subsequent developments in the philosophy of science, the distinction between natural and social science in this respect cannot be so sharply drawn as it was in the past. There has been sustained criticism of empiricist claims that science relies solely upon sense data, or observations of physical behaviour, that can be checked by others. It has been argued that this is impossible, and that natural science necessarily relies upon 'tacit knowledge' on the part of the researcher (Polanyi, 1959 and 1966); that perception is not a matter of sense-*impression*, that the organism plays an active role in producing what we perceive (Hanson, 1958; Gregory, 1970); and that all scientific data are assumption-laden (Kuhn, 1970).

Of course, the fact that the problem of producing reliable data is not unique to social science does not imply that it is easily resolved; or even that it does not take on a more severe form in that field. In my view, it is an area that still requires much greater methodological attention than it currently gets. That data are open to assessment by readers of research reports, and especially by fellow members of the relevant research community, remains essential to the way in which any science operates.

There are three important aspects to this problem in the case of qualitative research, given the absence of replicability.[101] First, it is rarely, if ever, possible to reproduce all of the relevant data collected in a social science project within the final research report. What is provided is almost always a very small proportion of the data, selected by the researcher in order to illustrate the nature of the data on which conclusions have been reached and perhaps also to establish key points in the argument.[102] Secondly, 're-presenting' data in textual form is by no means a simple matter. In fact, in literal terms, re-presentation is impossible. All that can be provided, at best, is a text that conveys to readers the relevant aspects of the situation(s) and people studied. In other words, what is presented must contain the cues necessary to generate appropriate contextual understanding on the part of readers who have not experienced the particular phenomena themselves. Thirdly, and following on from this, there is the problem that, presumably in order to make a sound interpretation of the data, readers of research reports must have the worldly wisdom, capacity for empathy, and knowledge of the culture required for them to interpret these data aright.

While these problems are a challenge, it is important to emphasise that what are required are pragmatic solutions in the context of particular studies, whereby the process of checking the reliability of data and the validity of conclusions is sufficient to produce worthwhile knowledge. It is probably a mistake to treat this issue as either needing or being open to some single, universal solution.

Comparative Method

The second problem, concerned with using the comparative method to determine what is generic, is perhaps even more challenging. In this area Blumer was, in effect, drawing on a long tradition of philosophical ideas going back through Mill and Bacon to Aristotle. While in his dissertation he recognises that social science cannot usually employ experimentation, following Znaniecki and others he suggests that there may be ways of using the comparative method via case study to achieve the same goal. However, he also expresses uncertainty about whether this will turn out to be possible. When he outlines a naturalistic approach in 1969, he explicitly labels this scientific, but as regards comparative

---

[101] Note that some kinds of qualitative research do claim replicability, notably conversation analysis: see Peräkylä, (1997).
[102] In this connection, we should note that *The Polish Peasant* was, to a large degree, a compendium of data. Moreover, it is now more possible, through archives, including online ones, to provide access for readers to the data from a study. However, this is still rarely done, and such provision is by no means straightforward, there are important ethical and other issues involved: see Hammersley, (1997).

method it does not seem to match the requirements for science he laid down in 1928. Moreover, it is not clear that he still sees the goal of science as the production of universal laws that capture the essence of the phenomena being studied.

A comparison with Znaniecki's position and analytic induction may be instructive here. Znaniecki saw the task of science as to develop concepts that capture causal relations in the cultural realm, in the form of laws that specify necessary and sufficient conditions for the occurrence of some type of phenomenon. He recognised that this involved abstraction both from many of the features of any particular case as it initially presents itself to an investigator *and* from the pragmatically-based commonsense concepts that people use to make sense of the world. While Znaniecki seems to have regarded this process of abstraction as occurring through detailed investigation of a single exemplary case, rather than through comparison, Lindesmith's later account of analytic induction did emphasise the comparative method. However, for the most part what is involved here is John Stuart Mill's method of agreement: examination of cases where the phenomenon to be explained occurred with a view to identifying those features that were also present and could offer an explanation.[103] Lindesmith did also give some attention to the method of difference, in the form of studying cases where the outcome was absent in order to determine whether the features that he had identified as necessary and sufficient were also absent. However, this was not done very systematically in his study of opiate addiction, and he did not seek to investigate cases where the conditions he had identified were met, in order to discover whether the outcome *always* occurred in these (Lindesmith, 1968).[104] So, even analytic induction does not, in fact, meet all the requirements needed to discover unique, law-like causal relations (Hammersley, 2008:ch4), but it goes much further in this direction than Blumer's naturalistic case study approach.

There are both practical and theoretical problems in applying the comparative method in social science. In practical terms, while the task of finding cases where the phenomenon to be explained occurs may be relatively straightforward, identifying cases in which the conditions specified in an emerging theory are met (in order to discover whether the phenomenon to be explained occurred in them) is much more challenging; especially when we remember that the sort of cases needed will change at each stage of the theory's development. If we also add the requirement that these cases must allow us to assess the effects of potentially confounding factors, the difficulties involved in finding and investigating appropriate cases becomes daunting.

The theoretical problems with using the comparative method focus on whether causal relations of the kind assumed by Blumer in 1928, and also by

---

[103] Mill's discussion of these methods is to be found in his *A System of Logic*, part VIII, see for example Nagel, (1950). For an excellent exposition and assessment, see Mackie, (1967).
[104] The same is true of Cressey's investigation of financial trust violation (Cressey, 1953).

Znaniecki and Lindesmith, actually operate in the social world.[105] The perspective of symbolic interactionism itself generates doubts about this: if human actions are contingent in character, because any effect of a causal factor is mediated by an emergent process of interpretation, then the outcome must be indeterminate, making the very notion of causal relations specified by necessary and sufficient conditions inapplicable. On this view, it seems likely that an ineradicable feature of the social world is that the same situation could generate different outcomes, and that the same outcome could be produced by different sets of factors. And the weaker form of causal relation that this implies would be probabilistic in character. It is worth noting that, if true, this would exacerbate the practical problems in carrying out comparative analyses in natural settings. In order to detect causal trends we would need to study a large number of cases at each stage in the process of investigation, no longer being able to treat a single exception as refuting a causal claim - a strategy that was central to analytic induction and Blumer's 1928 conception of science.

Of course, many qualitative researchers today would insist on the interpretative or constructive character of all social scientific analysis, and deny therefore that causal analysis is appropriate in studying the social world. In doing so, they draw, directly or indirectly, on a variety of influential philosophical sources, from philosophical hermeneutics to deconstruction. If applied to the research process, and taken to its logical conclusion, this sort of constructionism implies that in writing a research report we *create* the social phenomena we purport to represent.[106] Of course, most qualitative researchers do not adopt this extreme position in practice, but they are often at pains to emphasise that what they are documenting are contingent patterns of social construction; and that what they offer is simply one interpretation of the phenomena they have studied amongst others, and that this interpretation reflects their own personal and/or sociocultural characteristics. I have argued elsewhere that this kind of constructionism offers no resolution to the methodological problems facing social science (Hammersley, 2008). So, it seems to me that we still need to deal with the difficulties that Blumer identified as a dilemma for social science, even if their conceptualisation needs to be modified in light of more recent views about the nature of scientific, or any kind of academic, inquiry.

---

[105] In other words, causal relations specified in terms of necessary and sufficient conditions that identify unique connections in which the outcome category is causally homogeneous.

[106] This is not an implication following from either philosophical hermeneutics or deconstruction, but this conclusion does seem to have been drawn by some qualitative researchers. There is a sense in which Blumer's symbolic interactionism is constructionist, but he does not seem to have traced out the implications of applying this perspective to the research process itself. In his methodological writings he employs a form of pragmatist realism (Hammersley, 1989a). However, there is one place where he canvasses the possibility that social science fictions could be of value (see Blumer, 1979:xxxv).

Conclusion

In this chapter I have explored Blumer's dilemma in some detail. I have shown that he seems to have believed that it remained unresolved over the course of his long career, despite the fact that in the late 1960s he provided an account of how sociologists should go about their scientific work in which he did not mention this dilemma. I suggested he may have thought that naturalistic case study would generate the kind of conceptualisation of social phenomena necessary for applying the scientific approach he had outlined in his dissertation; though it is also possible that he had altered his conception of science, or that he remained genuinely uncertain about what it required in the case of studying the social world.[107]

In my view, Blumer's beliefs about these matters are less important than the question of whether the dilemma he identified still faces us today. I have argued that, while its terms need revision, the problems it highlights remain challenges for any approach to social research that aims at causal analysis. And, since I can see no justification for any claim to social science that does not acknowledge this goal, I conclude that these problems are serious ones and that Blumer was right to insist that, in the face of them, we should neither act like ostriches nor imagine ourselves to be magicians who can wish them away.

References

Blumer, H. (1928) *Method in Social Psychology*. unpublished doctoral dissertation, University of Chicago.

-----.(1930) 'Review of Lundberg's *Social Research*', *American Journal of Sociology*, 35:1101-11.

-----.(1939) *Critiques of Research in the Social Sciences: I. An Appraisal of Thomas and Znaniecki's 'The Polish Peasant in Europe and America'*. New York, Social Science Research Council.

-----.(1969) *Symbolic Interactionism: Perspective and Method*, Englewood Cliffs NJ, Prentice-Hall. [Reprinted by University of California Press, Berkeley, 1998]

-----.(1979[1939]) *An Appraisal of Thomas and Znaniecki's 'The Polish Peasant in Europe and America'*. Second edition, New Brunswick, NJ, Transaction Books.

Cressey, D. (1953) *Other People's Money*. Glenco Ill., Free Press.

Denzin, N.K. and Lincoln, Y. S. (eds.). (2005) *Handbook of Qualitative Research*. Third edition, Thousand Oaks CA, Sage.

Gregory, R. (1970) *The Intelligent Eye*. London, Weidenfeld & Nicolson.

---

[107] Of course, by no means all problems are resolvable at any particular time, and the appropriate attitude to adopt towards those that do not seem tractable is one of cautious uncertainty.

Haack, S. (2003) *Defending Science – Within Reason: Between Scientism and Cynicism*, Amherst NY, Prometheus Books

Hammersley, M. (1989a) *The Dilemma of Qualitative Method: Herbert Blumer and the Chicago Tradition*. London, Routledge.

-----.(1989b) 'The problem of the concept: Herbert Blumer on the Relationship between Concepts and Data', *Journal of Contemporary Ethnography*, 18, 2:133-59.

-----(1997) 'Qualitative Data Archiving: Some Reflections on its Prospects and Problems', *Sociology*, 31, 1, pp131-42.

-----.(2004) 'Towards a Usable Past for Qualitative Research', *International Journal of Social Research Methodology* (Special issue on 'Celebrating classic sociology'), 7,(1):19-27.

-----.(2008) *Questioning Qualitative Research*. London, Sage.

Hanson, N. (1958) *Patterns of Discovery*. Cambridge, Cambridge University Press.

Kaplan, A. (1964) *The Conduct of Inquiry*. New York, Chandler.

Kuhn, T. S. (1970) *The Structure of Scientific Revolutions*, Second edition, Chicago, University of Chicago Press.

Lindesmith, A. (1937) *The Nature of Opiate Addiction*. Chicago, University of Chicago Libraries.

-----.(1968) *Addiction and Opiates*. Chicago, Aldine.

-----.(1981) 'Symbolic Interactionism and Causality', *Symbolic Interaction*, 4, (1):87-96.

Lyman, S.M. and Vidich, A.J. (1988) *Social Order and the Public Philosophy: An Analysis and Interpretation of the Work of Herbert Blumer*. Fayetteville AS, University of Arkansas Press. (Republished as *Selected Works of Herbert Blumer: A Public Philosophy for Mass Society*. Urbana Ill, University of Illinois Press in 2000.)

Mackie, J.L. (1967) 'Mill's Methods of Induction', in Edwards, P. (ed.). *The Encyclopedia of Philosophy*. New York, Macmillan.

Maines, D.R. (1988) 'Myth, Text, and Interactionist Complicity in the Neglect of Blumer's Macrosociology', *Symbolic Interaction* 11:43-57

Maines, D. and Morrione, T.J. (1990) Introduction, in H. Blumer *Industrialization as and Agent of Social Change*. New York, Aldine de Gruyter.

Nagel, E. (ed.). (1950) *John Stuart Mill's Philosophy of Scientific Method*. New York: Hafner.

Peräkylä, A. (1997) 'Validity and Reliability in Research Based on Tapes and Transcripts', in Silverman, D. (ed). *Qualitative Analysis: Issues of Theory and Method*. London: Sage.

Polanyi, M. (1959) *Personal Knowledge*. Chicago: University of Chicago Press

-----.(1966) *The Tacit Dimension*. Garden City NY: Doubleday.

Schmaus, W. (1994) *Durkheim's Philosophy of Science and the Sociology of Knowledge*, Chicago, University of Chicago Press.

Shapin, S. (1994) *A Social History of Truth: Civility and Science in Seventeenth-century England*, Chicago, University of Chicago Press.

Thomas, W. I. and Znaniecki, F. (1918/20a) *The Polish Peasant in Europe*

and America, Chicago, University of Chicago Press/Boston, Badger Press.
Thomas, W. I. and Znaniecki, F. 'Methodological Note', in Thomas and Znaniecki (1918/20a). Reprinted in Bierstedt, R. (ed.). (1969) *Florian Znaniecki on Humanistic Sociology*, Chicago, University of Chicago Press.
Znaniecki, F. (1934) *The Method of Sociology*, New York, Farrar and Rinehart.

CHAPTER 7

'All Life is Experimentation': The Chicago School and the Experimenting Society

Matthias Gross
Department of Urban and Environmental Sociology
Helmholtz Centre for Environmental Research – UFZ,
Permoserstr, Leipzig, Germany

Introduction

Experimentation is generally regarded as a constitutive element of modern science and is understood as its distinguishing characteristic when compared with methods of discovery prior to the 17th century. Its predominant features are the artificial set-up of an experimental system, the inducement of changes by external control of certain parameters and the measurements of observable effects. As a scientific method, experimentation aims not only at manipulating the mechanisms and functions of the experimental system but at understanding segments of reality represented by it. In a different sense, in the 19th century the label of 'social experimentation' was occasionally used by authors such as Auguste Comte, John Stuart Mill, George Cornewall Lewis, Adolphe Quetelet for observation of events happening anyway rather than manipulation of variables by researchers (cf. Brown 1997; Dehue 2001). These events could be natural disasters such as a flooding, but also administrative actions.

Whether the social sciences in general and sociology in particular could ever be experimental sciences that model themselves on the natural sciences has been controversially debated since the beginning of the institutionalization of the social sciences in the late 19th century up until the current day. Comte for instance believed that the experimental investigation would be "wholly inapplicable in Social Science; but we shall find that the science is not entirely deprived of this resource though it must be one of inferior value." He continued:

> There are two kinds of experimentation – the direct and the indirect: and that it is not necessary to the philosophical character of this method that the

circumstances of the phenomenon in question should be, as is vulgarly supposed in the learned world, artificially instituted. Whether the case is natural or factitious, experimentation takes place whenever the regular course of the phenomenon is interfered with in any determinate manner. The spontaneous nature of the alteration has no effect on the scientific value of the case, if the elements are known. It is in this sense that experimentation is possible in sociology. (Comte, 1854:70).

Nevertheless, Comte's ideas could not stop the experimental method to remain marginal in sociology. To a certain degree, the marginalized status of experiment in sociology also goes back to the duality between the natural sciences and the human sciences in the German tradition of idealistic philosophy dating from the 19th century. This tradition viewed *Naturwissenschaft* (natural science) and *Geisteswissenschaft* (humanities and social sciences) as qualitatively different. Natural laws, it was contended, had no place in the study of human culture. Human culture represents the realm of individual freedom, moral norms, and historical uniqueness, but not of some kind of determinism. Nature and culture were essentially different realms of being and thus the natural scientific idea of experimenting with the object of study seemed inappropriate. If nature and culture are essentially different, so must be the instruments of research.

Perhaps most prominently Stuart Chapin (1947) introduced the category of 'ex post facto experiment', where an observed fact should be traced back to its causes. For Chapin, this was an attempt to adapt as good as possible the sociological method to the experimental method of the natural sciences (cf. Greenwood 1976:46-47). However, the most common objections to the experimental method have always been (1) the argument that there are no causal laws to be found in the realm of social relations constituted by meaning, intention, reflexivity, and institutions, (2) that social phenomena rule out any control by the experimenter, (3) that the subject matter of sociology is far too complex for experimentation, and finally (4) that artificial experiments on society would be ethically untenable.

It was not before the early 1900s that a clear definition of experiment as a comparative measurement of experimental and control groups emerged and it was not until the 1950s that randomly controlled trials became a sort of ideal type experiment in the social sciences. Most prominently experimentations on a larger societal scale have been proposed since the 1960s by Donald Campbell and his respective co-authors. They introduced the concepts of quasi-experiments, which signify that an experimenter does not have complete control and thus cannot "schedule treatments and measurements for optimal statistical efficiency, with complexity emerging only from that goal of efficiency" (Campbell and Stanley 1963:1). Here experiment is understood as "that portion of research in which variables are manipulated and their effects upon other variables observed" (ibid.). Even if these experiments do not always include random assignments to various treatments, they are nevertheless based upon deliberate interventions which serve to describe and understand causal effects.

Large scale social experimentation hit its first peak in the 1970s and it never seized to play a part in public reform projects. However, from a methodological point of view these "quasi-experiments" always have been considered as more or less deficient models of laboratory experiments. Thus for Campbell the dominant question was how to compensate the "threats to experimental validity" (Campbell 1969:409, cf. Bulmer 1986).

In this chapter I will introduce a notion of experiment that is neither modeled along the 19th century idea of 'experiment by chance' nor along the ideal of a randomized controlled trial, but rather a notion of a self-experimenting society. This concept, and at least the seed of a theory, is based on Robert E. Parks and some of his Chicago colleagues' concept of "laboratory" and "experiment." In a sense, their idea of experiment can be seen as a hybrid concept between the 19th century understanding of social experiment and post World War II ideas on experiments as social reforms.

The Study of Society and Experimentation in
Social Science Research

From the beginning of the institutionalization of American sociology as a university discipline, sociologists have tried to make their approaches more objective by attempting to adopt the language and methodology of the natural sciences.[108] Included in this endeavor is the perspective in which society or the city are viewed as a laboratory. This metaphor has been in use at least since the founding of the Department of Sociology at the University of Chicago in 1892. When the University of Chicago was established that same year, the potential of sociological research for providing insights that would offer guidance for society was regarded as considerable. As a matter of fact, the idea of the city of Chicago as a social laboratory *par excellence* was one of the key suggestions of the first professor of the Department, Albion W. Small (1854-1926), for an approach to the study of society.

This idea can be followed in the first American textbook of sociology, a monograph entitled *An Introduction to the Study of Society* (1894), which Small co-authored with George E. Vincent. In the introduction Small and Vincent described their book bluntly as a 'laboratory guide' to studying people in their 'every-day occupations' (1894:15).

In a similar way John Dewey (1859-1952), set out his pragmatist idea that the experimental methods of modern science provided a most useful approach to the development of current social change. Dewey considered the relationship between knowledge and action by applying the methods of experimental sciences to social learning. However, one should remember that the ideas set

---

[108] This and the following section takes up ideas put forth in Gross (2001, 2003, 2004) and Gross and Krohn (2005), and extends and develops them further.

forth by Small and colleagues was well before John Dewey coined his usage of the notion of experimentation as an essential part of humans' everyday experience. Indeed, at this time (mid-1890s), when Dewey spoke of experiment, he still had in mind the natural science ideal of an experiment, where the boundary conditions are controllable and a dependent variable reflects the phenomenon under study (cf. Dewey, 1969).

Small and Vincent indeed believe that their "book is to be compared with laboratory guides in biology" (ibid.:17). In other words, it was a guidebook by means of which students of sociology could study the experiments going on in society, very much designed like a laboratory manual, a collection of chapters or "units" describing the procedure for specific experiments or observations. This also included ready-made experiments, or experiments that were 'set up' by others. The perception of the city as a kind of laboratory and the study of human society as work in this laboratory was even presented in the university catalogue of the University of Chicago in 1899/1900. It was claimed that "the city of Chicago is one of the most complete social laboratories in the world... No city represents a wider variety of typical social problems than Chicago" (Tolman, 1902: 116). Small and Vincent, together with other sociologists of their day, believed that sociological investigation should be understood as taking place inside a social laboratory. This social laboratory, however, is a place, where knowledge gain and practical work need to be combined (Vincent, 1905). To Small every outcome of a social process is based on an experiment. In 1921, in an article on "The Future of Sociology," Small stated:

> All life is experimentation. Every spontaneous or voluntary association is an experiment. Every conscious or unconscious acquiescence in a habit is an experiment. [...] Each civilization in the world today, each mode of living side by side within or in between the several civilizations is an experiment. (Small, 1921:187).

He goes on to point out what that might mean for sociological research:

> All the laboratories in the world could not carry on enough experiments to measure a thimbleful compared with the world of experimentation open to the observation of social science. The radical difference is that the laboratory scientists can arrange their own experiments while we social scientists for the most part have our experiments arranged for us. (Small, 1921:188).

This powerful statement of all social life being exposed to experimental settings and engaged in experimental performances needs some qualification, since viewing all purposeful action as bound to risks of trial and error would not provide a conceptual basis for "sociological experimentation." In fact, it would partially fall back to the 19th century usage of the term, when experimentation was related to human calamities, natural disasters, as well as acts of governments. It cries out for a more precise specification of the societal and cultural conditions which give social life its experimental characteristics. However, already in 1905 George Vincent felt that the experimental character of life in general could only be meaningfully succeed when everyday practices were combined with sociological training. Systematically linking internal factors of academic training to the outside world, what Vincent called a combination of "practical experience with academic tastes" (1905:310) meant for him to actually push an experiment farther (1905:302). It is this cyclically linked process between knowledge-informed strategic action and methodically guided observation of practical development that gives the natural experiment approach a sociological flavor.

Is all Life Experimentation?

Although the notion of society as a laboratory was first assigned to social settlements and later mainly used with reference to cities, other sociologists of the Chicago department from the 1890s, like Charles Henderson or Charles Zueblin, used the term sociological laboratory to indicate the mixture of social settlements and sociological research as a unified part of the progressive development of society. For them the significance of scientific observation of society, that is, the sociological production of knowledge, and the relevance of social reform, went hand in hand.[109] For instance, the application of newly gained knowledge to society and the design of strategies that would feed knowledge directly back into society, was practiced in studies on deviance, research on the ecological basis of society, on social insurance, journalism, on alleviation of unemployment, or the study of the impact of immigrants on social change (e.g. Addams, 1970; Henderson, 1898; Lathrop, 1894; Small and Vincent, 1894; Vincent, 1905; Zueblin, 1899).

Taking up the notion of experiment embraced by the early founders of the discipline, but also his earlier work in Tuskegee, Robert E. Park marshaled the early Chicago ideas into a widely respected research program. Already during his participation in a program for African-American farmers for improving agricultural methods in Tuskegee, Park calls the program "one detail of an experiment in social upbuilding" (Park, 1908:826). However, after he left Tuskegee for Chicago, it was especially the modern city in Park's view that was seen as a social laboratory. In this laboratory, all parts of the environment are

---

[109] Mary Jo Deegan (1988:36) has prominently argued that the improvement of settlements was associated with social work, which at that time was mainly undertaken by women. The detached observers' position of the sociologists, in Deegan's view, was the male perspective on the social laboratory, that woman were not able to take. While Deegan's analysis of early women sociologists is important, the usage and meanings of 'experiment' and 'laboratory' in the development of early Chicago sociology shows a different picture. For another important attempt to correct the view that woman were not allowed to be part of the sociology community, but did not want to be part of it, see Coghlan (2005).

interdependent and are moved by individual, collective, and ecological forces. In order to understand the development of the great cities it was, as Park later termed it, the natural areas that should be investigated. For Park, the city is a constellation of natural areas. Planning the development of theses natural areas, would be an attempt to direct the ecological basis of society and indeed, this is not as easy as it seems. "Cities," Park wrote, "are always getting out of hand. The actual plan of the city is never a mere artifact, it is always quite as much a product of nature as of design" (Park, 1925a: 674). Harvey Zorbaugh, one of Park's students, also observed that

> the city is curiously resistant to the fiats of man. Like the robot, created by man, it goes its own way indifferent to the will of its creator. Reformers have stormed, the avaricious have speculated, and thoughtful have planned. But again and again their programs have met with obstacles. Human nature offers some opposition; traditions and institutions offer more; and – of especial significance – the very physical configuration of the city is unyielding to change. (Zorbaugh, 1926:188).

In Park's and his student's understanding the modern city and thus modern society in general were understood as a partial natural phenomenon. Pointing to the 'natural' side of the city, is simply calling special attention to modern society's very own dynamics, which result from modern means of planning and production. Every plan humans set out is actually tested within their own society. Natural areas are made by humans, but their dynamics appear to be 'natural'.

In Park's approach the societal dynamic is always perceived in terms of its dependency on the material environment. The requirements of a city therefore lay in all the materials and commodities needed to sustain the city's inhabitants. The activities of the inhabitants can have unplanned or 'chaotic' consequences. In the chaotic city-jungle Park's unity of research was what he has termed the 'natural area.' Natural areas can be regarded as poles of order in an otherwise disordered world. In that context he often stressed the complexity and complication of social relations in modern societies, but at the same time he believed that this offered new possibilities, especially in cities (Park, 1915: 608). This is, for Park, that which justifies the view that would make the city a laboratory or a clinic in which human nature and social processes may be most conveniently and profitably studied (1915:612). In the revised version of his classic piece on "The City" Park stated:

> The city, especially the great city, in which more than elsewhere human relations are likely to be impersonal and rational . . . is in a very real sense a laboratory for the investigation of collective behavior. (Park, 1925b: 31).

In terms of Park's perceptions, the development of the city and of society at large can thus be understood to be associated with processes that 'experimentally' result in a better understanding of how society 'works'. Consequently, for Park sociology is on its way to becoming 'an experimental science', and he went on to clarify that

> experiments are going on in every field of social life, in industry, in politics, and in religion. In all these fields men are *guided* by some implicit or explicit *theory* of the situation, but this theory is not often stated in the form of a hypothesis and subjected to a test of the negative instances. (Park, 1921:180).

Here Park is elaborating the idea articulated by Small that society itself is operative in designing social experiments.

In 1929, in a volume entitled *Chicago: An Experiment in Social Science Research*, the editors Thomas Smith and Leslie White gathered twelve articles on the research done in and on the city of Chicago. The lead article was Robert Park's "The City as a Social Laboratory," where again he described the city as "the natural habitat of civilized man." The city, for Park, represents modern society's most consistent and most successful attempt to remake the world people live in. However, he goes on to state:

> If the city is the world which man created, it is the world in which he is henceforth condemned to live. Thus, indirectly and without any clear sense of the nature of his task, in making the city man has remade himself. It is in some such sense and in some such connection as this that we may think of the city as a social laboratory. (Park, 1929:1).

That in modern society the experimenter is becoming part if the experiment is also captured in the preface to Nels Anderson's monograph *The Hobo*, where Park stated: "If it is true that man made the city, it is quite as true that the city is now making man" (Park, 1923:v). In Park's view it is especially urban life where human society becomes more and more complex and, as he called it, human institutions grow rapidly: "They grow under our very eyes, and the processes by which they grow are open to observation and so, eventually, to experimentation" (Park, 1929:19). In general, for Park the city is "an advantageous place to study social life." The urban environment gives social life the character of a laboratory, since "in the city every characteristic of human nature is not only visible but is magnified." Since the city "magnifies, spreads out, and advertises human nature in all its various manifestations" it is "of all places the one in which to discover the secrets of human hearts, and to study human nature and society" (ibid.). Park believed that by magnifying human society in its various incarnations, it could be studied almost as if it were being looked at through a microscope. The microscopic tool, however, is only made available to the observing sociologist by society itself. Again, for Park the city is the most prominent place for creating and supporting the experimental spirit.

For the purpose of these experiments the city, with its natural regions, becomes a "frame of reference", i.e., a device for controlling our observations of social conditions in their relation to human behavior. (Park, 1929:11).

But if experimentation is to mean more than simple trial and error, theory and design of action have to be taken seriously. It is this move that gives Park's reflection upon experiments performed in all fields of society a further boost.

In order to gain from the observation of these experiments, Park wants to discover the "relation of cause and effect." In his idea it "is the business of sociology, in studying human affairs, to look for these same relations of cause and effect; to lay down general rules which enable us to predict from the existence of the situation A the succeeding situation B" (Park, 1914:167), and he goes on: "The method to which I refer is the intensive study of the typical and individual" (ibid:168). It is interesting to note here, that Park, referring to Wilhelm Windelband's distinction between the nomothetic and the idiosyncratic, on the one hand wants to "push the scientific investigation and extend and improve our technique as far as possible," since this "is the main business of sociology as a science and a method." On the other hand "it is necessary, in order to deal practically with human beings, to understand individual men and women" (Park, 1914:167). For Park, implicitly, the sociological method would have to be understood as a way of getting inside group behavior and generating data in 'naturally' occurring contexts that can be generalized. In Park's method, the Weberian approach of a "verstehende sociology" of trying to understand the typical and the nomothetic scientific approach of performing experiments are linked together. What Park contended here, was that modern society has turned itself into a place that can be understood as the laboratory for investigating sociologists. With this type of experiment going on, the sociologist as experimenter is bound to participate in complex networks of actors imbedded in institutional and natural environments the actors cannot completely control. Even less could they be controlled by sociologists.

Uncontrolled Experiments and the Development of Modern Society

The development of modern society, in the sense outlined by Robert Park would mean a society that builds its existence on certain kinds of experiments, practiced outside the special domain of science. It is this view in Robert Park's understanding that presented a concept of experiment taking place in society and – even more important – is performed by society itself. What the early Chicago sociologists were indicating was the increasingly experimental character of modern social life in general. When characterizing the city as an experiment, Robert Park did not merely mean the experiments of city planners or social workers who take society as their object of study, but rather the experimental character of social action and societal development, which – taken full strength – takes the form of an open ended experiment. Modern society thus would be a society of self-experimentation.

The experimental nature of society, understood in this way, changes from an evolutionary process or, as Park termed it, a natural history, into an institutionalized strategy which includes all kinds of political, cultural, or aesthetic components. Their outcomes are not predictable and they can cause constant adjustments rather than end in a final goal. The notion of experiment as explored here serves as a means to understand modern societies' social practices that increasingly present themselves as experiments via a willingness to remain open to new forms of experience. This, of course, is most likely to happen in the modern city.

Two core insights based on the discussion above shall be emphasized: *Firstly*, the notion of experiment postulated here can be understood as comprising a deliberate intervention undertaken by a rapidly developing society which persistently sets up institutional conditions of action without being able to completely control the 'natural dynamics' of growth and decay. *Secondly*, the Chicagoan approach of viewing settlements as social laboratories places the sociological experimenter right in the middle of experimental practices. The production of sociological knowledge and its application are thus able to coincide in an ongoing process of recursive learning. This recursive process successively guides the sociological observer to learn more about the fundamental constitution of society.

An experimental performance in the Parkian idea of social experiment comprises mutual action and reaction without allocating any fixed position to an independent 'scientific' experimenter. This perspective of an experimental society is not to be understood as a utopian theory or a design for a future society, but rather as a sociological means to understand and analyze contemporary society's self-experimental character.

Today, observers of scientific research in the age of increasing uncertainty in knowledge production increasingly claim that the boundaries between the laboratory and the life world become blurred. As authors such as Bruno Latour, Ulrich Beck and others have claimed (Beck, 1995, Latour, 2004, Krohn and Weyer, 1994), today scientific experiments are increasingly less conducted in the laboratory, but have become collective experiments that concern each and every one of us. It thus seems to be critical to realize that from the very beginning of American sociology, social scientists have not only been actively been involved in conflicts about social change, inequality or different reform attempts, but they saw the laboratory experiment as a special case of the general or the "real" experiment in society – and not vice versa, where experiments in society are seen as an inferior version of the laboratory experiment. Small's, Vincent's, and Park's idea of experimentation thus appears to be much ahead if its time.

References

Addams, J. (1970 [1895]) 'Prefatory Note', in *Hull-House Maps and Papers: Residents of Hull-House.* New York: Arno Press:vii-viii.

Beck, U. (1995 [1988]): *Ecological Politics in an Age of Risk.* Cambridge, UK: Polity Press.

Brown, R. (1997) 'The Delayed Birth of Social Experiments.' *History of the Human Sciences,* 10 (2):1-23.

Bulmer, M. (1986) 'Evaluation Research and Social Experimentation', in Bulmer, Martin (ed.). *Social Science and Social Policy.* London: Allen & Unwin:155-179.

Campbell, D.T. (1969) 'Reforms as Experiments.' *American Psychologist,* 24 (4): 409-429.

Campbell, D.T. and Stanley, J.C. (1963) *Experimental and Quasi-Experimental Design for Research.* Chicago: Rand McNally.

Chapin, F, S. (1947) *Experimental Designs in Sociological Research.* New York: Harper.

Coghlan, C.L. (2005). '"Please Don't Think of me as a Sociologist": Sophonisba Preston Breckinridge and the Early Chicago School', *The American Sociologist,* 36 (1):3-22.

Comte, A. (1854) *The Positive Philosophy of Auguste Comte.* New York: Appleton.

Deegan, M. Jo. (1988) *Jane Addams and the Men of the Chicago School, 1892-1918.* New Brunswick, NJ: Transaction Publishers.

Dehue, T. (2001) 'Establishing the Experimenting Society: The Historical Origination of Social Experimentation According to the Randomized Controlled Design', *American Journal of Psychology,* 114 (2):283-302.

Dewey, J. (1969) *The Early Works of John Dewey, 1882-1898.* Carbondale, IL: Southern Illinois University Press.

Greenwood, E. (1976 [1945]). *Experimental Sociology: A Study in Method.* New York: Octagon Books.

Gross, M. (2001) *Die Natur der Gesellschaft: Eine Geschichte der Umweltsoziologie.* Weinheim: Juventa Verlag.

-----.(2003). *Inventing Nature: Ecological Restoration by Public Experiments.* Lanham, MD: Rowman & Littlefield.

-----.(2004) 'Human Geography and Ecological Sociology: The Unfolding of a Human Ecology, 1890 to 1930 – and Beyond', *Social Science History,* 28 (4):575-605.

Gross, M. and Krohn, W. (2005) 'Society as Experiment: Sociological Foundations for a Self-experimental Society.' *History of the Human Sciences* 18 (2): 63-86.

Henderson, Charles R. (1899) *Social Settlements.* New York: Lentilhon & Co.

Krohn, W. and Weyer, J. (1994) 'Society as a Laboratory: The Social Risks of Experimental Research.' *Science and Public Policy,* 21 (3):173-183.

Lathrop, J. C. (1894) 'Discussion: Hull-House as a Laboratory of Sociological Investigation.' *Proceedings of the National Conference of Charities* 21:313-320.

Latour, B. (2004) *Politics of Nature: How to Bring the Sciences into Democracy.* Cambridge, MA: Harvard University Press.

Park, Robert E. (1908) 'Agricultural Extension among the Negroes.' *The World To-Day*, 15 (8):820-826.

-----.(1914) 'Organization of Social Surveys.' *Publications of the American Sociological Society*, 8:167-168.

-----.(1915) 'The City: Suggestions for the Investigation of Human Behavior in the City Environment.' *American Journal of Sociology*, 20 (5):577-612.

-----.(1921) 'Sociology and the Social Sciences: The Group Concept and Social Research.' *American Journal of Sociology*, 27 (2):169-183

----.(1923) "Editor's Preface." In Anderson, Nels, *The Hobo: The Sociology of the Homeless Man*. Chicago: University of Chicago Press:v-viii.

-----.(1925a) 'Community Organization and the Romantic Temper.' *Social Forces*, 3 (4):673-677.

-----.(1925b) 'The City: Suggestions for the Investigation of Human Behavior in the Urban Environment', in Park, Robert E., Burgess, Ernest W. and McKenzie, R.D. (eds.)., *The City*. Chicago: University of Chicago Press:1-46.

-----.(1929) 'The City as a Social Laboratory.' In Smith, Thomas V. and White, L. D. (eds.), *Chicago: An Experiment in Social Science Research*. Chicago: University of Chicago Press:1-19.

Small, Albion, W. (1921) "The Future of Sociology." *Publications of the American Sociological Society*, 15: 174-193.

Small, Albion, W. and Vincent, George E. (1894) *An Introduction to the Science of Society*. New York: American Book Co.

Smith, Thomas V. and White, Leslie D. (eds.), (1929) *Chicago: An Experiment in Social Science Research*. Chicago: University of Chicago Press.

Tolman, F. L. (1902) "The Study of Sociology in Institutions of Learning in the United States. Pt. II." *American Journal of Sociology*, 8 (1): 85-121.

Vincent, George, E. (1905) "A Laboratory Experiment in Journalism." *American Journal of Sociology*, 11 (3): 297-311.

Zorbaugh, Harvey, W. (1926) "The Natural Areas of the City." *Publications of the American Sociological Society*, 20: 188-197.

Zueblin, C. (1899) "The World's First Sociological Laboratory." *American Journal of Sociology*, 4 (3): 577-592.

CHAPTER 8

The Art of Comparison: Lessons from the Master, Everett C. Hughes

Howard S. Becker
San Francisco, USA

Introduction

Comparison has always been the backbone, acknowledged or not, of good sociological thinking. Finding two or more things that are alike in some important way yet differ in other ways, looking for the further differences that create those you first noticed, looking for the deeper processes these surface differences embody--these operations create sociological knowledge of the world and give us the more abstract theories that tell us what to look for the next time out.

Finding things that are alike sounds easier than it is. There are traps. Most commonly, we think two things are alike because they have the same name: all things called schools must be alike, all things called families are the same in all important respects. Why else would we call them by the same name? But, in fact, schools differ in crucial ways and most especially in what they actually do. Some may be engaged in an activity that could charitably called "education," but many others are far more custodial in their operation. And other organizations which go by different names--prisons, for example--can easily be seen to do a great deal of educating, both the kind prison officials organize to teach inmates a useful trade and the kind inmates organize to teach each other potentially more useful trades. I leave to you the similar exercise to be done about families.

If we can't take names at face value, how do we find similar things to compare? We can do what Goffman did (in *Asylums* 1961, see also Becker 2007) choose a trait that defines the category to investigate and stick with it, no matter how counter-intuitive the collection of cases it produces. But the same problem arises: how to find a trait that identifies a category about which we can make sociological interesting remarks. Goffman's example tells us to choose a trait that constrains social interaction: total institutions, on his definition, prevent the between inmates and staff who live and work in them from interacting with the outside world, and strictly regulate and minimize interaction between these two categories of inhabitants. These characteristics are easy to discover and "measure," and provoke no definitional arguments.

Why not? Because they do not coincide with our conventional categories of moral judgment, which make sure to place "incongruous cases" in their morally relevant slot. We routinely make moral judgments, one way or another, about prisons and mental hospitals, which we conventionally know to be wicked places filled with wicked people (whether we mean the inmates or the custodians), and about places like convents or military training centers, which we conventionally know to be respectable organizations. But we have no such ready-made judgments about a category which contains those four organizations, as well as submarines, ships at sea and all the other varied phenomena Goffman's definition assembles. The morally disparate character (from a conventional point of view) of these organizations which are so clearly alike in their limitation of interaction frees analysis from having to conform to conventional ideas of good and bad.

Having found a category whose interactional similarities promise to produce sociological insight, we then look for other interactionally interesting differences between them. And we look for the conditions of such differences and for their consequences. Goffman's example doesn't help here, because he did not make such a differentiated analysis of members of the category of total institutions. He didn't pursue the differences between convents, submarines, mental hospitals, and jails. We find an example of this more complicated form of comparative analysis in Everett Hughes' probing dissection of the process of industrialization.

Some Background

Everett Hughes - student of Robert E. Park, a sociologist with a truly global perspective when that was rare - went to Germany after he finished his dissertation on real estate salesmen, and studied ethnic and religious variations in the industrial labor force (Hughes, 1935). Then he went to teach in Canada and soon interested himself in similar problems there, first in the larger economic setting of the country, then in the province of Quebec (Hughes, 1941), and finally in a year of intensive fieldwork in the small city of Drummondville, which had recently become home to two textile factories. This work produced what is probably the first major sociological study (though seldom mentioned in the history of that subdiscipline) of industrialization (Hughes, 1943).

He moved to Chicago and then World War II arrived. He was immediately interested in the general question of how a war (or any other major historical event) would affect institutions, a word he used synonymously with organizations (Hughes, 1942). This overlapped with a practical problem University of Chicago researchers had been asked to help with: how to deal with an industrial labor force which managers, desperate for workers, had racially integrated over the objections of its white members. Hughes collaborated with other researchers at the University on several studies of race relations in the various war industries operating in and around Chicago (Hughes, 1946). These studies, enriched by his wide reading on a variety of related topics, provided the basis for the specific and detailed analysis presented in his book on French Canada, and for the paper I'm concerned with here, which generalized his findings in this area.

The Basic Analysis

In 1949, Hughes published a paper with an accurate but unconventionally, for the time, long title: "Queries Concerning Industry and Society Growing out of Study of Ethnic Relations in Industry," which integrates the findings of his field studies and his extensive reading in a comparative analysis of processes of industrialization around the world.

He first identifies two related questions, superficially different, but similar in the underlying structures they refer to. The first is factual: what is the ethnic division of labor in former colonies which have been penetrated by European and North American based industry?

The second question arises in the context of a more practical and parochial concern: how to make the fullest use of the total American labor force? More bluntly, how to get rid of inequities and inefficiencies due to ethnic and racial prejudice and discrimination?

He connects these specifics, vaguely for the moment, to the most general theoretical perspective possible, saying: "Whenever one scratches a problem of racial and ethnic relations, he uncovers problems concerning society itself; and in this case, concerning industry and society." Fair warning. He will look for the most general phenomena in the specifics of a case.

To that end, he makes three sweeping generalizations, factual statements asserted as indisputably true, which serve as the major premises of the argument orienting the rest of the paper. Though few people recognize it, Hughes thought in an essentially mathematical way, frequently reasoning from a few basic premises to a variety of interesting, unexpected, but logically connected consequences. Of course, he chose premises his knowledge of this area of human activity ensured would be analytically fruitful. I don't mean that he simply deduced logical results which he then tested empirically. Of course not. Rather, he created a logical structure from which these results followed. Induction as much as deduction, seasoned with a healthy dose of intimate knowledge of the phenomenon.

The first generalization is: "Industry is always and everywhere a grand mixer of peoples." When a local area first acquires industrial organizations and forms of work, an inevitable result is ethnic and racial mixing. This seemingly innocuous observation motivates all the analysis which follows and puts the specific examples he refers to in a framework in which they stand for more than they appear to be superficially.

The generalization is supported by its own chain of reasoning. Industry always precipitates a grand mixing of peoples because the indigenous population, working in a pre-industrial agricultural economy, cannot provide as many workers as industry needs. Land used for agriculture can't support the number of people an industrial plant needs, so the work force has to be imported from elsewhere. Geographically separated populations almost always differ from one another racially and/or ethnically, so the imported workers inevitably differ from the indigenes in culture as well. Slight geographical distances produce noticeable cultural differences in understandings and practices with respect to work, money, and other things that affect industrial operations (even in ethnically similar populations).

Hughes then makes a crucial distinction: between industrialization as it occurred in the mother countries of industry (in which the industrial revolution first occurred) and their colonial outposts, to which the mother countries have exported industrial patterns of organization and work which the indigenous population has no experience at all of. He immediately finds a characteristic organizational difference between the two situations in the patterns of ethnic recruitment to the industrial ranks in them.

The mother countries provide the matrix of law, customs and institutions industry needs, which are already there and working. Managers, technicians, and core skilled workers, who occupy the top positions of the industrial hierarchy, live where the factories are and are immediately available when one is built. Native to the area, and originally from the same ethnic stock, they share cultural understandings about work and, especially, the discipline of wage work. However, often enough, the new factories have to import the lower echelons of the labor force, who will do the actual factory work. These imported workers at first come from nearby, and cultural and ethnic differences, though real enough, are essentially those between various European nations. Older, pre-industrial elites (landed, commercial and professional) may be jealous of the new industrial leaders, especially when they differ ethnically. The ethnically different industrial workers may be successfully mobile, perhaps in a second generation; or they may be more or less permanently locked into a lower position. In the latter case, politics may take on an ethnic flavor. But mobility in the factory ranks is usually some kind of possibility.

In colonies and ex-colonies, on the other hand, the people who will make up an industrial labor force already live there, but require training in the skills and discipline of industrial work. Or similarly untrained people will be imported from a third country. The upper echelons of technical and managerial people must be imported as well, since no indigenous people have the training or attitudes owners and top managers think necessary for these positions. The distinction between mother country and colony is embodied in such pairs of terms as England vs. Africa, Netherlands vs. Dutch East Indies, the United States vs. the Philippines. A minor variant occurs when rural people from the same country are imported to an urban setting to do industrial work (the situation Hughes encountered in his research in Quebec).

This distinction gives Hughes, as we will see, what he needs to understand many phenomena of industry in the colonies and then, working the comparison in both directions, in the mother countries as well. How do you pick a difference that is so analytically productive? Goffman looked for traits that affected possibilities of interaction. Hughes focused on differences between these basic situations of industrialization that affected patterns of interaction, in this case differing patterns of ethnic recruitment and their immediate consequences in the distribution of ethnicities among organizational ranks.

His second generalization says: "Modern industry, by virtue of being the great mixer, has inevitably been a colossal agent of racial, ethnic and religious segregation" (Hughes, 1949:212) He defines segregation statistically: wherever the ethnic distribution among ranks and kinds of work differs from what might have occurred through a random assignment of people to these categories, you have segregation. Note that that this makes the term a technical rather than a moral category; in this understanding of segregation, it is not by definition a "bad" thing. Using a technical statistical definition lets Hughes note something of interest and importance, that ordinarily carries a moral charge, without having to engage in polemics about it. We shouldn't be diverted by the feeling that we must make immediate moral judgment. Time enough for those judgments when we have a full understanding of the dynamics of the situation and of the possibilities for action of all the participants.

Many kinds of distributions can result. At an extreme, people of differing ethnicity and culture fill each rank and specialty in the industrial organization. And they remain that way, because industries seldom provide opportunities for mobility to the racially and ethnically different occupants of lower ranks. Although some may occasionally allow or even encourage such mobility, these organizations more often resemble caste systems, allowing no mobility beyond the ethnically assigned limits. Which Hughes flags as a question that needs an answer.

In the relations between industrial ranks, marked by potential and often enough actual trouble, industrial, political, religious, and ethnic conflicts can and often do merge. The empirical possibilities for misunderstandings range from simple confusions about the meaning of words to open warfare and the development of racially and ethnically based politics, with many in-between steps Hughes makes good analytic use of.

His third generalization is: "Industry is almost universally an agent of racial and ethnic discrimination. People who hire industrial workers almost always have to choose from an ethnically differentiated applicant pool, so any choice they make is inevitably an ethnic choice" (Hughes, 1949:212) If segregation is a deviation from a chance distribution, discrimination produces a deviation because the chooser considers ethnic traits even though they are irrelevant to work behavior. But segregation is not in itself evidence of discrimination. The industrial experience and training of people varies with their ethnicity, and a choice based on ethnicity may result from taking into account relevant traits which are in fact correlated with ethnicity. That makes it difficult to know when discrimination occurs. Even the person who makes the may not know whether or not he is discriminating.

The distinction between mother countries and colonial situations is the right comparison to make, because it emphasizes striking differences in the way what are essentially the same industrial activities are organized. Ethnic distribution among industrial ranks is the right choice for the major dimension of analysis because it affects all the other facets of interaction in the factories and communities where industrialization occurs. Hughes adds one more crucial feature: the political and social organization of the community the new factory's owners plant it in.

What We Get From Comparison

With the groundwork laid, Hughes now produces - like a magician taking flowers and rabbits out of an empty hat - a complex analysis of the relations between industrial ranks, work organization, and community structure, covering such questions as mobility, ambition, sponsorship, nepotism, and trust, and the role of government. The basic operation is simple: suppose that whatever you find in the one case will be present in the others, probably in a form different enough that we wouldn't notice it if its presence in the first case hadn't alerted us to the possibility. It's what Goffman did in "Cooling the Mark Out": if confidence men have to quiet the potentially destructive actions of an angry mark whose sense of himself has been rudely disappointed, other situations in which people experience that kind of disappointment should display similar personnel and similar operations. Which he finds, for instance, in greeters in restaurants (who calm patrons who aren't going to get think the special treatment they think they deserve), and in the work of psychiatrists, who he suggests do the cooling out of people society has disappointed in a more general way. Hughes works his comparisons between industrial settings in both directions, letting phenomena in the colonies tell him what to look for in the mother countries, and vice versa. A good example is his analysis of the practice and meaning of mobility between ranks in industry.

Although all Western countries have ethnically differentiated hierarchies of power, skill and prestige (in some the ethnic differences may have withered away over the years), the open class systems of the mother countries encourage mobility, so rising through the ranks is, at least in principle, possible. Workers are encouraged to be ambitious and there is perhaps just enough mobility to make that not quite foolish.

Not so in colonies, where no indigenes gain entry into the inner circles of industrial prestige and control. Which has several consequences, most importantly that neither group will grasp the other's meanings and intentions. And this produces the anomalous position of the "straw boss": a management person marginal to both indigenes and the ethnically different bosses, perhaps a person of mixed ancestry, but in any case someone who knows and understands the ideas and thinking of both groups. The bosses tell him what to tell the workers and he does that, just as he lets the bosses know what the workers are thinking and saying.

> [S]uch a person will know the peculiar ways of the workers, and will deal with them accordingly. He is a liaison man, a go-between. And wherever there are workers of some kind extremely alien to industry and to the managers of industry, someone is given this function. He documents, in effect, the gap between the higher positions and the lower; and symbolizes the fact that there is no easy ladder of mobility from the lower position to the higher.
> (Hughes, 1949:218)

The straw boss is bilingual both literally and culturally, translating the meanings industry takes for granted into language understandable to people of a different culture. Does that job, that function, exist in the mother countries? Not by that name, but it does. Looking for it, Hughes uncovers a web of connections between ethnicity, mobility, ambition, and trust that appears, in one form or another, in both kinds of settings.

> [In the colonial situation] the straw-boss symbolizes limited mobility. He is himself mobile, and ambitious. But the nature of his job rests on the lack of mobility of the masses. In the mother-countries, the straw-boss turns up, too. He is found wherever some new and strange element is introduced into the labor force in number. The Negro personnel man [in U.S. industry in the 1940s] is one of the latest strawbosses; he acts as a liaison man between management and Negro help. He cannot himself be considered a candidate for any higher position or for any line position in industry; his is a staff position which exists only so long as Negroes are hired in fairly large numbers, and so long as Negro help is considered sufficiently different from other help to require special liaison. If the race line disappeared, or tended to disappear in industry, there would be no need of the Negro personnel man.
> (Hughes, 1949:218)

Hughes transforms "straw boss" from a term of industrial argot into an analytic concept applicable in all industrial settings where people of differing cultures meet--and remember that his first big generalization was that industry always produces cultural mixing.

Hughes compared examples from his own research in Chicago industry in wartime (the example of the Negro personnel man) and from his work in the textile factories of quasi-colonial Quebec to generate a new concept for understanding industrial organization, a new "telltale" which alerts us to basic organizational phenomena. In addition, he surely relied on what he learned from the work of his students (e.g. Dalton: 1959:199) research on the kinds of ethnic loyalties or lack thereof required in U.S. business organizations) as well as on his voluminous reading in the literature of colonialism.

The straw boss provokes questions about ambition: just how ambitious is it appropriate for workers to be? Industry thinks workers should be ambitious--

sometimes. But industry (like society more generally) is ambivalent about ambition (a topic Hughes returned to repeatedly, complaining when it's absent and also complaining when people are too ambitious (Hughes, 1947). Does industry really want the ambition it claims to look for in everyone? What proportion of ambitious people can an organization absorb without trouble? He notes an organization in which managers speak of the "Thank God for people," who are content to remain where they are.

Controlling groups want to be able to trust their members,

> In the colonial or semicolonial industrial regions, management often quite frankly talks of the necessity of keeping management in loyal hands; that is, in the hands of people closely identified with one another by national sentiment as well as by general cultural background. In the mother-countries of industry, one does not hear such talk, but it is possible that the mechanism operates without people being aware of it. It may operate through the mechanism of sponsoring, by which promising young people are picked and encouraged in their mobility efforts by their superiors. In the course of their rise, they are not merely given a technical training, but also are initiated into the ways and sentiments of the managerial group and are judged by their internal acceptance of them.
> (Hughes, 1949:218)

The highest, most powerful ranks in industry confine power in the hands of people thought to be loyal not merely to the particular organization but to the managerial class and its culture. They take ethnicity as an accurate indication of that cultural loyalty.

Having raised the question of sponsoring power, Hughes looks for it elsewhere and, sure enough, points out the sponsoring power of lower ranks, who often control recruitment to their own ranks by suggesting "trustworthy" people from their village or family as recruits when openings at their own level occur. Stereotypes about what different groups are "good at" grow and persist.

Hughes covers other topics in this short paper, though by no means all those dealt with at length in the monograph on Quebec, which also analyzes religion, family structure, class structure, community organization in and between ethnic groups, and politics. All of these are amenable to the same kind of comparative development (and in fact many are dealt with in some of the other papers in his comprehensive collection *The Sociological Eye* (1984[1971]).

Questions of Method

I've identified some of the crucial steps in the process of comparison, but have not begun to answer all the questions raised by Hughes' practice, and will not here; it's a big topic. These seem to me the chief operations calling for further exploration and specification:

1. How do we choose the right cases to compare? How do we find oppositions as fruitful as mother country of industry and colonial setting?
2. How do we choose the right dimensions to compare, dimensions as fruitful as the ethnic division of labor?
3. Most difficult, perhaps, how do we find the sometimes seemingly insignificant events or social types that connect a variety of general phenomena fruitfully, as the phenomenon of the straw boss did for Hughes?

It's clear, when you read Hughes or Goffman, both masters of this kind of comparison, that they knew all sorts of odd facts, esoteric stories, historical oddities - things we don't have to know to set examinations for our students, didn't have to know for the examinations we took ourselves when we were students, the things we think "every sociologist ought to know." Those conventional requirements, while no doubt necessary for some purposes, mirror the limited range of things sociologists already think important, and are unlikely to contain the kinds of references that not only enlivened the prose of these masters, but also gave them the theoretical purchase that produced new ideas and connections. Since students inevitably spend so much time learning what they "must know," it's no surprise that they don't read widely in other areas (particularly as the "literature" of conventional sociology continues to increase exponentially).

Nor, as Harvey Molotch (1994) has pointed out, do students have the time or inclination to venture beyond the walls of their own quasi-total institution, the university. Such ventures would give them the breadth of examples fruitful comparisons demand.

Not only do students not have the breadth of experience and knowledge to produce unconventional comparisons, they surely have learned, as would-be professionals, to ignore their own random impulses of unconventional comparison. It's hard to imagine a student today who would compare, as Hughes loved to do, prostitutes, priests, and psychiatrists, and so discover the dimension of "guilty knowledge" he found so interesting (knowledge of their client's secrets and possibly illicit behavior). I think, rather, that students would consult the literature on professions and come up with a list of conventionally defined professions as the basis for a comparative analysis.

I can't produce any formulae that will solve these problems automatically. The requirements for doing comparisons well are irreducibly idiosyncratic, time-consuming, and dependent on possessing a sort of random array of knowledge that conventional graduate training does not give us.

References

Becker, Howard, S. (2007) *Telling About Society*. Chicago: University of Chicago Press.

Dalton, M. (1959) *Men Who Manage*. New York: Wiley.

Goffman, E. (1961) *Asylums: Essays on the Social Situation of Mental Patients and Other Inmates*. New York, Doubleday

Hughes, Everett C. (1935) "The Industrial Revolution and the Catholic Movement in Germany." *Social Forces*, 14.

-----.(1941) "French and English in the Economic Structure of Montreal." *Canadian Journal of Economics and Political Science*, 7:493-505.

-----.(1942) "The Impact of War on American Institutions." *American Journal of Sociology*, XLVIII.

-----.(1943) *French Canada in Transition*. Chicago: University of Chicago Press.

-----.(1946) "The Knitting of Racial Groups in Industry." *American Sociological Review*, XI.

-----.(1947) "Principle and Rationalization in Race Relations." *The American Catholic Sociological Review*, 8:3-11.

-----.(1949) "Queries Concerning Industry and Society Growing Out of Study of Ethnic Relations in Industry." *American Sociological Review*, 14:211-220.

-----.(1984[1971]) *The Sociological Eye: Selected Papers*. New Brunswick, NJ: Transaction Books.

Molotch, H. (1994) "Going Out." *Sociological Forum*, 9:229-239.

CHAPTER 9

'The Ethnographic Mosaic' of the Chicago School: Critically Locating Vivien Palmer, Clifford Shaw and Frederic Thrasher's Research Methods in Contemporary Reflexive Sociological Interpretation.

Shane Blackman
Canterbury Christ Church University, England

Introduction

Contemporary accounts of ethnography as a research method usually cite the Chicago School of Sociology[110] under Robert Park and Ernest Burgess as the starting point for urban participant observation, the use of life history and the gathering of personal documents as valid sources of ethnographic data collection (O'Reilly, 2005, Brewer, 2000). In contrast, Platt (1983) and Harvey (1987) have argued that the work of the Chicago School has been misunderstood, contending that to attribute the origin of participant observation to the Chicago School is historically misleading. These two contrasting positions on the Chicago School not only present an unclear picture but also fail to demonstrate the sociological value of the early studies in the development of understanding ethnographic data collection, analysis and writing. Through a close reading of the work of Vivien Palmer, Clifford Shaw and Frederic Thrasher, I want to suggest that these sociologists were advancing new qualitative research procedures. Sociological researchers at the Chicago School were experimentally employing some of the key empathetic strategies

---

[110] The Chicago School were a mixture of teaching and research staff such as W. I. Thomas, Robert Park, Ernest Burgess, Clifford Shaw and Henry McKay, graduate students undertaking MAs or Ph.D for example Nels Anderson and Paul Cressey, then Frederic Thrasher, Ruth Shone, Everett Hughes, Vivien Palmer and Harvey Zorbaugh, while others such as Vivien Palmer and Louis Wirth were both graduates students and staff.

which would later define urban ethnographic practice, through the use of narrative, biography, autobiography, personal documents, dialogue, participation observation, life stories, rapport and voice. These features of qualitative methods are now seen as part of what Bourdieu and Wacqaunt (1992) call the 'reflexive' turn in ethnographic fieldwork accounts.

Howard Becker (1966:viii) in his introduction to *The Jack-Roller*, describes research at the Chicago School in terms of "the image of the mosaic." The idea of a combination of different qualitative methods is mentioned by Martin Bulmer (1984:104) who states: "The blend of informal interviewing and observation mark several of the Chicago studies as pioneering works of participant observation." I want to argue that the early Chicago School research tradition can be understood as employing an 'ethnographic mosaic' approach, where triangulation of different methods and diverse pieces of data in naturalistic settings mark the beginning of participant observation and use of the sociological ethnographic imagination (Bulmer, 1983). For David Matza (1969: 24) the Chicago School contribution went beyond method because their vision of research subjects was in terms of possessing agency within structural constraints in terms of a first hand 'appreciation' of the subjective view "to describe with fidelity and without violating its integrity." Vivien Palmer (1928: 173-74) says the aim of sociological fieldwork is "to unlock the subject's treasure chest" it is not about the 'reform' of subjects or 'enlisting their support' it is about "a dignity to the interview which aids rapport." Brian Roberts (2006: 18) critically locates the Chicago School contribution within three approaches, 'natural areas,' 'natural history,' and 'naturalism.' This chapter is argues that members of the Chicago School were experimenting with research methods applying a 'naturalistic orientation' through anthropological fieldwork driven by the passion to develop sociology to challenge social inequality. Indeed, from Albion Small, W. I. Thomas and Robert Park onwards the Chicago School were involved in practical political programmes and campaigns of social reform but were also criticised by C. Wright Mills (1943) and Alvin Gouldner (1968, 1970) for being liberal apologists for capitalism (Smith, 1988). However, their paramount commitment was the ongoing challenge of establishing a rigorous and reflexive discipline of sociology to report on and engage with social change (Abbott, 1999).

Myths, Falsehoods and Participant Observation

This chapter will initially examine the so-called myth of origin and assess the assertion that this myth has created a false history of the sociological research methods. Traditionally, in accounts of sociological research methods, the work of the Chicago School of Sociology is introduced as the formalised beginning of urban ethnographic approaches in the discipline. In Britain, for example, Robert Burgess (1984:16), David Silverman (1985:16) and Paul Atkinson (1990:28) speak about the success of participant observation studies and the importance placed upon gathering detail, first-hand data and knowledge of people's lives.

Although the work of the Chicago School has received critical attention since it began, this established mainstream position within Sociology has been largely unquestioned (Abbott, 1999:14). During the 1980s and 1990s critical questioning of the Chicago School legacy emerged in Britain from Jennifer Platt and Lee Harvey. The accusation was that in sociology a myth had been created about the Chicago School and their contribution to the development of qualitative research methods. Jennifer Platt's (1983, 1994, 1998) argument is that there is a common misunderstanding about the ancestry of participant observation which she calls an 'origin myth.' She maintains that there is a false history concerning the development of qualitative fieldwork, which incorrectly attributes the Chicago School of Sociology as the beginning of participant observation. There are two central points to Platt's claim, firstly that there is an exaggeration of the amount of first hand data they collected and secondly, she asserts that participant observation was not used at Chicago during the Park and Burgess years.

Part of her analysis is a development of the detailed investigation by Lee Harvey (1986, 1987) who questions in some detail the first-hand ethnographic observation undertaken by Anderson, Thrasher, Cressey and Zorbaugh. Harvey (1987:66) states "participant observation was not a recognisable Chicago research practice until at least into the 1940s." The major part of Platt and Harvey's argument is that the Neo-Chicago ethnographers romantically repositioned the original work of the Chicago School. For Lee Harvey part of this argument derives from Ruth Cavan (1983:415) who sees Norman Denzin's interpretation of participant observation as giving 'more formal shape' to the development of participant observation. In support, Platt (1983:389) states "that those who have written the history have looked backward from the standpoint of the present, searching for ideas now familiar and hence have failed to notice the ways in which categories have changed". Platt identifies Rosalie Wax, Howard Becker and Everett Hughes as taking part in this 're-conceptualisation' as a result of the intellectual challenge from the post war quantitative survey method. Platt (1983:393) goes further to argue that the Chicago School work has been subject to a "retrospective construct, which distorts the historical reality." For Howard Becker (1999:10) the origin myth requires more direct critical assessment and reflection. For him sociology at Chicago should be understood as a 'school of activity' where diversity was pursued and confusion was apparent and the legacy is "the mixture of things that characterize the school of activity at every period." Where Becker does see degrees of commonality is in terms of the emergence and subsequent influence of symbolic interactionism through the work of Herbert Bulmer in combination with Robert Park's passion for urban fieldwork studies championed by Everett Hughes, "the real descendant of Park."

Platt and Harvey's analysis is held together by some valid evidence and detailed argument, but there are significant weaknesses derived from their narrow preoccupation towards participant observation. Both critiques are informed by a positivistic obsession with counting how many life histories, interviews or observations Thrasher or Anderson undertook. Their mathematical reading fails to be sensitive towards an ethnographic approach in that it does not recognize the depth of knowledge and experience of the Chicago researchers who were concerned to give priority to their research subjects both during fieldwork and writing.

Both Platt and Harvey focus on the use of the term participant observation and argue that the Chicago School are found wanting. However, they do admit that it is used by a number of the Chicago School although they insist that its use is different from that of today. A key assumption in Platt's (1983:389) argument is that the Chicago School researcher's did not employ: "participant observation in the full modern sense." Here Platt and Harvey's position is confused because contemporary understanding of participant observation is as a set of research strategies, which aim to gain a close, intimate familiarity with a social group in a naturalistic setting, and it is this very combination of qualitative research techniques which the Chicago School researchers applied. Thus, the Chicago School approach of an 'ethnographic mosaic' conforms to Martin Bulmer's idea of combining methods at Chicago including interviewing, observation, participant observation, personal documents, narrative and life history within the context of naturalistic settings (Ellen, 1984:19).

Today this broad qualitative set of strategies is called participant observation, or ethnography. Few of the Chicago School did what could be called 'pure participant observation.' They had a mosaic style in order to capture diverse sets of data. It appears that for Platt and Harvey it is not just a question of whether the Chicago School originated the use of participant observation. Harvey (1987: 213-216) asserts that the contribution of the Chicago School in the sociology of knowledge should be down graded from a paradigm to a unit. Platt (1994) has further accusations to put before the Chicago School. Her critique is more than just an argument over the original use of the term participant observation. Her insistence is that the empirical work of the Chicago School was nothing new or original in terms of topics for investigation, it had already been undertaken elsewhere, for example at Hull House[111]. Platt also adds that they were not pioneering new methods, she maintains that others were doing this before; neither were the Chicago School the first to use first hand data. Platt (1994:61) ideological project is revealed when she states that Robert Park offered a "misleading sense of directness" derived from his journalistic experience. For her Robert Park's "attractive programmatic statements" (1994:74) have been misleadingly understood to mean an ethnographic 'call to arms' in qualitative research. Mary Jo Deegan (2001:20) notes that Platt has a "careful series of critiques of the Chicago School", but she ignored most of Burgesses writings on

---

[111] Deegan, (1988).

methodology and undervalued the importance of Vivien Palmer's work on field studies. Also, Deegan (2001:20) challenges Martin Bulmer's argument that in Vivien Palmer's work "too few examples were given from actual research." She states (2001:20) "Palmer drew frequently on the core ethnographies" demonstrating that the work of Palmer, Shaw and Thrasher were integrated into the local community. For Ken Plummer (2001:111) the Chicago School approach while not wholly new, was experimentally seeking to make urban ethnographic methods "academically acceptable" and this he states, "required institutional and intellectual legitimation and this is what Chicago accomplished."

The issue of using the term participant observation is more complex than Harvey and Platt allow, in that reflections presented by surviving members of the Chicago School can appear inconsistent or linked to personal ambitions. Reflecting on working with Park and Burgess, Ruth Cavan (1983:414) states that participant observation "was not formalised nor named at the time, but was the basis for a number of studies." In his Introduction to the 1967 edition, Nels Anderson (Cavan, 1983:xiii) states that he had not heard "the term participant observer, yet at Chicago that type of research was gaining a vogue". Also Anderson argues, "While this method was faithfully followed in my work, it was not in the usual sense of the term." He talks about moving out from the experience of being a hobo to that of being a graduate researcher: "I was in the process of moving out of the hobo world" (Cavan, 1983:xiii) into a new role. Anderson clearly wants to talk about his successful social mobility. But, at a later point, Anderson (1983:403) talks in much more detail about his past experience of living as a hobo and when as a graduate student his personal financial struggles resulted in him getting a job at the Chicago Home for Incurables: "I was forced to take a room in a workingman's hotel in Hobohemia, where I slept and worked." Anderson's approach is closely expressed as an ethnographic mosaic in his use of different means to gather data, and he was fully engaged with his research subjects and felt very close to them because he had been one of them. Pauline Young (1951:203) who worked under Park and Burgess describes Nels Anderson as an intimate participant observer of the life of the hobo on the road, in the jungle, in lodging houses, at Hobohemia, at work and at Hobo College in Chicago. He identified himself with the life of the hobo for an extended period and gained insight into the inner life, which would have been impossible, had he not been able to eliminate social and mental distance through intimate participation.

Of Pauline Young's (1932) own study *The Pilgrims of Russian Town*, under the guidance of Park, it was suggested that she "think and feel Molokon,"[112] Robert Faris (1967:71) states "although her approach was essentially descriptive, it involved what came to be called participant observation, which meant taking

---

[112] Faris, R. (1967:71)

some part in the lives of the members of the community." Junker (1960:174) maintains that participant observation was a key tool for the Chicago School and notes the importance of Vivien Palmer's work. She has considerable clarity about the purpose of participant observation, which is as useful as any contemporary definition. Palmer states:

> A participant observer can obtain more revealing data concerning a group than an outsider. And an individual can usually learn more sociology by getting a new point of view concerning groups with which he is already familiar through an impartial investigation of them, than by studying groups with which he has no intimate contacts.
> (1928:107)

To support her argument Palmer (1928: 167) refers to Eduard Lindeman's *Social Discovery* (1924: 191) who stresses that participant observation is a research tool to look at group behaviour and states "the term implies, not that the observers are participating in the study but that they are participating in the activities of the group being observed." Furthermore, Mary Jo Deegan (2001:20) argues that Ernest Burgess "was training students in this technique, documented by Albert Blumenthal's (1933) ethnography of a small town". Whilst Martin Bulmer (1984:101) suggests that many of the Chicago studies were not always explicit about their use of different methods, it is Harvey and Platt's intention to challenge the idea that the Chicago School can be seen as an originator of participant observation fieldwork. Some of Harvey and Platt's points are of value in refocusing attention on the diverse and different fieldwork techniques employed by the Chicago School. One way of understanding the force of their critique of the Chicago School is to consider Susan Sontag's (1963/1966) idea of the 'anthropologist as hero.' Many of the studies undertaken by the Chicago School researchers have the status of a 'modern classic' (Short, 1963:xv). The Chicago School focus on the Durkheimian project of legitimating sociology and giving voice to research participants meant that they became in Sontag's terms 'sociological heroes' because under Park and Burgess' guidance they changed the discipline of sociology into what it is today (Faris, 1967:37).

Critically Situating the Chicago School

Over twenty years ago Jim Thomas (1983:387) stated, "The legacy of Chicago sociology continues to be neglected". In the 21st century, this is still the case although admittedly the resurgence of ethnographic work can be seen in Paul Atkinson et al *Handbook of Ethnography* (2001), which has brought legitimacy and renewed interest, but for Jim Thomas what we have lost is "the spirit that guided the research of the early Chicagoans." In this chapter my approach is influenced by Lyn Lofland's (1983:492) comment that she is "interested in what the Chicago School taught us". Chris Jenks (2005:68) states the Chicago School was "unashamedly micro in its approach" and through the integration of symbolic interactionism and ethnographic fieldwork their sociological eye became more local and focused on the culture and actions of groups and individuals in naturalistic settings.

When undertaking my own Ph.D field studies and subsequent research I found that the Chicago School could be a positive guide in fieldwork and how I would write the text (Blackman 1990, 1995). This is similar to David Matza (1969) who in *Becoming Deviant* engaged with the Chicago School work at the level of critical reading and understanding. As a doctoral student when I read the methodological accounts of Palmer, Shaw and Thrasher it did not occur to me to think of these accounts as old, or sociological heritage, something not relevant or a museum piece. Through their explanations of fieldwork success and difficulties I could appreciate my own ethnographic issues and I sensed that the Chicago School researchers were struggling to grasp the meaning of their fieldwork, participants and direction. As a Ph.D student who completed in 1990 I identified with the Chicago School researchers who employed an experimental ethnographic mosaic approach guided by theoretical concerns. For example, Vivien Palmer put priority on the development of interactive dialogue between observer and participant and promoted the idea that the sociologists work with a creative imagination. Clifford Shaw elaborated the life history method specifically enabling the disenfranchised to make their voice heard within an intimate setting and created a text that used the language of the participant. Frederic Thrasher employed participant observation techniques alongside other qualitative methods where it was his ambition to put himself in the classic Malinowski position of being an apprentice to the culture under study in order to learn from the participants. My common bond with Chicago School sociologists was undertaking ethnographic fieldwork, namely the collection of data through participant observation of young people in naturalistic settings (Dewalt and Dewalt, 2002:2).

Mary Jo Deegan (2001:15) demonstrates that the Chicago studies themselves were refining Park and Burgess' understanding of Chicago's social mosaic. These social researchers were some of the first sociologists who were active creators of meaning through their creative imagination of presenting narrative and lived culture. The ethnographic mosaic approach fits with the notion of contemporary ethnography, as a 'hybrid reality' where multiple truths are socially constructed by participants and observers who are energised to build narratives (Denzin, 1997). Creative sociological thinking under the guidance of Park and Burgess was described by Everett Hughes (1969:165-169) as directly linked to the new impetus to be part of a great social movement for the investigation of human societies to develop sociology as a discipline.

On a practical level a significant influence on the development of the Chicago School urban ethnography was the close institutional relation between Sociology and Anthropology. Ned Polsky (1997:277) states "although the departments of sociology and anthropology were formally separate, there was enormous cross fertilization between the two: graduate students in one department were encouraged in all sorts of informal ways to take courses in the other departments."[113] Herbert Bulmer reinforces the idea of "crossing over from one department to another."[114] This is supported by Ruth Cavan (1983:410) who states "Sociology and anthropology constituted a dual department until 1929." For her this "opportunity afforded sociology students to broaden their knowledge." Furthermore, the connection with anthropology can be seen in the 'Green Bible' with its many anthropological references for example to Franz Boas and J. G. Frazer. In terms of the institutional development of sociology in the United Kingdom, Vivien Palmer (1927:759) speaks of a similar relationship at the London School of Economics[115] "the department of sociology is naturally very close to the social anthropology field, and the two lines of approach are inherently related." This is not to deny that the Chicago School were involved in gathering quantitative data (Bulmer, 1984)[116] and also that Park and Burgess were influenced by positivism. The 'Green Bible' is very much concerned with the science of sociology and the application of scientific techniques to systematically collect, analyse data and generate theory. Within this is a Durkheimian project of wanting to establish sociology as an independent discipline, separate from other social sciences, such as psychology. Housed within the scientific framework outlined by Park and Burgess and elaborated by their students is an emergent grounded and interactionist approach to the study of social and cultural life, which places an emphasis on subjectivity and promotes disciplinary imagination.

One of the most significant contributions by C. Wright Mills (1959:14) to sociology was to argue that sociology was a craft, whereby the sociologist applies their intellectual imagination to produce "new ways of thinking." Mills wanted the discipline to be critical but also aware through the sociologists' biographical 'reflection' and for sensibility to be open to the 'capacity for astonishment.' In terms of ethnography, Paul Atkinson (1990:88) takes up this idea to argue that qualitative data, though rich in itself, is subject to the ethnographic imagination whereby the writer uses techniques of persuasion to produce a coherent text. What Mills and Atkinson are arguing is that good sociological studies do not produce themselves; the writer has to be creative. The contribution of the Chicago School can be described using Michael Agar's concept of 'rich points'. Agar (1997:1157) suggests that ethnographic fieldwork offers surprises, things which are unexpected, gaps between the world of the participant and that of the observer. He states: "When a rich point occurs, an ethnographer learns that his or her assumptions about how the world works, usually implicit and out of awareness, are inadequate to understand something that happened." One key intellectual strand that links the work of Palmer,

---

[113] Lofland, (1997).
[114] Lofland, (1997) and Shone (1983:410).
[115] Bronislaw Malinowski was at the LSE from 1910 and appointed to its first Chair of Social Anthropology in 1927.
[116] Bulmer, (1984), chapter 10.

Shaw and Thrasher is the use of 'rich points' to fight against pathological views of social behaviour especially focused on young people's activities labelled deviant (Blackman, 2005). As with other members of the Chicago School they were struggling with the political and theoretical issue of how to represent the authentic voice of the research subject within a context of social reform. Their theoretical understanding of reflexive sociology was understandably emergent, however, without the theoretical support, which we have today, they relied on their creative sociological imagination and sensitive interactive fieldwork guided by theory.

The following sections seek to capture some of the essence of Jim Thomas' 'spirit' to demonstrate the insight of the studies undertaken at the Chicago School with special attention on the work of Vivien Palmer (1926, 1927, 1928), Clifford Shaw (1927, 1930) and Frederic Thrasher (1927, 1928, 1928a).

Vivien Palmer: The Creative Sociological Imagination

From 1925 Vivien Marie Palmer began work on *Field Studies in Sociology: a Student's Manual*, which was set-up by the Local Community Research Committee at the university of Chicago, "to test the feasibility of the use of the city of Chicago as a laboratory for research in the social sciences"[117]. She directed the day-to-day work of the 'Social History of the Local Communities of Chicago' project, coordinating the disparate research efforts to divide the city according to its natural areas. In 1932 Vivien Palmer gained her doctorate on *The Primary Settlement as a Unit of Urban Growth and Organization*. Palmer's book on *Field Studies* applied to sociology was meant as a compliment to the 'Green Bible'. Martin Bulmer (1984:120) is positive about her study. He thought its main legacy was in terms of a "codification of the practices of the urban research programme." However, it is important to look inside Vivien Palmer's introduction to *Field Studies* to assess its value because it offers what C. Wright Mills called 'the promise.'[118] Jennifer Platt (1997:46) is correct to suggest sociologists who have written the history of the discipline sometimes tend to look backward through 'rose-tinted' glasses. However, the danger of romanticism is curbed when Vivien Palmer (1928:6) reminds us that qualitative fieldwork can be unexciting, routine and certainly not exotic. She urges a realistic understanding of fieldwork for the "researcher must follow many blind trails, make unfruitful excursions." She is keenly aware of this irony because in fieldwork she states "a great deal of miscellaneous material is constantly discovered" (1928:182) she further notes "this store of miscellaneous materials represent the outposts of the research work and upon its richness depends much of the progress of the study."

---

[117] Palmer, (1928:vii)
[118] Mills, (1959), Chapter 1.

In order to produce a useful sociological study Palmer (1928:200) states: "the results depend upon the creative imagination of the investigator, upon his ability to detect new relationships in his data and invent new formulas to account for his concert discoveries." In her first paper Palmer (1926) advocated the importance to sociology of doing field studies and she is aware of the formal pressures impacting on sociology to present itself as a scientific discipline, yet she still argues that successful fieldwork is dependent on 'human subjectivity' and 'creativity'. Palmer (1926:342) states "skill in investigation must always remain, in the last analysis, an art gained through practice." She argues against formal or rigid procedures, insisting that the ethnographic field diary is crucial in not merely recording but shaping the writers approach. Palmer (1926:347) insists that the researcher must be in possession of the "feel of the problem before he goes into the field."

For her fieldwork is really about capturing activities in action as a form of participant observation. She states: "human beings are everywhere so continually performing their own experiments in group life that the investigator can always find social experiments of many kinds in progress." Palmer (1928:170) sees qualitative interviewing as both an introspective account to gain 'subjective data' but also governed by "a process of continuous spiral interaction" and stimulation. Thus she states: "the skillfully conducted interview assumes the appearance of a natural conversation". She insists the idea is "to secure the habitual reactions of the person... to slip so completely into his world, into his universe." (1928:171). In order for the free flow of information to occur equal respect has to be established as the basis for exchange. Palmer (1928:173) insists that the research subjects have to possess the feeling "that the aim of the research is worth while" and to have "something worth while to contribute. This recognition of the informant's importance creates a status for him which is one of the most valuable assists in conducting the interview." Any instrumental or coercive action by the sociologist is seen by Vivien Palmer (1928:173) as to be "avoided" and not "demanded" and certainly nothing should be "forced upon the informant."

In her pursuit of rigour in outlining qualitative fieldwork procedures Palmer (1928:8-9) was aware that 'introspective accounts' and the sociological researcher's interest in gaining participants subjective data "is frequently challenged." To her credit she wants to work within a scientific approach albeit a type of positivism, which is reflexive. Palmer (1928:9) states: "Every scientific observation has its subjective aspects" and "with the increasing use of subjective materials in studying group behaviour" the result is a requirement for "definition of concepts contained in the subjective narratives of behaviour" to be part of sociological analysis.

Here her concern is for an authentic voice of participants, which is not only argued in terms of data collection but also has high priority in the process of data analysis and theorisation. Her qualitative sensitivities are clear when she speaks about how to interpret data: "One of the most difficult problems in analysis is that of lifting specific facts from the context in which they appear without destroying their meaning." This methodological problem has been at the centre of how to write up all ethnographic studies (Becker, 1986). It is the weight given to the power of the imagination within sociology which marks Vivien Palmer's (1928: 14) approach as experimental and different. She states when sociologists make generalisations the key thing is the "transition from the actual to the conceptual belongs to reflective thinking, is dependent upon constructive imagination." Palmer is outlining procedures and practices for qualitative interpretation, which demonstrate the personal depth of the Chicago School ethnographic mosaic where they walked and lived inside the locale. Within the sociological analysis, Palmer (1928:203) argues, "The research worker reconstructs in his imagination the interrelationships in which the phenomena represented by the items actually occurred." The concern with sharp analytical understanding and sensitivity towards interpreting the whole and parts of the data clearly provide evidence that Vivien Palmer's approach is an early form of grounded theory in ethnography. It is not merely her movement towards systematic coding of the data but her recognition that creativity is required during analysis and the writing, as integral features to the construction of an ethnographic account.

Shaw: The Participants' Voice

In 1909 the first director of Institute for Juvenile Research, then called The Juvenile Psychopathic Institute, Chicago, was William Healy. In 1926 on the recommendation of Ernest Burgess a new sociological research section was created within the organisation, now titled the Institute of Juvenile Research, and its director was Clifford Shaw.

The Chicago School were preoccupied with the idea of studying the 'total situation,'[119] through a range of fieldwork approaches, this ethnographic mosaic was concerned with documenting the practical feature of ordinary interactions within the community to show real life struggles. Clifford Shaw was influenced by William Healy's study (1915:130) The *Individual Delinquent*, which put forward the research method of the case study focusing on the individual through empirical data. Healy's movement towards autobiographical accounts derived from his frustration with quantitative data, not offering more causal data to understand deviance. He stated: "Statistics will never tell the whole story."

In Shaw's 1927 paper he advances Healy's initial method of the case study and combines Burgess' (1923:680) argument that the delinquent is a person, that is, "an individual with the wishes common to all human beings and with a conception of his role in group life." Shaw placed the young people's stories at the centre of understanding the close relationship between biography, locality and community, to emphasize that social and cultural factors were responsible

---

[119] Shaw, (1927:149); Thrasher, (1928) *The Study of the Total Situation.*

for delinquency. Shaw (1927:157) argues that individual case study material is representative of "larger cultural conflicts between family and the prevailing social patterns of the community." In Shaw's paper he sets out to employ the 'life-history' method as case study material within the context of an ethnographic study. This first *Boy's Own Story* of Angie (Angelus) a fourteen-year-old boy, has all the hallmarks of participant observation. Interview data is collected from all the family and extended family members and neighbours within the locality. The data is highly contextual and naturalistic, everyday life within the family is discussed and participants use argot in their descriptions. The data reveals personal and family struggles, and we move from a series of accusations to actual violence in the presence of Shaw.[120] This short paper is packed with live culture, experience and amounts to a preliminary piece of work before Clifford Shaw wrote *The Jack-Roller* in 1930.

The Jack-Roller is the natural history life story of Stanley, a young delinquent boy. Shaw first met Stanley in 1921 when he was aged 14. Ken Plummer (2001:106) notes "they established a very close and mutual affection for each other, one that lasted throughout their lives." Clifford Shaw followed Stanley as he moved from institution to institution to record his views and experiences of his life. In *The Jack-Roller*, Burgess (1930:194-195) argues: "Mr. Shaw pays attention to the powerful factors of group and neighborhood influence" and at all times Shaw is looking towards social factors to explain delinquency. The success of Shaw's ethnographic mosaic is his attention to detail he (1930:34) states: "The air in the neighbourhood is smoky and always filled with disagreeable odor from the yard stock." Moreover for Burgess the validity of the study derives from Shaw's approach:

> To see life as the boy conceived it rather than as an adult might imagine it. Empathy means entering into the experience of another person by the human and democratic method of sharing experiences. In this and other ways rapport is established. Sympathy is the attempt through imagination to put one's self in another person's place with all the fallacies, which are almost necessarily involved.
> Burgess, 1930:194-195)

Shaw was the first to recognize that his study was not original. He cites the academic influences, but also the more popular culture autobiographies of criminals.[121]

This emphasis on the boy's own subjective story, Shaw (1930:3) argues is derived from the work of Healy, the Thomas's and Znaniecki, where it is "desired that his story will reflect his own personal attitudes and

---

[120] What Clifford Shaw's response was to the actual aggressive and violent behaviour is not explained.
[121] Shaw 1930: 2.

interpretations". Shaw (1930:3) is fully aware of the potential bias in an account, and seeks to see the value of placing objective information with subjective accounts. Shaw (1930:21) suggests: "rationalizations, fabrications, prejudices, exaggerations are quite as valuable as objective descriptions, provided, of course that these reactions be properly identified and classified."

For Ken Plummer (2001:115) *The Polish Peasant* study by Thomas and Znaniecki (1918) and Clifford Shaw's (1930) *The Jack-Roller* are the key innovative texts in the development of the personal documentary approach, but for him they remain "naive." More critically, Norman Denzin (1992:39) argues that *The Jack-Roller* is not a biographical text, it is an empirical and textual study written primarily by Clifford Shaw not the research subject Stanley. Denzin insists that *The Jack-Roller* is a personal account by Shaw of Stanley and cannot be understood as objective[i]. Norman Denzin (1992:41) critically argues that Shaw "turned Stanley into a sociological version of a screen hero," maintaining that *The Jack-Roller* is a romantised account of the subjects where sociology allowed the deviant outsider a chance to project their voice, to tell their story but "it transformed subject's into sociology's image of who they should be." In contrast, Brian Roberts (2006:20-22) sees the natural history and personal documentary approaches as pioneered by Robert Park at Chicago as a compromise which sought to remove blaming the population for their condition, while seeking to ethnographically develop an understanding of culture as performed in groups demonstrating forms of solidarity under conditions of social and economic pressure (Blackman, 2007).

Within Vivien Palmer's (1928:176) analysis there is an implicit understanding of wanting to develop grounded theory. For example for her the use of the research subjects own words is fundamental. She argues if qualitative data "is reported in the first person, in the actual phrases and language used by the informants, it will furnish better data for scientific analysis." Palmer wants authenticity and originality stating further that if the sociologist "translates the expressions of informants into his own language or summarises them in trite generalisations or common concepts, he makes a less objective record." She states, "subjective descriptions of life-experience reveal indispensable facts about groups." (1928:9). Vivien Palmer is making the case for the sociologist to show commitment and dedication towards the research subjects in the collection of ethnographic data. This is demonstrated by Jon Snodgrass (1982: 173) who reveals that Clifford Shaw gave all his royalties from the book to Stanley (Michael Majer) for his hospital treatment when he was seriously ill in hospital and later died in 1982.

Roger Salerno (2007:158) does not see an issue with Shaw undertaking revision of Stanley's words. He states, "It would be in keeping with the Chicago school tradition to modify such transcriptions." The legacy of Shaw's text is that it became an academic and popular text, which set the standard in terms of projecting the research subject's voice in the context of their culture (Roberts 2006). Shaw's methodological procedures become ethnographic when he reflects on the young person's actions combined with the deviant's narrative of their own activities, set in the context of the locality. For Shaw (1930:22) the boy's own story, "is recorded in the exact language of the interviewee." Shaw (1930:21) states "The task of securing complete and useful documents by this technique usually necessitates a series of interviews, which in some cases extend over a relatively long period of time." For Shaw (1930:22) the value of the boy's own story is that it can be "secured with a minimum of guidance and control on the part of the investigator." This allows what Glaser and Strauss (1967) saw as the slow emergence of grounded theory where control of the research allows the participants the chance to voice their understanding beyond the direction of the researcher. *The Jack-Roller* does not merely offer the chance for the deviant to speak their own story. Burgess (1930:197) reveals that through Shaw's uncoloured translation of the language of the participant "the materials stand on their own footing and may be interpreted variously by other students." Thus, Clifford Shaw's use of the 'delinquent boy's own story' in the study *The Jack-Roller*, can be seen as a landmark in modern reflexive ethnography which seeks to advance the voice of the research participant as we write the text. As Jim Thomas (1983:773) concludes: "Oral histories thus sensitise researchers to methodological problems by providing knowledge of a subculture to which we bring a set of self-centric assumption."

Frederic Thrasher: Rapport and the Ethnographer's Apprenticeship

Before Frederic Thrasher undertook his qualitative investigation into gangs, he did an MA in 1918, at Chicago with a thesis on "The Boy Scout Movement as A Socializing Agency." James Short (1963:xviii) in his introduction to the abridged edition of *The Gang* states: "We do not know specifically how Thrasher collected his materials... and we do not know precisely how Thrasher chose his informants." Due to this lack of detail, it is my intention to use two of Thrasher's 1928 papers: 'How to study the boys' gang in the open' and 'The Study of the Total Situation' as a way to understand his ethnographic contribution to the Chicago School. However, in *The Gang* Thrasher (1927: xii) did say that: "the task of collecting and preparing the data prsented... occupied a period of about seven years." Although participant observation was only one research method of many he employed during fieldwork for *The Gang*, in the two subsequent studies, Thrasher (1928a:490) makes it clear that participant observation was a major form of data collection; he states that this method was used in the "intimate first hand observational study" on boy's gangs in the open. James Short (1963:xviii) argues that because of these post - *The Gang* studies "confidence in what is reported as fact in the book seems justified." It is clear from Thrasher's 'How to Study the Boy's Gang in the Open', that he is skilled in fieldwork techniques, especially in relation to gaining rapport through strategies of empathy employing an ethnographic mosaic approach.

In the 'Boy's Gang in the Open' study he befriended a gang of six youths. He documents how over a period of several weeks he began to develop positive field relations. From his field diary Thrasher (1928:246) describes taking some of the boys out in his car: "We made our way to Tenth Avenue where I went as fast as I dare, making the ride as wild and exciting as possible by dodging in and out among the cars." At a later part of the fieldwork he took the boys on a long trip to Forest Hills, a sort of short holiday.

The close contact and emotional side of participant observation is reflected in the work of Clifford Shaw and Frederic Thrasher's methodological explanations. In Jon Snodgrass's (1982:26, 33, 171) follow-up to *The Jack-Roller*, we see Stanley talk of "the many visits with Shaw and his family, which I enjoyed greatly"... he continues, "It would not be far-fetched to state that the Shaw's were my real parents." In a similar vein, from the field diary, Frederic Thrasher (1928:246-247) states "All right, boys! Come to my house. We'll stop there on the way back from the garage so that you'll know just where to come." The boys state "Sure." He continues: "They took charge of my brief case while I made a purchase and then carried it up to my apartment where they were ushered in and introduced to my wife. "This is my gang, aren't you boys?" "Sure." "All right, boys, see you Sunday afternoon at 2.30." Thrasher further elaborates how the boys arrived the following day, sat in the living room and decided on their group name and what activities to undertake. Shaw and Thrasher adopted roles with their participants as a way to smooth their involvement whereby solidarity was attainable with the research subjects who became human personal documents.

Thrasher describes his ethnographic approach "having participated in such undertakings with the boys, further opportunities... permits the investigator to participate and to retain their interest while observing their behavoiur." It is through Thrasher's detailed experience of fieldwork that he reflects:

> Almost any information desired may be elicited after the ground has been prepared. Rapport may be established more quickly and with the whole gang, however, if the investigator is alert to take advantage of opportunities which may arise.
> (Thrasher, 1928:245)

Thrasher's (1928: 247) use of collective interviews during fieldwork offered him substantial data from participants "with fewer inhibitions." What is very productive in Thrasher's ethnographic fieldwork is the way he employs rapport to not merely gain rich data; he looks beyond it in an anthropological sense of ethnography to gain first-hand ethnographic knowledge. Thrasher states:

> Taking the group for occasional rides is also valuable in promoting rapport with the boys by creating a body of common experiences to which the boys can refer - obstacles overcome, dangers passed through together, etc. It gets the investigator 'in solid' with the boys... It gives the investigator an opportunity to put himself in the position of being instructed by the boys.
> (Thrasher, 1928:250)

These quotations demonstrate Thrasher's focus on empathy and his personal contact with participants, in contrast, Chris Jenks (2005:66) maintains "Thrasher felt and expressed an intense level of moral repugnance for gang members and their nefarious activities". Jenks offers no evidence to support this assertion and from the methodological explanation put forward by Thrasher (1928:251) in the 'How to Study the Boy's Gang in the Open,' Thrasher voices no negative moral views when describing the lads profane language, dirty jokes, stories about being with the girls, violence, gambling and masculine bravado. Clearly, he is struggling in an intimate fieldwork setting with young men who are lively and pepped up on cigarettes, but he remains the sociological researcher trying to gain solid grounded data and maintain the boy's respect. According to Patricia Clough (1992:33) "If the participant observer is to grasp the actors' points of view so as to make them public, these viewpoints must be depicted in terms of social action." From the field diary extracts we see Thrasher (1928:251) direct his research subjects but at the same time he is open and honest in his methodological account. For example, he drank wine while being with the boy's and then drove them home. He stated subsequently "our wild ride back to the Village through the terrific incoming traffic was full of thrills." He concludes (Thrasher, 1928:251) the end result of this fieldwork adventure was that "rapport was pretty well established."

Thrasher explains how the power relations within fieldwork can alter whereby the researched are now directing the research and influencing its progression, a strategy which successful ethnographers have consistently applied but have to be careful to monitor and adjust when fieldwork relations change. The dialogic or participatory style of Thrasher's ethnography demonstrates that he is in a learning mode and is seeking collaborative data. The Chicago School approach was in opposition to that of the received view, "with researcher and researched in a more egalitarian relationship" Michael Agar (1997:1165). Thrasher's discussion and the boys' comments from the field diary reveal an exciting and intense period of fieldwork for both the researcher and the researched. The sensitivity by which Thrasher undertook his ethnographic fieldwork is clear from the passage below, focusing on the degree to which the ethnographer has to be flexible towards the group. Thrasher says:

> Incidents of a disconcerting sort are common occurrences in doing this type of research and have to be laughed off and considered as 'part of the game.' The sacrifice of a piece of furniture, dinner, part of the finish on one's car, and so on, must be taken stoically and with good humour.
> (1928:245)

What is particularly relevant in Thrasher's methodological account is that he decided to undertake the ethnographic fieldwork with the boys first, and then at a later point when he had achieved successful immersion with participants, he considered getting data from others within the community. He states (Thrasher: 1928:254) "Interviews with outside boys, with social workers, with teachers, and others should enable the investigator to complete a picture which would be very helpful." What is of value in this comment is that critics of Thrasher's approach, such as Platt and Harvey suggest that he was not involved in close forms of ethnography and relied on formal agencies to gather data. Here we see Thrasher put priority on participant observation with young people first. Furthermore, although Thrasher is reticent about his research methods in *The Gang* (1927) he does offer one comment, which is very similar to his later studies. Thrasher (1927:96) states: "To understand the gang boy one must enter into his world with a comprehension, on the one hand, of this seriousness behind his mask of flippancy or bravado, and on the other, of the role of the romantic in his activities and in his interpretation of the larger world of reality." Thrasher's aim of wanting to feel the real experience in the form of an apprenticeship of learning from participants can be seen as a significant development in modern reflexive ethnography where he sets up through empathy the chance of research friendship on the basis of free dialogue.

Conclusion

A key priority in the early work of the Chicago School was to establish a holistic understanding of culture, but within it they were concerned with respecting the integrity of difference, showing sensitivity towards the research subjects and gaining a theoretical understanding of research methods. In this chapter I have suggested that the Chicago School approach was about the use of a combination of different research tools, from an interdisciplinary position i.e. sociology and anthropology which can be understood as creating an ethnographic mosaic. According to Howard Becker (1999:10) it is this mixture rather than a unified approach, which characterise the Chicago legacy. Furthermore, Morris Janowitz (1966:iv) maintains that initially under W.I. Thomas and then developed further by Robert Park the Chicago School tried to advance intellectual emancipation for Sociology using an ethnographic approach concerned with social control and social change. Behind their reformist pronouncements was a commitment to anthropological fieldwork in an urban setting and the use of participant observation was one key research tool within their ethnographic mosaic approach

Norman Denzin presents two positions to understand the Chicago School contribution to modern reflexive sociology. Firstly Denzin, (1997:xiv-xv) states: "The ethnographic tale is a utopian tale of self and social redemption, a tale that brings a moral compass back into the readers and writer's life." Secondly, Denzin (1995:123) accuses the Chicago School of complicity whereby their focus on realism "functions to perpetuate the status quo. It brings to the inteactionist the halo of the one who identifies with the downtrodden of the world." For him the Chicago School ethnography is a 'romantic ideology', which creates 'comforting illusions' of 'pure fantasy' "which make individuals responsible for their own problems." While the Chicago School did perhaps overemphasize their preoccupation with the 'underdog' or outsiders, it was this identification with and authentic fieldwork on participants, that remains significant in modern ethnography. Denzin's critique is both useful and limited, in the sense that it highlights the liberal agendas that the Chicago School had to work within. But Denzin fails to acknowledge the wider social mosaic within which Robert Park assigned social problems to sociological researchers on the basis that there could be no equality until there was justice (Hughes 1969:169)

Kamala Visweswaran (1994:15) argues that a key part of contemporary ethnography "is founded on the fiction of restoring lost voices." This chapter has suggested that it is possible to restore the methodological contribution of the Chicago School. The ethnographies of the Chicago School can be seen in a nostalgic sense theoretically described by James Clifford (1986:112) as 'salvage ethnography': they saved us something from an older 'disappearing world' before modern rationality absorbed all. Such an assessment would be partial. This chapter has set out to argue that the ethnographic writing and work of Vivien Palmer, Clifford Shaw and Frederic Thrasher should not be seen as part of an ethnographic requiem. They remain live examples of ethnographic struggle through theory and fieldwork, and in their methodological accounts we experience dialogue with them to locate, assess, reflect and resolve their and our own fieldwork issues, problems and successes.

References

Abbott, A. (1999) *Department and Discipline: Chicago Sociology at One Hundred*. Chicago: University of Chicago Press.
Agar, M. (1997) 'Ethnography: An Overview'. *Substance Use and Misuse*, 32, (9): 1155-1173.
Anderson, N. (1923/1967) *The Hobo*. Chicago: University of Chicago Press.
-----.(1983) 'Stranger at the Gate: Reflections on the Chicago School of Sociology', *Urban Life*, Vol.11, No.4:396-406.
Atkinson, P. (1990) *The Ethnographic Imagination*. London: Routledge.
Atkinson, P. Coffey, A. Delamont, S. Lofland, J. and Lofland, L. (2001) (eds.). *Handbook of Ethnography*. London: Sage.
Becker, H. S. (1963) *Outsiders*. New York: Free Press.
-----.(1966) 'Introduction', Shaw, C. *The Jack- Roller: A Delinquent Boy's Own Story*. Chicago: University of Chicago Press: v-xviii.
-----.(1986) *Writing for Social Scientists*. Chicago: University of Chicago Press.
-----.(1999) 'The Chicago School, So-Called', *Qualitative Sociology*, 22 (1):3-12.
-----.(1966) Introduction, Shaw, C. *The Jack- Roller: A Delinquent Boy's Own Story*. Chicago: University of Chicago Press:v-xviii.
Blackman, S. J. (1990) 'Youth and Pupil Groups: An Ethnographic Study of Their Pedagogic Relations and Resistant Practices'. Unpublished Ph.D Thesis, Institute of Education, University of London.
-----.(1995) *Youth: Positions and Oppositions - Style, Sexuality and Schooling*. Aldershot, Avebury Press.

-----.(2005) 'Youth Sub-cultural Theory: A critical Engagement with the Concept, Its Origins and Politics, From the Chicago School to Post Modernism', *Journal of Youth Studies*, 8, (1):1-20.

-----.(2007) 'Hidden Ethnography': Crossing Emotional Borders in Qualitative Accounts of Young People's Lives', *Sociology*, 41, (4):699-716.

Blumenthal, A. (1933) *A Sociological Study of a Small Town*. Chicago: University of Chicago Press.

Bourdieu, P. and Wacquant, L. (1992) *An Invitation to Reflexive Sociology*. Cambridge: Polity Press.

Brewer, J. (2000) *Ethnography*. London: Sage

Bulmer, M. (1983) 'The Methodology of The Taxi-Dance Hall', *Urban Life*, Vol.12, (1):95-101.

-----.(1984) *The Chicago School of Sociology*. Chicago: University of Chicago Press.

Burgess, E. W. (1923) 'The Study of the Delinquent as a Person', *American Journal of Sociology*, Vol. XXVIII. (6):657-679.

-----.(1930/1966) 'Discussion', in Shaw, C. *The Jack-Roller: A Delinquent Boy's Own Story*. Chicago: University of Chicago Press.

Burgess, R. (1984) *In the Field*. London: Allen and Unwin.

Cavan, R. (1928) *Suicide*. Chicago: University of Chicago Press.

-----.(1983) 'The Chicago School of Sociology: 1918-1933'. *Urban Life*, 11, (4):407-420.

Clifford, J. (1986) 'On Ethnographic Allegory', in Clifford, J. and Marcus, G. (eds.). *Writing Culture: The Poetics and Politics of Ethnography*. Berkeley. University of California Press.

Clough, P. (1992) *The End(s) of Ethnography: From Social Realism to Social Criticism*. London: Sage.

Coffey, A. (1999) *The Ethnographic Self*. London: Sage.

Cressey, P. G. (1927/1983) 'A Comparison of the Role of the Sociological Stranger and the Anonymous Stranger in Field Research', *Urban Life*, 12, (1):102-120.

Deegan, M. J. (1988) *Jane Addams and the Men of the Chicago School*. New Brunswick, N. J: Transaction.

-----.(2001) 'The Chicago School of Ethnography', in Atkinson, P. Coffey, A. Delamont, S. Lofland, J. and Lofland, L. (eds.). *Handbook of Ethnography*: London: Sage:11-25.

Denzin, N. (1989) *Interpretive Biography*. Sage University Paper series on Qualitative Research Methods. Vol. 17: Beverly Hills, CA: Sage.

-----.(1992) *Symbolic Interactionism and Cultural Studies: The Politics of Interpretation*. Oxford: Blackwell.

-----.(1995) 'Stanley and Clifford: Undoing an Interactionist Text'. *Current Sociology*. Vol.43, PT2:115-123.

-----.(1997) *Interpretive Ethnography: Ethnographic Practices for the 21st Century*. London: Sage.

Dewalt, K. and Dewalt, B. (2002) *Participant Observation: A guide For Fieldworkers*. Walnut Creek, CA: Altamira Press.

Ellen, R. F. (1984) (ed.). *Ethnographic Research: A Guide to General Conduct.* Academic Press: London.

Faris, R. (1967) *Chicago Sociology 1920-1932.* San Francisco: Chandler.

Gieryn, T. (2006) 'City as Truth-Spots: Laboratories and Filed Sites in Urban Studies', *Social Studies of Science*, Vol. 36, (1):5-38.

Glaser, B. and Strauss, A. (1967) *The Discovery of Grounded Theory.* Chicago: Aldine.

Gouldner, A. (1970) *The Coming Crisis in Western Sociology.* London: Heinmann.

-----.(1968) 'The sociologist as partisan: sociology and the welfare state', *The American Sociologist*, 3. May:103-116.

Hammersley, M. and Atkinson, P. (1983/2008) *Ethnography: Principles in Practice.* London, Tavistock.

Healy, W. (1915) The *Individual Delinquent*, Little, Brown and Co: Boston.

Hughes, E. (1969) 'Robert E. Park', in Raison, T. (ed.). *The Founding Fathers of Social Science.* Harmondsworth: Penguin:162-169.

-----.(1971) *The Sociological Eye: Selected Papers on Work, Self and the Study of Society.* Chicago: Aldine. Atherton.

Janowitz, M. (1966) 'Introduction', in W.I. Thomas, *On Social Organisation and Social Personality.* Chicago: University of Chicago Press.

Jenks, C. (2005) *Subculture: The Fragmentation of the Social.* London: Sage

Junker, B. (1960) *Fieldwork.* Chicago: University of Chicago Press.

Lee, H. (1986) 'Schools in the Sociology of Knowledge: the Chicago School as a Case Study', *Sociological Review*, 35:245-278.

-----.(1987) *Myths of the Chicago School of Sociology*, Aldershot: Avebury.

Lofland, L. (1983) 'Understanding Urban Life: the Chicago Legacy', *Urban Life*, Vol. 11, (4):491-511.

-----.(1997) 'Reminiscences of Classic Chicago: the Blumer-Hughes Talk', in Plummer, K. (ed.). *The Chicago School: Critical Assessment, Vol. 4.* Routledge. London:182-204. (originally in *Urban Life*, No. 3, October 1980).

Matza, D. (1969) *Becoming Deviant.* Prentice-Hall, Inc. Englewood Cliffe: New Jersey.

Mills, C.W. (1959) *The Sociological Imagination.* Oxford University Press: New York.

-----.(1943) 'The Professional Ideology of Social Pathologists'. *American Journal of Sociology*, Vol. 49:165-180.

O'Reilly, K. (2005) *Ethnographic Methods.* London: Routledge

Palmer, V. (1926) 'Field Studies for Introductory Sociology: An Experiment', *Journal of Applied Sociology*, Vol. X. March:341-348.

-----.(1927) 'Impressions of Sociology in Great Britain', *American Journal of Sociology*, Vol. 32, (5):756-761.

-----.(1928) *Field Studies in Sociology: A Student's Manual.* Chicago: University of Chicago Press.

Park, R.E. and Burgess, E.W. (1921) (eds.) *Introduction to the Science of Sociology.* Chicago, University of Chicago Press.

Platt, J. (1983) 'The Development of the Participant Observation Method in

Sociology: Origins, Myths and History', *Journal of the History of the Behavioural Sciences*, Vol. 19, October:379-393.

-----.(1994) 'The Chicago School and Firsthand Data'. *History of the Human Sciences*, Vol.7, (1):57-80.

-----.(1998) 'Chicago Methods: Reputations and Realities', in Tomasi, L. (ed.). *The Tradition of the Chicago School of Sociology*. Aldershot: Avebury:89-103.

Plummer, K, (2001) *Documents of Life 2*. London: Sage

Roberts, B. (2006) *Micro Social Theory*. London: Palgrave Macmillan.

Salerno, R. (2007) *Sociology Noir: Studies at the University of Chicago in Loneliness, Marginality and Deviance, 1915-1935*. North Carolina: McFarland & Company, Inc: Jefferson.

Shaw, C. (1927) 'Case Study Method'. *Publication of the American Sociological Society*, Vol. 21: 149-157.

-----.(1930/1966) *The Jack-Roller: A Delinquent Boy's Own Story*. Chicago: University of Chicago Press.

Short, J. (1963) 'Introduction' to the abridge Edition, in Thrasher, F. (1927/1963) *The Gang*. Chicago: University of Chicago Press.

Silverman, D. (1985) *Qualitative Methodology and Sociology*. Aldershot: Gower.

Smith, D. (1988) *The Chicago School: A Liberal Critique of Capitalism*. London: Macmillan.

Snodgrass, J. (1982) *The Jack-Roller at Seventy: A Fifty-year Follow-up*. Lexington: Lexington Books

Sontag, S. (1963/1966) 'The Anthropologist as Hero', in *Against Interpretation and Other Essays*. New York: Farrar, Strauss & Giroux.

Thrasher, F. (1927/1963) *The Gang*. Chicago: University of Chicago Press.

-----.(1928) 'How to Study the Boys' Gang in the Open', *Journal of Educational Sociology*, Vol.1, (5):244-254.

-----.(1928a) 'The Study of the Total Situation', *Journal of Educational Sociology*, Vol. 1, (2):477-490.

Thomas, J. (1983) 'Chicago Sociology: An Introduction', *Urban Life*, 11, (4): 387-395.

-----.(1983a) 'Towards a Critical Ethnography: A Re-examination of the Chicago Legacy', *Urban Life*, 11, (4): 477-490.

Thomas, W.I. and Znaniecki, F. (1918-20) *The polish Peasant in Europe and America*, 5 vols. . Chicago: University of Chicago Press.

Visweswaran, K. (1994) *Fictions of Feminist Ethnography*. Minneapolis: University of Minneapolis.

Young, P. (1932) *The Pilgrims of Russian-Town: The Community of Christian Spiritual Jumpers in America*. Chicago: University of Chicago Press.

-----.(1951) *Scientific Social Surveys and Research*. New York: Prentice-Hall.

CHAPTER 10

Communication: an Inheritance of the Chicago School of Social Thought

Filipa Subtil
Escola Superior de Comunicação Social,
Polytechnic Institute of Lisbon, Portugal

José Luís Garcia
University of Lisbon,
Instituto de Ciências Sociais, Portugal

(Translated by Richard Wall)

Introduction

From its founders at the end of the nineteenth century to its major figures in the early years of the twentieth, the Chicago School of Social Thought is an essential point of reference, by reason of its work on human ecology, the city, immigration, ethnic relations, delinquency, social control and the human self – work which is today regarded as part of the sociological canon. In this chapter we argue that these thinkers were pioneers, undertaking research of major significance on the topics of communication and the media in society, helping to make them a focus of attention for social theory and sociology. It is true that the thought of one of the leading thinkers of the Chicago School, the social psychologist G. H. Mead, on the communicative nature of the human self and on social interaction led to sociological approaches, such as symbolic interactionism, which grant crucial importance to communicative processes. It was also incorporated into major contemporary theoretical edifices, the leading example of which is the work of Habermas (1987 [1981]). But recognition of Mead's theories is not enough for a proper understanding of the enormous and in many respects distinctive contribution made by thinkers such as Small, Dewey, Mead, Thomas and Znaniecki, Park and Burgess to social scientific research on communication. It was above all researchers in the field of communication research who investigated this legacy. They identified gaps in this area which social theory and sociology, however, still need to address.

This chapter has two main objectives. First, to examine the work done in the Chicago School of Social Thought on two fundamental aspects of the study of communication and modern information media. Focusing specifically on the work of Small, Dewey, Mead, Thomas and Znaniecki, and Park and Burgess, we aim to explore their profound insights, on the one hand, into the connections between communication and social interaction, and on the other, and the relations between communication, culture and democracy. Secondly, to show how, following a time, from the interwar period until the end of the 1960s, in which its theoretical contribution to the study of communication, democracy and the media suffered some neglect, this legacy was a source of inspiration for a hermeneutic approach to communication, as an alternative to positivist, utilitarian and functional approaches. To provide a closer focus for this approach, the article offers the specific example of the ritual or cultural theory of communication associated with the influential work of James W. Carey. The debate on these key issues, which relate more particularly to the intellectual history of communication research, is viewed here as an integral part of the tensions in the social sciences generally over how social life is made possible by communication, and how communication can be a support for common public life and democracy.

The Contributions of Albion Small and George Vincent to Early Sociological Thought on Communication and the Press in the USA

In the United States, it was only towards the end of the nineteenth century that any signs of reflection on communication appeared, as precursors of later research work. Until then, references to communication in the young American nation had been limited to intellectually stimulating meditations which produced a random literature focused on topics such as the press, freedom of expression, censorship, the public, the telegraph, advertising, and the economic power of the newspapers (Lang, 1989:369; Carey, 1997 [1996]:20).

At the turn of the century, some of the founders of sociology in the United States developed original thinking within their discipline on both the role of communication in society and the emergence of the mass media. This took place during a period of profound social upheaval – roughly between 1890 and the First World War. It was a period which saw the closing of the frontier, the end of agriculture as the dominant form of living, the huge growth of cities, the creation and growth of electricity grids, expanding industrialization, the maturing of industrial capitalism and the growth of international trade and communications, the expansion of the national press, and the powerful emergence of marketing and advertising.

As in Europe, the final decade of the nineteenth century is a key period in the development of the social sciences in the US, and for the institutionalization of sociology and anthropology in American universities. Albion Small (1854-

1926), the founder of the Department of Sociology and Anthropology at the University of Chicago, in 1892, was one of the main driving forces in this new field of study, in which William Sumner (1840-1910) and Edward Ross (1866-1951), professors of sociology at the universities of Yale and Wisconsin respectively, were also dedicated participants. The precursors of sociology in the US came together in their research on communication and the press under the intellectual and cultural influence of turn-of-the-century German political economy.[122] Political economists Albert Schäffle, Karl Knies and Karl Bücher developed a conception of communication as a binding force in society, and of the press as a social and cultural form of circulation of symbols and of transmission of ideas and information which actively incorporated the context of expanding industrial capitalism and the growth of trade. In sociology, Ferdinand Tönnies examined in depth the role of journalism in forming public opinion, and Max Weber highlighted the importance of the social scientific study of the press (Hardt, 2001:43-168; Simonson and Peters, 2008; Pietilä, 2008:205-223).

Small was part of a vast intellectual movement of social reform in the US, the main concepts of which rest on the assumption that scientific theories are closely tied to the problems of public life. The social sciences should not be limited to drawing up abstract models of society. In particular, the task of sociology was to help to find practical solutions for the problems emerging as advanced industrial society took shape in the US. Sociology took on strong ethical and civic commitments, in order to help achieve a better and fairer society

The press, as the most influential link between communication and society, was torn between its cultural mission and private business interests. The press did not remain unaffected by the process through which the market became disembedded from other social institutions – the great transformation which constitutes the political and economic origins of our time, to quote Polanyi (1944) – until it becomes a world with claims to control the rest of society. The aim of achieving high advertising revenues and an ever-increasing number of readers generated increasing uneasiness and suspicion as to the true role of the press, giving rise to a wide-ranging debate on the economic and social aspects of the emerging media industry. Many scientific and literary journals took up the theme, in particular the *The American Journal of Sociology*, where Small and other pioneers of sociology published several articles on the press, public opinion, the effects on culture of the way reporting was being carried out, and the

---

[122] Hanno Hardt's book, *Social Theories of the Press: constituents of communication research, 1840s to 1920s*, first published in 1979, continues to be the best-researched source on the relationships between communication, media and society in the work of the German academic political economists, which had a powerful impact on the early American sociologists (Hardt, 2001).

relationships between journalism, democracy and press ethics (Small, 1915; Ross, 1903a; 1903b: 1903c; 1904: 189-207; 1910: 303-311; 1917-1918:620-632)

In *An Introduction to the Study of Society* (1894), which he wrote in collaboration with George Vincent, Small examines in depth, on the one hand the meaning of communication for human and social life and, on the other, the paths taken by the press at the end of the nineteenth century in the US. Small and Vincent drew up a communication model which extends the importance which Schäffle attributed to communication as the primordial element in social development, within an organismic understanding of the social environment. Under Schäffle influence, they defined communication as part of society's regulatory system, penetrating the social system and operating like the nerve fibres of the animal organism. This is how communication takes place between individuals, making each subject a part of multiple and distinct psycho-physical channels of the social nervous system. At the same time as they perform the function of mediation, individuals also operate as 'terminal cells' in the process of communication. The subject is a 'connecting cell' and also a 'terminal cell' for all the channels of communication which radiate into society, to adopt Small and Vincent's terminology.

To initiate the process of communicating, individuals arm themselves with a multiplicity of symbols. Symbols are the external expression of psychical phenomena essential to the preservation of ideas, customs and conventions, that is to say, to archive and disseminate human experience. Among the symbols used to communicate, Small and Vincent include language (oral, written and printed), vocal and instrumental music, gestures, drawings, photographs, and painting, with language being the most adaptable medium for circulating human experience (Small and Vincent, 1894: 219). It is through that multiplicity of symbols that the infrastructure of discussion, dissemination and transmission of knowledge and information in social life arises, producing society's general system of communication. The system incorporates various elements: the press, commerce, trade, public address, education, church and government. Each of these parts has a permanent relationship to the others. Through a number of examples, Small and Vincent demonstrate the role which each of these specific communication systems plays in society: the press is interwoven in all aspects of the psycho-physical communication apparatus, and its reach is almost as extensive as that of the mails; in business organizations, the communication process facilitates the coordination of production, transportation and exchange of wealth; in schools, communication processes are key elements in increasing and communicating knowledge; the church communicates 'peculiar psychical impulses' from a religious standpoint; and finally, government is described as 'the clearest and most complete example of a social communicating structure' (Small and Vincent, 1894:232). In the specific case of the press, Small and Vincent show how it is the prototype for the multiple possibilities of communication channels: the press is able to collect ideas, transform them into printed symbols and distribute them to all social groups. The press is a convergence of psycho-physical channels towards a centre. In this centre there are devices for making symbols, which are then distributed by various means of transport between the various different segments of society.

Small and Vincent, for whom the press had the crucial function of disseminating knowledge in social and public systems of communication, were particularly interested in analysing the profound changes in the media in the second half of the nineteenth century. They observed that the increasing demand for books and magazines, not just in cities but also in smaller communities, which had been brought about by, amongst other factors, the division of labour, was facilitated by increased transportation. They realized that in a context of growing industrialization and urban expansion, the press had increased its power, becoming an influential social institution and the most significant vehicle for the communication of ideas. They concluded that the press was the most powerful medium for communicating ideas between the institutions of public power (political parties, unions, the university, the church, and social groups) and the rest of the population.

In highlighting the increasing social and cultural role of the press in the nineteenth century, Small and Vincent drew attention to the possibility that it might be used by different interests for the purposes of manipulation, or be controlled by other means. From this awareness of the press' and the newspapers strong social influence on public communication they argued for a critical assessment of press corporations and the services they provide, including a review of their professional practices and precise observations on the public duties and responsibilities of the newspapers. Their diagnosis was somewhat critical of the press in the late nineteenth century: the press was not providing adequate services in reporting facts, in guiding public opinion, and in observing the form and content of the information published; despite its organized character, the press was unsatisfactory in its coverage of news; it was increasingly affected by the world of business, and tended to follow the path of sensationalism; the combination of self-interest and, occasionally, corruption was leading to distortion of the facts. Small and Vincent concluded that these tendencies were becoming widespread, so that it was becoming increasingly difficult to derive from the newspapers an understanding of social activities and a proper sense of ethical behaviour. Nevertheless, despite these pathologies, they regarded the press as an integral part of a system of public communication, the main mission of which was to collect and disseminate information in the service of a broader concept of democracy. Critical research on the media system is justified by the important role it plays in social life and democratic politics (see Hardt, 2001:150-155).

Communication, Conversation, Community Life and Democracy in John Dewey

Although Small and Vincent's work was an important milestone, in that it introduced both communication and the press as foundational topics in American sociology[123], John Dewey's pragmatist philosophy is widely acknowledged for its merit in having contributed to a more comprehensive and sophisticated understanding of the concept of communication in the history of modern thought (Carey, 1989 [1975]:13-36; Peters, 1986:527-559; 1989:199-220; 2000 [1999]:16-22; Schiller, 1996:24). Dewey was head of the department of philosophy at the University of Chicago between 1894 and 1904, and one of the most influential American thinkers and educators of the early decades of the twentieth century. While the German tradition of political economy is evident in Small, the epistemological importance Dewey attributes to communication owes more to his Aristotelian-Hegelian background and to his engagement with naturalist pragmatism (Depew and Peters 2001:14). Dewey had a vigorous intellectual influence on the Chicago School of Social Thought, as demonstrated in the various relational aspects of communication and in the understanding that social life is a process which ties together the self, communication, community life and democracy.

There is one permanent thread to Dewey's ideas on communication. 'Of all affairs', he wrote, 'communication is the most wonderful' (Dewey, 2004 [1925]: 35). In his speculations on the origins of human society, Dewey argues that it is the outcome of the transformation of purely organic behaviour of human groups into behaviour marked by intellectual properties, through language and conversation – these being defined as practical activity. These properties derive from the emerging influence of language which, beyond its material basis in acts of signalling, implies cooperation and empathy. Language is eminently a form of activity, an instrument for action, and should not be confused with a mere system of representation, nor does it serve a simple function of representation. Words do not take on meaning on account of their representative nature, but rather because of their relationships to other words and to social engagement consubstantiated in the act of conversation. Because it is a process of sharing common meanings, symbolic action is inextricable from associative action. The intentional action of human subjects is 'trans-actional' in nature. In order for acts or behaviour not to be mere physical occurrences of an organic symbiosis, individuals must understand and communicate each other's meanings and, through this combined action, modify and adjust their conduct accordingly (see Dewey 2004 [1925]:35-36; 1938). What defines communication is that it is a shared experience. Hence it is an experience which congenitally, according to Dewey, has a unique moral character.

---

[123] For the reasons given earlier, the same can be said for Sumner and Ross.

In line with his emphasis on the social aspect of communication processes, Dewey also argues that knowledge is attained in the context of symbolic communication as a communal event. Going counter to philosophical positions which hold that ideas and knowledge are the functions of an individual and isolated mind or conscience, he argues that 'knowledge is a function of association and communication; it depends upon tradition, upon tools and methods socially transmitted, developed and sanctioned' (1981 [1927]:158). Communication, knowledge and understanding are essentially identical phenomena (Dewey 1981 [1927]:176). Moreover, communication also embodies an ideal. Communication, which is a shared experience, creates and conveys symbols, thought and culture, and gives access to sharing other experiences, expectations, moral values, emotions and interests, thus providing the foundations for a democratic way of life. Dewey distinguished between democracy as a social idea and political democracy as a system of government, and for him, associated life, community and democracy were names for the same thing (see 1981 [1927]:143-184).

It is appropriate in this context to quote at length from the beginning of his work *Democracy and Education*, written in 1916, which illustrates Dewey's notion of communication as a cultural, social and political principle:

'Society not only continues to exist by transmission, by communication, but it may fairly be said to exist in transmission, in communication. There is more than a verbal tie between the words common, community, and communication. Men live in a community in virtue of the things which they have in common; and communication is the way in which they come to possess things in common. What they must have in common in order to form a community or society are aims, beliefs, aspirations, knowledge – a common understanding – like-mindedness as the sociologists say. Such things cannot be passed physically from one to another, like bricks; they cannot be shared as persons would share a pie by dividing it into physical pieces. The communication which insures participation in a common understanding is one which secures similar emotional and intellectual dispositions – like ways of responding to expectations and requirements.' (1916:4)

Dewey's persistent idea is that communication is not just a medium for symbolic transmission, but also, and above all, a socio-symbolic process occurring at different social levels which maintains, produces and culturally transforms society. While the significance of his thought on the role of communication in the creation of the human self, of society, and of social life has been widely acknowledged, less recognition has been given to his judgments on the press and modern technical information media in real life, a reality in which he analyses trends in commodification, complex technological systems, and political action. Dewey's definition of communication as a ritual of sharing, participation, and possession of common beliefs, on the one hand, and as transmission and remote dissemination of signs and messages, on the other, produced an intellectual legacy that would later, as we shall see below, be imaginatively reinvented by James W. Carey (1934-2006), a key figure in US communication theory and cultural studies during the second half of the twentieth century.

A modern society, a Great Society in Deweyian terms, needs mechanisms to implement conversation and systematic discussion on a different scale to traditional societies, in order to promote a democratic social order, a Great Community. To this end, the media and the news are an opportunity for public debate and for action, the body through which a pubic is constituted and public opinion is formed. The role of the genuine press is to promote conversation in modern culture, generating the ability to follow an argument, understand other positions in depth, extend the limits of comprehension, discuss viable alternative proposals, and to contribute to a common civic moral disposition (Dewey, 1981 [1927]:143-184).

Communication, for Dewey, consists of building the identity of peoples, just as art, architecture, custom and ritual do, and thus sets up a relationship which is intrinsic to the nature of public life. It is here that the technical information media, and newspapers in particular, have an added responsibility to create an informed and enlightened public opinion, containing within it the germ of rational and critical action. There is a clear ethical principle in this conception of communication, to the extent that any obstacle to communication, sharing and expanding experience must be overcome. The media offer Dewey an ample space for learning, in which the largest number of citizens can be brought together, without sacrificing their identities as members of particular social groups. With the concept of instrumentalism, which Dewey saw as embodying an evolutionary notion of progress through technological development, information techniques are regarded as instruments whose main function is to solve problems and, as these change, so they (the technologies) must adapt to such change. As Peters states, communication is seen as the solution for social disorganization and for the difficulties which democracy faces in a period of enormous change (Peters, 1989:205).

Years later, Dewey's vision becomes increasingly nuanced. In *The Public and its Problems*, published in 1927, Dewey, who is far from being regarded as a critic of industrial civilization, shows signs of some discomfort with the paradoxes emerging from the paths taken by American society since the World War. The work reveals a Dewey who is no longer an optimistic and patriotic liberal, the defender of the civilizing force of industrialization who had supported American participation in the first large-scale world war.[124] In several passages, he is much more ambiguous regarding the social conditions produced by large, impersonal organizations and by the techniques of communication. They

---

[124] After the Second World War, Dewey wrote an 'Afterword' to *The Public and its Problems*, dated 22 July 1946. In it, Dewey reflected on war and international relations, and argued for his persistent approach in favour of finding areas of common interest. His comments on the dominance of economics in the political organization of social life are noticeably critical, as is the link he makes between modern technological methods and the destruction brought about by war.

emerge as both offering liberating potential and presenting a problem. On the one hand, communication techniques help to multiply and enlarge those connections (freely circulating opinions and facts) which are essential to public life, but on the other, they paralyze and disturb the extraordinary reach of those connections. It is not Dewey's intention in this interpretation to make technology the scapegoat; on the contrary. In his view, the problem lies not in technology *per se*, but in the weakening or absence of ideas and moral values to accompany technological factors. As he wrote: 'We have the physical tools of communication as never before. The thought and aspirations congruous with them are not communicated, and hence are not common. Without such communication the public remain shadowy and formless, seeking spasmodically for itself, but seizing and holding its shadow rather than it substance. Till the Great Society is converted into a Great Community, the Public will remain in eclipse' (Dewey, 1981 [1927]:142). The press is one of the large and impersonal organizations which, in focusing on its own interests, seriously hinders the possibility of establishing community.

This short summary of Dewey's thought shows how his viewpoint established communication as the central element of human life and human societies, using a poly-faceted and multidimensional idea. Through his interpretation of individual thought as the outcome of a communicational exchange which the subject makes in a context of association, Dewey drew up a hypothesis on the social nature of the dialogical roots of thought. Consequently, he located the process of communication between individuals in a framework which is both sociological and normative, a notion which would be creatively adopted by George H. Mead. Dewey pointed to the need to think about mass communication. That task was inseparable from his wider concerns with social, political and moral order, in a word, with democracy, ideas which we will come across in the work of both Thomas and Znaniecki, and Park. We agree with Peters when he states that Dewey provides the elements for a theory of mass communication (even though he does not call it that) preceding the emergence of the mass media as we know them (Peters, 1989:201). However, one cannot avoid noting the idealistic nature of Dewey's views. On the one hand, he sought to emphasize communication's potential contribution to a sense of community, while on the other he argued that the press should be seen as the civic part of conversational process.

A Polyphony of Hypotheses on Communication: George Herbert Mead, William Thomas and Florian Znaniecki, Ernest Burgess and Robert Park

Based on the pioneering work of Small and Dewey at the University of Chicago, the next generation of social theorists, in particular, Mead, Thomas and Znaniecki, Park and Burgess, further explored the communicational conceptions of human rationality and society. Whether in developing the theoretical approach which puts interpersonal communication at the heart of the formation and transformation of the human character and of social interaction, or in addressing the possibilities and contradictions which modern means of communication (particularly the press) offer for public life, these thinkers made fundamental contributions to positioning communication as an essential category in sociology.

At Dewey's invitation, the social psychologist George H. Mead (1863-1931), a distinguished exemplar of the philosophical school of pragmatism in the social sciences in North America, lectured in the Department of Philosophy at the University of Chicago between 1894 and 1931. He has become a classic figure in sociology, recognized above all for his reflections on the social nature of human subjectivity. Mead's work is widely acknowledged as having creatively extended Dewey's reasoning whereby human identity, and sociality itself, arise from, and develop with, communication. In fact, those parts of his work which are most often cited are his explanations of the social nature of the human self and the micro-sociological levels of social interaction. Mead developed in detail the idea that communication consists of a process of creating and expressing symbols through which the human self becomes both object and product of its own experience and interaction with other members of society. He fruitfully explored the idea that communication is a constitutive concept of the self and of the common life of individuals and societies. The key process of development of the human subject as a social subject is based on a complex interplay in which the subjects are able to engage when, in pursuing their intentions, they succeed in adjusting them according to how well they anticipate the possible responses of others in relation to those intentions. The complexity of that interactive exercise, which is communicational and thus constitutes social interaction, derives from the fact that human communication is not merely an exchange of signs, gestures or abstract ideas, but a process in which each one adjusts his own behaviour to the attitudes of others. This type of cooperative action between subjects is possible because human beings are able to draw on a particular kind of gesture – which Mead called significant symbols – in their communicative interaction. Certain gestures, which only humans can make, become significant symbols when they are responses to a given meaning in the experience of one individual and that same meaning is in turn evoked in another individual. Amongst the gestures which humans can draw on, those which are most likely to become significant symbols are vocal gestures or vocalizations and, within these, language. When gesture becomes language, that is to say when it adopts the form of rational cooperative activity, it becomes a significant symbol which invokes a particular meaning.

Mead developed some important ideas, which have become part of the social science heritage, on the role of language as a mechanism for socialization and the organization of action. Mead's arguments highlight the fact that, unlike a mere conversation of unconscious or non-significant gestures, language involves the communication of meanings or, in other words, significant gestures. These do not produce an immediate or direct response, but need to be interpreted in order that an answer may be obtained. This is the essential space for symbolic interaction, the domain in which individuals, in order to respond to the gestures and actions of others, are compelled to use and interpret the symbols which those gestures and actions represent. For social interaction to take place, which means the same thing as human communication, symbols alone are not sufficient. It is of fundamental importance that the symbols be significant for the actors involved, that they have a common meaning shared by all members of a society or particular social group.

Significant symbols which human beings are able to create prolifically make it possible to produce complex webs of communication, out of which history and culture emerge. Subjects share a culture, an elaborate set of significations and values which governs most actions and makes it possible, to a large extent, to foresee how other individuals will behave. It is precisely in the sharing of common meanings that society becomes a cooperative activity. In order for individuals to form a cohesive social unit – and according to Mead this is the ideal of human societies – a system of communication is required in which those who carry out specific functions take on the attitudes of those whom those functions affect (Mead, 1934:327). In this interpretation, society is only possible, and is only maintained, through communication, the ideal form of which would be a universal discourse. If communication could be enhanced, then there would be a kind of democracy in which each individual could find, within himself, that which he seeks in the community (Mead, 1934:327-328). Democracy would be a community's process of enlightened self-government and self-regulation through communication between its members on the common problems which emerge in the exercise of inter-subjective praxis, and who demand the continuous normative revision of what constitutes a sense of duty. Mead was convinced, however, that in existing democratic systems communication had not developed in this way: individuals did not place themselves in the position of those they affected. In Mead therefore, communication is understood as the heart of a theoretical approach – and one which has a visible influence on modern thought – which reinforces the intrinsic relationship between moral development of society and the human personality of its members. The extent to which Jürgen Habermas adopted core aspects of Mead's thought in his monumental work *The Theory of Communicative Action* (2007a [1981]; 2007b [1981] particularly in Volume Two) is widely acknowledged, as is the contribution that incorporation of Mead by Habermas made to enshrining Mead's work in the canon, albeit at the cost of confining Mead to research into the micro levels of social interaction (Silva, 2007). While we cannot here embark on a more complex discussion of the way Habermas incorporated Mead's approach and the extent of its effect on the development of a concept of radical democracy which Dewey did not achieve, we should nonetheless recall that Mead had already expanded the connection between communicational and democratic rationality to topics such as political democracy, war, international relations, industrialization and social reform.[125]

In addition to having been the main defining principle of social interaction, communication in Chicago was also granted a crucial role in re-establishing social cohesion and control as part of a process of social change brought about by vast economic, demographic and technological transformations. Both the new techniques of transportation (railroad, automobile, airplane), and new communication devices (the telegraph, the newspaper, the telephone, cinema and radio) were seen as instruments through which modern society was being formed by communication. These devices, and their growth, were viewed as a condition for the creation of a democratic community in a context of social change. This standpoint, strongly indicative of Dewey's influence, can clearly be seen in the now classic work of William Thomas and Florian Znaniecki, *The Polish Peasant in Europe and America* (1984 [1918-1920]), and in the work of Robert Park (on his own as well as with Ernest Burgess) which one can interpret as part of a joint effort to structure and organize the new cities which had arisen as a result of large migration flows, mass industrialization, and the growth of civic life.

In the face of an accelerating process of social disorganization, a term used by Thomas and Znaniecki to describe the decline in relations of proximity (primary groups) and the loss of ties of solidarity brought about by a shifting population, the breaking-up of families, and the proliferation of market relations, communication is redefined as the principle for re-establishing order and social cohesion, key concepts of Chicago sociology, not only in small local communities, but also at a national level. For these sociologists, 'social reorganization,' or modern social organization, can only be achieved by way of active processes of communication. Communication is an antidote to 'social disorganization' (Thomas and Znaniecki, 1984:218-219).

This is the direction in which Thomas and Znaniecki's references to the role of the press in modern society point. In an excerpt from *The Polish Peasant in Europe and America*, where they discuss the possibilities of social reorganization of peasant communities, which faced isolation as a result of increasing and ever-deepening contact with the outside world (wider, more complex and inter-cultural human spaces), they describe how, given the impossibility of forging harmonious cooperation on a large scale, communication through the press had taken the place of direct contact, and how abstract moral solidarity had given way to concrete social solidarity (1984:218). In Thomas and Znaniecki – and this goes for other Chicago thinkers too – we find a diffuse and very

---

[125] Silva's recent research (2007:291-313) into the unpublished Mead archive shows that Mead's thought goes beyond the already well-known original contributions he made at the micro-sociological level of social interaction and how his theoretical assumptions expanded to include these topics.

characteristic conception of the American imaginary – the hope that information technologies would somehow play a redeeming role, as part of the phenomenon which Leo Marx called the 'technological sublime'. David Depew and John Durham Peters have summarized that spirit very appropriately: 'Each new medium of communication, from the telegraph to the Internet, has been greeted not only as a more efficient means of sending signals, but as reordering, for good and ill, the tissues of the democratic order itself. The question of communication and community in the United States is thus not only a fascinating theoretical issue; it is entangled in a long and deep history of political anxieties and wishes' (2001:6).

The connection between social change, planning and resettlement, and communicative action was also one of the persistent themes in the work of Robert Park. The works of Park, one of the sociologists closest to the philosophical-communicational thought of John Dewey, who also had an in-depth knowledge of European social theory, particularly the German, became classics of urban sociology. Communication, however, is the key concept on which he built his sociological approach. Acknowledgement of the significance of his work on communication came rather late, only in the 1980s (Frazer and Gaziano, 1979:1-47; Czitrom, 1982:91-121; Saperas, 1992:160-168; Rogers, 1994:172-190; Berganza Conde, 2000; Buxton, 2008:345-362; Muhlmann and Plenel, 2008), even though his doctoral thesis, published in German in 1904 and translated into English only in 1972, had addressed theoretical problems which are ever-present in communication studies, and which are constant elements in all his thought – collective behaviour (the masses and the public), the media, the nature of sociology, and social ties.

His interest in the topic goes back to the final decade of the nineteenth century (between 1891 and 1892), when he was still a journalist. At Dewey's invitation he took part in a publishing venture entitled *Thought News, a Journal of Inquiry and a Record of Fact*. The main objective of *Thought News*, which was never published, was to help make clear to the public the ways in which social laws produce what are conventionally defined as 'problems'. According to Willinda Savage, writing in 1892, Dewey and the journalist Franklin Ford, another of the project's mentors, had described the *Thought News* project as follows: 'This will be a newspaper and will aim to perform the function of newspaper (...) which shall not discuss philosophic ideas *per se* but use them as tools in interpreting the movements of thought; which shall treat questions of science, letters, state, school and church as parts of the one moving life of man and hence of common interest, and not relegate them to departments of merely technical interest; which shall note new contributions to thought, whether by book or magazine, from the standpoint of the news in them, and not from that of patron or censor'[126] (Savage *in* Czitrom, 1982:107). In facilitating a better understanding of events, this higher journalism would provide the knowledge that must precede effective action (Matthews, 1977:27). The power of the press would thus reside in the ability to publicize the meaning of the relationships between facts, and more generally, their own relations to the movement of life. Only in this way could one make the transition from opinion to intelligence, providing a scientific basis for social action. An apt quotation from Dewey summarizes their ideas: 'A proper daily newspaper would be the only possible social science' (Dewey in Matthews, 1977:20-30).[127]

Park's involvement in the *Thought News* project left an indelible mark on his vision for sociological research, and on his thinking about news, journalism, and the influence of public opinion. That vision sought to make a close connection between the two forms of knowledge which he believed had much in common, journalism and sociology. In this he belongs with the German sociologist and journalist Siegfried Kracauer, who also attended Georg Simmel's lectures in Berlin. The final words of an autobiographical note he dictated to his secretary at the Fisk University, found among his papers after his death, express his belief that he always saw the sociologist as a kind of 'super-reporter', a reporter who was a bit more precise and operated with a little more detachment than the average, and recalls his friend Franklin Ford's use of the term 'Information with a capital I' (see Park, 1950). Park believes that the news is the public's main source of knowledge of the surrounding environment. Following Dewey, he argues for the existence of ties between indispensable, rigorous and plentiful information, and the democracy anchored in conversation and the creation of a public which such information makes possible. Hence the major responsibility he assigns to the press in building that democratic public, as well as in reinforcing the quality of democracy. According to Park, the conditions for achieving these objectives were exceptional, on account of the technological developments which had enabled the new means of communication to overcome physical and psychological obstacles between people (giving them the opportunity to recreate their face-to-face relationships on a large scale), while at the same time enabling the dissemination of the truth to increasing numbers of people. His experience with that project and his work as a journalist strengthened his conviction that communication was the main cohesive force in modern society.

In Park and Ernest Burgess' book, *Introduction to the Science of Sociology* (1970 [1921]) communication is viewed as the central element in sociology. In this

---

[126] The excerpt cited by Czitrom is in a 1950 article, published by Willinda Savage, 'John Dewey and 'Thought News' at University of Michigan', *Michigan Review* 56, Spring:204-205 based on the *Michigan Daily*, 16 March, 1892.

[127] The excerpt cited by Matthews is in Charles Cooley, Notes on Lectures by John Dewey at Michigan. University of Michigan Historical Collections. On the *Thought News* project, see also Czitrom (1982:104-108), Berganza Conde (2000:14-20) and Muhlmann (2008:26).

book, which many see as the most influential work of sociology of the inter-war period in the US, sociology is seen as 'the science of collective behaviour', which studies minds in social relation, as opposed to psychology, which focuses on minds in isolation (Park and Burgess, 1970:42). Further on in the book the authors write: 'Sociology, as collective psychology deals with communication' (1970:132). Communication is the process whereby one individual's experience is conveyed to another, and at the same time the means by which individuals achieve common experience (see 1970:36-37). It is this experience which establishes the conditions for a common, public life, and for a consensus in which the individual participates, to a greater or lesser degree, and of which he is himself a part. The social organization of human beings, the various types of social groups, and the changes which take place within them at different times and under different conditions are determined not only by instincts and by competition, but by a social heritage – made up of customs, tradition, public opinion, and contract – which is created in and transmitted by communication (see 1970: 80-81). 'The continuity and life of a society depend upon its success in transmitting from one generation to the next its folkways, mores, techniques and ideals. From the standpoint of collective behavior these cultural traits may all be reduced to the one term, 'consensus'. Society viewed abstractly is an organization of individuals; considered concretely it is a complex of organized habits, sentiments, and social attitudes – in short, consensus' (1970:81). In this *sui generis* reality of communication, Park and Burgess perceived, as Peters rightly observes, a 'new possible foundation for the social sciences', in particular, for the emergence of the new disciplinary oxymoron which goes by the name of social psychology (Peters, 1986:533).

In a later essay entitled 'Reflections on Communication and Culture' (Park, 1972 [1938]:98-116), the link between communication and society is even stronger, when he insists that communication performs several essential functions in holding society together. Communication builds consensus and understanding between individuals in a given social group. These are fundamental principles for building a society, and also for cultural unity; communication forges and encourages a network of customs and mutual expectations which bring together the various social entities (family, work organization, etc.); it helps to maintain the order and cooperation which are vital for the continuity of society; it passes on the cultural legacy, the history and traditions of social groups, in the sense that it not only ensures that common undertakings are pursued, but that social institutions endure on a day to day basis and from generation to generation (see Park, 1972:102).

The cultural dynamics of the social group by means of communication are the key to his concept of social control. Parkian social theory assigns importance to two kinds of social order: first, the biotic or ecological order, governed by involuntary relations and symbiotic interaction – as in competition, conflict, adaptation and assimilation. This is the order of the external world, of the commercial world, and also to a lesser extent of politics, in which the free and socially and morally unconstrained individual pursues his individual interests. Secondly, the moral order, in which communication is the dominant form of interaction, which produces conscious meanings and voluntary institutions. The moral order is found in the more intimate world of community and family. Within it, the individual is confronted by the interests, expectations and demands of others. In primary groups, communication and personal influences are the principles of order. Park's intent is to suggest that these two kinds of social order, governed by competition and communication, are mutually reinforcing and complementary, even though they perform different social functions.

In putting forward a model of society as being governed by the two kinds of social order simultaneously, Park – adopting the archetype of the naturalistic theory of social evolution – sees society as always being moulded by the inherent dynamism of a structure which is constantly adjusting to the social needs of individuals and groups, constantly in a state of 'unstable equilibrium' or 'dynamic disequilibrium'. This shifting compromise is only realized when consensus, built through communication, attenuates relations of competition and conflict. Whereas competition differentiates individuals and groups, communication unites them. This approach is also the framework for his research on the press.

In *The Immigrant Press and its Control* (1922), Park puts forward the hypothesis that the foreign-language press is a changing and ambivalent force. While it inevitably leads to assimilation of American culture, it also preserves the group's cultural heritage[128]. The press is the tie which binds the immigrant with his ethnic group, the community in which he lives and the world around him, that is to say, the nation which welcomes him. As its title suggests, the book also touches on the importance of the concept of social control, a central notion of Parkian theory. Aware of the American government's concern that the immigrant press might spread propaganda or opinions prejudicial to national security (over half the foreign-language newspapers published in the US were in German), Park advocated close collaboration with the institutions of the immigrant communities, particularly the press, in order to encourage integration and the assimilation of the American culture. For Park, the foreign-language press could be regarded as an instrument of 'Americanization.'

In his essay on the natural history of the press, an historic achievement of a 'surviving species, (...) an account of the conditions under which the existing newspaper has grown up and taken form' (Park, 1923:274), he traces the historical development of newspapers in four main phases – newsletters, party papers, independent papers and the yellow press. Guided by the idea that the press is an institution moulded by an unceasing process of adjustment to the

---

[128]*The Immigrant Press and its Control* was a work commissioned by the Carnegie Corporation, of New York, on ways to Americanize the immigrant population of the US in the 1920s. The project was entitled *Americanization Studies for the Acculturation of Immigrant Groups into American Society,*

needs of individual subjects and groups, in a framework of the change brought about by each historical period, Park argues that in the modern city the newspaper has come to replace the personal contacts and organized gossip of the small community (the village), as the main source of social control and formation of pubic opinion. For Park, the newspaper and the news in the big city are mechanisms of social control and for the formation of public opinion in the sense that they are a guide to reality, systematically emphasizing that which is unusual and 'supplying topics for conversation': 'the press is asked to create a mystical force called 'public opinion' that will take up the slack in public institutions' (1923:278). In this essay, he also sets out the hopes placed in the potential role of the newspaper in building community spirit in the urban societies of the early twentieth century, although he does point out the difficulties in such an undertaking: 'It is evident that a newspaper cannot do for community of 1,000,000 inhabitants what the village did spontaneously for itself through the medium of gossip and personal contact. Nevertheless, the efforts of the newspaper to achieve this impossible result are an interesting chapter in the history of politics as well as the press' (Park, 1923:278-279).

Park traces the history of those difficulties, which is also the history of the newspaper. It is implicit in the essay that the paths taken were not those which best matched his hopes for the press. Park concludes that if history did not follow the path he might have wished it to follow, the fault lay not with institutions, but with the people chosen to lead them, and with incorrigible human nature. Thus one cannot expect newspapers to be more than they actually are: 'newspapers are about as good as they can be'. In his view, it would only be possible to achieve a better press by educating people and organizing political information and intelligence (Park, 1923:289).

In the many articles he wrote on the press over two decades, one can detect his increasing discomfort with the kind of journalism which threatened to come to the fore in the twentieth century. He started out believing that news and the circulation of news are fundamental for the process of cultural dissemination, but could not help being aware that the chosen formula for increasing newspaper readership was to add a touch of literature to the news: to write news so that it would appeal to the emotions. With this aim in mind, the formula became love and romance for women, sport and politics for men (Park, 1923: 287). This was what the founders of the so-called yellow press, Joseph Pulitzer and William Randolph Hearst, had gambled on, the main contribution of the former being muckraking and the second 'jazz' or noise. Before Pulitzer and Hearst, newspapers had adopted the principle that their business was to educate. After them, they appealed to the heart rather than to the mind. From then on, not everything printed in the newspaper belonged to the realm of news. It was printed as news, but was read as if it were cheap literature – published because it incited the emotions and excited the imagination, and not because the message was urgent and a call to action. While the news is essentially located in time and space, in art and literature time and space do not limit circulation (Park, 1927:806-813; 1972 [1938]:115, 116).

The way Park argued it, the new trends in the penny press, and later the yellow press, produced a type of journalism which, instead of educating a democratic public and encouraging the formation of public opinion, the press became increasingly a 'controlling mechanism for directing attention' (1972 [1904]:46). The opinion thus formed was a judgment made at the precise moment the information was received, and this could only produce immediate and unthinking perceptions. These trends led Park to fear that modern readers would regress into the emotional, uniform and intolerant crowd described by Gustave Le Bon. In his analysis, the drastic changes which had occurred in the modern world had led to a loss of historical perspective, and to a tendency to live in an eternal 'illusory present.' Together with early critics of the cinema, Park made a ferocious attack on modern media-based pastimes: 'This restlessness and thirst for adventure is, for the most part, barren and illusory, because it is uncreative (...) It is in the improvident use of our leisure, I suspect, that the greatest wastes in American life occurs.' (Park, 1925:675). Years later he refers to symbolic and expressive forms of communication – literature, cinema and the fine arts – as 'subversive cultural influences' (Park, 1972 [1938]:115). Park concludes, '(...) the function of art and of the cinema, is on the whole, in spite of the use that has been made of it for educational purposes, definitely symbolic, and as such it profoundly influences sentiment and attitudes even when it does not make any real contribution to knowledge' (1972 [1938]:116).

By virtue of the extent and diversity of his empirical research, and the significance of his insights for intellectual thought, we may rightfully consider Park to be the first sociologist of communication and the media. Other Chicago thinkers granted an essential role to communication in creating social ties, and left valuable contributions to sociological explanation in this area, but it was society and its organization, and the profound changes then taking place which focused their attentions. Park, on the hand, combined these concerns and his civic ideals with the concrete study of how communication and the media developed and operated in the real world during that period. The later research which two of his pupils, Paul Cressey and Frederic Thrasher, did on cinema in the 1930s, confirm his strong attachment to the media (Buxton, 2008:345-352).

James Carey's Cultural Theory of Communication
and the Chicago School of Social Thought

In the period between the two world wars communication studies became established institutionally in the US as a scientific and academic field. The theoretical framework within which this institutionalization took place was very different to the theories developed by the Chicago School of Social Thought. It focused on quantitative and qualitative descriptions of audiences, with the aim of measuring the short-term effectiveness of the media on different publics, and became the mainstream research paradigm in a political context of world conflicts and later, over two decades, in the social context of mass consumption which emerged in its wake. This kind of research studied directly and indirectly perceptible social and psychological effects – influence, persuasion, attitude change, opinion formation, and individual decision-making, changes in electoral behaviour, consumption patterns and use of the various media.

From around the 1920s, two generations of researchers were active in the scientific field of mass communication studies, studying the effects of communication. Two philosophical and ideological attitudes influenced the study of the effects of mass communication and were powerful factors in shaping academic research. On the one hand there was the liberal tradition, with its utilitarian and economicist bent. On the other, there was the legacy of logical positivism on the concept of science. The first of these attitudes, whereby human societies are governed by the social contract and the natural laws of the market, stresses a view of communication focused on the options and effects facing individuals when they make their choices as readers, listeners or spectators and are guided by utility or satisfaction of individual desires. The key theoretical question here is the conditions of freedom which sustain individual decision-making. During the period mass communication studies were becoming institutionalized, the logical positivism-influenced attitude held that communication phenomena should be explained according to the general and universal laws of the physical and natural sciences, and interpreted these laws as valid and meaningful propositions susceptible to empirical verification. This epistemological position implied, to a certain extent, that communication research which was not based on those assumptions was not to be regarded as scientific knowledge worthy of the name, but was considered to be merely speculative. The central task of the process of communication was defined and limited to audience observation and analysis.

The principal current which opposed this orientation, established by the German intellectuals of the Frankfurt school, some of them exiled in the US, also adopted an attitude very different to that of the Chicago tradition. The Critical Theory of Horkheimer, Adorno, Marcuse and Lowenthal sought to renovate the Marxist critique by shifting the target from economic power to symbolic power, and by sharply criticizing the consequences of capitalism and industrialization for social organization and the culture of advanced modernity. Other thinkers in the US, such as Clement Greenberg and Dwight Macdonald, also interpreted those consequences on the basis of a reductionist concept of mass culture which limited culture to ideology, action to reproduction, and communication to coercion.

In the troubled period at the end of the 1960s and the beginning of the 1970s, a group of scholars revolted against what Jefferson Pooley called 'natural science envy and blind faith in quantitative methods' (2007:469), as well as reacting to the post-war confidence in scientism. James Carey was one of those from within communication studies in the US who took an active part in the protest movement in the social sciences in the 1970s. To support and legitimate his developing cultural approach, interacting with other hermeneutic alternatives such as Clifford Geertz's cultural anthropology, Richard Rorty's neo-Pragmatism, and British cultural studies under Hoggart and Williams, Carey reclaimed the key concepts of the Chicago School of Social Thought: the commitment to an understanding of knowledge as a project which is both epistemological and ethical; and the sharing of a concept of communication as a symbolic process in which societal reality is made possible and can be transformed. The following excerpt shows his debt to the Chicago School of Social Thought: 'Education in mass communication begins where research on mass communication began: the University of Chicago. Just before the turn of the century, the first systematic work on mass communication was initiated by John Dewey and carried on later by a distinguished group of philosophers and sociologists: G. H. Mead, Robert Park, W. I. Thomas, Franklin Giddings, Herbert Blumer. As a whole, the group showed an interest in German social theory, in an interpretative sociology, and in methods that were broadly historical and comparative, and observational. While it never did engage Marxism directly, it did find itself in tension with Marxism because it was interested in similar problems and operated at the same level of engagement. It was a movement we would describe as broadly humanistic. Its work contributed, on the one hand, to the theory of mass society and, on the other, to the development of what is known today as symbolic interactionism. While the latter is often formulated in rather too interpersonal a way, it continues to provide for many an entrance into the world of mass communication that is a broadly historical, interpretative, empirical and critical.' (1979:288-289).

The reclamation of this legacy, always present in his work, intensified from the beginning of the 1980s onwards, as part of the response to the collapse of a view of communication expressed in behavioural, utilitarian and functional terms. In addition to being based on the pragmatism of the Chicago School of Social Thought, his cultural conception of communication draws on the theory of symbolic forms of Max Weber and Ernest Cassirer, and on Harold Innis' cultural theory of media technology. It also has ties to the cultural critique of figures such as Lewis Mumford. In the interplay of all these traditions, Carey not only fights the reductionism of the scientific view of communication, but also provides important guidelines for integrating hermeneutic approaches into what he believed were the contradictions emerging from the immense transformations in the communication system and the cultural fragmentation of post-modernity (1997b:324).

Reality is brought into existence, says Carey, through the immeasurable symbolic forms with which human beings make sense of the world, using their own intellectual capacities (1992a [1975]:26-27). For Carey as for Dewey, this process is communication. Communication gives meaning to the chaos of the world and puts society into action, offering shared identities, guiding us into common models of interpretation, and encouraging relations of mutual respect. Carey also saw conversation as the existential ritual *par excellence*, in which social experience is shared and becomes the common culture. He rejected the idea that human societies come into being from a contract of association or by agreement between individuals. On the contrary, he believed that human societies are continuously built up through language, but it is a language which, unlike that of animals, conveys values, conceptions of good and evil, of justice and injustice, advantage and disadvantage – which go beyond mere individual sensibility. It is precisely on those values or ideas that the principles of common life rest. It is such shared notions which create family and society. Thus Carey rejects the liberal doctrine according to which society is formed by potentially egotistical individuals and survives through the 'invisible hand of Providence'. He does not believe that the market keeps individuals together, coordinates their actions, and ensures freedom. Still less does he believe that social harmony is the result of competition between individuals – or that competition is the primary value of society (Carey, 2001:ix-xiii).

Carey suggests two contrasting and potentially competing forms and practices of communication: the 'transmissive' and the 'ritual'. The former is more widely disseminated in the industrial cultures, and refers to terms such as 'sending', 'transmitting' or 'giving information to others'. This conception follows conventional models of signals transmission and messaging over long distances. Although its origins lie in the past, it is this model of communication which was boosted when transportation and technology came to the fore in the nineteenth century, and it provided the framework for theoretical developments in the twentieth century (Carey, 1992a:15). The ritual version of communication refers to notions such as 'sharing', 'participation', 'association', 'communion', and owes a debt to participation ceremonies, building experience, and the feeling of belonging to a community (Carey, 1992a:18). Carey argues that neither of these approaches necessarily denies what the other asserts. But while the ritual approach does exclude the transmission of information, Carey sees the original meaning, or the highest form of communication, not as the transmission of intelligent information, but in the construction and maintenance of a cultural world which has meaning for human action (1992a:18-22).

Carey's ritual or cultural theory of communication, and his view of human life as being symbolically constructed and at the same time experienced, provides social theory with valuable explanatory ideas on the relevance of communication in modern societies. Under the influence of an Innisian approach to social history and technology, he explored the notion that the bias of communication technologies affects social, economic, political, and cultural organization, as well as conceptions of time and space. 'Media of communication are not merely instruments of will and purpose but definite forms of life: organisms, so to say, that reproduce in miniature the contradictions in our thought, action, and social relations' (Carey, 1992a: 9). One of Carey's main contributions was to demonstrate clearly how journalism and the media are not one and the same. The media reflect the various ways in which people experience messages and information, and are subject to strong commercial and power interests. Journalism, on the other hand, for Carey as for Dewey and Park, is seen as having an inalienable commitment to democracy; it is part of the process of the conversation of the community, its goal being to strengthen the conversational foundations of community life and to fulfil democratic ideals. From this point of view, the news is a form of cultural expression. Journalism is the practice of that cultural expression, helping to establish social ties and maintain a community, and exists independently of any media system. Technology and bureaucracy do not define the practice of an activity: rather, it is the exercise of a set of skills for achieving improvement and elevation of public life, a common life which can be shared by all as citizens. Carey believed that journalism as practiced in society has been increasingly and seriously threatened by a market-driven media industry, by the brave new world of information technology, by a readership which no longer believes in the press, by a political climate which alienates citizens from politics and journalism, and by other problems deriving from the professional culture of the press itself (see Carey 1979:234, 241, 249).

Among the intersecting traditions which Carey so originally reclaimed, the ethical and epistemological commitment of the Chicago School of Social Thought to the possibility of a democratic public life finds an echo in several modern intellectual movements – cultural studies (e.g. *Cultural Studies*, vol. 23, n° 2, March de 2009), media ecology (e.g. *Explorations in Media Ecology*, vol. 5, n°2, 2006), the civic journalism movement –, in the philosophical theory of communication found in thinkers such as John Durham Peters (1986;1989; 2000), and in the historiography of research into media and communication in the US (Park and Pooley, 2008).

Conclusion

Small, Dewey, Mead, Thomas and Znaniecky, Park and Burgess, the thinkers of the Chicago school, developed their ideas under the influence and impact of the social-democratic and reform movement in American public life after the second industrial revolution. They placed communication and the subjective life at the heart of their understanding of human beings and of sociological explanation. Moreover, they added a normative aspect to this interpretation of human communication: communication is a moral foundation for collective life and the condition for democracy as a social ideal. Persuaded of the validity of this approach, they believed in the possibilities of democratization and social progress offered by modern communication technologies.

For the purposes of this essay, we have pointed out some common elements in the ideas of members of Chicago School of Social Thought, although we are well aware there are some discontinuities between them as well. Three main aspects of their ideas stand out for an understanding of communication.

First, the concept of communication was synonymous with connection, with bonds between human beings. Socialization, and the process of formation of the self, take place through communication. Distancing themselves conceptually from instinctive interpretations of human behaviour, the Chicago thinkers established a theoretical viewpoint which places interpersonal communication at the heart of the formation and transformation of the human personality. This line of reasoning opened the way for the research for which Blumer coined the term symbolic interactionism. This concept of communication is based on a trans-actional approach to the symbolic activity of individuals at several interconnected levels, from the inner being of one individual to the interpersonal and inter-group levels, right up to global society. In connecting communication closely to the social sphere, this approach also gave sociology a potential level of analysis – the intra-individual – which had hitherto been confined to psychology, one which was creatively pursued by the tradition of symbolic interactionism. At the same time, it provided a powerful hypothesis to counter the causal logic of the French tradition of sociology as developed by Durkheim, which limited sociological explanation to the group *qua* group.

Secondly, communication was regarded as the potential key to solving the social problems of urban, cosmopolitan, industrialized societies. Communication and community were used as discourses to protest and resolve the contradictions brought about by advanced industrialization and the enormous growth of cities during that period of history. They were also used as a formula for humanizing those factors and producing consensus as a democratic way of life (Peters and Simonson, 2004:16). In the Chicago tradition, the possibility of democratic rationality lies in the communicative character of human rationality, which can be incorporated by the structures of power and is revealed in the democratic forms of political organization

Thirdly, the Chicago thinkers shared a point of view which included the study of modern means of communication, their technologies, and their institutions. They were thus pioneers in research into newspapers, public opinion, transportation and communication infrastructure and flows, networks, and interactive groups. However, their engagement with social reform tended to run ahead of the concrete study of the ways in which communication and the media were developing, and they neglected issues such as conflict, authority and domination. This approach, which had also been a feature of German political economy and Weberian sociology, meant that they lost sight of some of the darker realities of modern communication.

Drawing on the US experience of establishing its advanced industrial society, the Chicago School of Social Thought made a strong contribution in social theory to a communicative and cultural approach to subjectivity, social relations, and public life. The theoretical core of this contribution is in line with a normative representation of man which goes beyond the monism of egotistical interest and instrumentalism, and the nature of *homo economicus*. These ideas intersect with others generated in different latitudes during more or less the same period, such as those of the anthropologist Marcel Mauss and political economist Karl Polanyi. Whether we continue to draw on the Chicago thinkers, like James W. Carey, or on the various cultural studies approaches which have flourished in Canada, Europe and elsewhere in the world, it is still an important task today to think about where modern society is headed by examining the links between communication and culture, and adopting an ethical approach to democracy and public life[129].

References

Belman, L. S. (1977) 'John Dewey's Concept of Communication', *Journal of Communication*: 27, Winter: 29-37.

Berganza, C. and M. Rosa (2000) *Comunicación, Opinión Pública y Prensa en la Sociologia de Robert E. Park*. Madrid: CIS.

Bulmer, M. (1984) *The Chicago School of Sociology. Institutionalization, Diversity and the Rise of Sociological Research*. Chicago: Macmillan.

Buxton, W. J. (2008) 'From Park to Cressey: Chicago Sociology's Engagement with Media and Mass Culture', in David Park and Jefferson Pooley, *The History of Media and Communication Research. Contested Memories*, Oxford, New York and Viena: Peter Lang: 345-362.

Carey, J. W. (2001) 'Foreword', in Hanno Hardt, *Social Theories of the Press. Constituents of Communication Research 1840s to 1920s*. New York and Oxford: Rowman & Littlefield Publishers inc.:ix-xiii.

-----.(1999) 'Innis 'in' Chicago. Hope as the Sire of Discovery', in C. Acland and W. Buxton (eds.). *Harold Innis in the New Century. Reflections and Refractions*. Montreal & Kingston, London and Ithaca: McGill-Queen's University Press:81-104.

-----.(1997a [1996]) 'The Chicago School and the History of Mass Communication Research', in Eve S. Munson and Catherine A. Warren (eds.), *James Carey. A Critical Reader*. Minneapolis and London: University of Minnesota Press:14-33.

-----.(1997b) 'Afterword/The Culture in Question', in Eve S. Munson and Catherine A. Warren (eds.), *James Carey. A Critical Reader*. Minneapolis and London: University of Minnesota Press:308-339.

-----.(1992a [1975]) 'A Cultural Approach of Communication', in *Communication as Culture. Essays on Media and Society*. London: Routledge:13-36.

-----.(1992b [1982]) 'Reconceiving 'Mass' and 'Media'', in *Communication as Culture. Essays on Media and Society*. London: Routledge: 69-88.

-----.(1992c [1981]) 'Space, Time, and Communications. A Tribute to

---

[129] We would like to acknowledge the valuable comments made on an earlier version of this chapter by participants in *The Legacy of the First Chicago School of Sociology. Social Theorists, Methodologies and Methods Conference* (September, 2007), particularly Howard Becker and Svetlana Bankouskaya. The authors also wish to thank Daniel Pooley and Daniel Carey for their comments and discussion on James W. Carey's thought.

Harold Innis', in *Communication as Culture. Essays on Media and Society*. London: Routledge:142-172.

-----.(1979) 'Graduate Education in Mass Communication', *Communication Education*. vol. 28, September:282-293.

-----.(1974) 'Journalism and Criticism: The Case of an Undeveloped Profession', *The Review of Politics*, Vol. 36:2 (April): 227-249.

Castilho, R. del (2004) 'Érase una vez en América John Dewey y la Crisis de la Democracia', in John Dewey, *La Opinión Pública y sus Problemas*. Madrid: Ediciones Morata:11-54.

Chapouie, J-M. (2001) *La Tradition Sociologique de Chicago 1892-1961*. Paris: Seuil.

Czitrom, D. J. (1982) 'Toward a New Community? Modern Communication in the Social Thought of Charles Horton Cooley, John Dewey, and Robert Park', in *Media and the American Mind. From Morse to McLuhan*. Chapel Hill: University of North Carolina Press:91-121.

Depew, D. and J. D. Peters (2001) 'Community and Communication: The Conceptual Background', in Gregory J. Shepherd and Eric W. Rothenbuhler (eds.), *Communication and Community*. Mahwah, New Jersey, and London: Lawrence Erlbaum Associates Publishers:3-21.

Dewey, J. (2004 [1925]) 'Nature, Communication, and Meaning', in John D. Peters and P. Simonson (eds.), *Mass Communication and American Social Thought. Key Texts, 1919-1968*. Lanham, Boulder, New York, Toronto and Oxford: Rowman & Littlefield Publishers, inc.: 35-36.

-----.(1981 [1927]) *The Public and Its Problems*. Athens: Swallow Press and Ohio University Press.

-----.(1938) *Logic. The Theory of Inquiry*. New York: Holt, Rinehart and Winston.

Dewey, J. (1915) *Democracy and Education*. New York: Macmillan.

Frazier, P. J. and C. Gaziano (1979), 'Robert Ezra Park's Theory of News, Public Opinion and Social Control', *Journalism Monographs*:64, November: 1-47.

Habermas, J. (2007a [1981]) *The Theory of Communicative Action, vol 2: Lifeworld and System : A Critique of Functionalist Reason*. Boston : Beacon Press.

-----.(2007b [1981]) *The Theory of Communicative Action, vol: Reason and Rationalization of Society*. Boston: Beacon Press.

Hardt, H. (2009) 'James Carey. Communication, Conversation, Democracy', *Cultural Studies*. vol. 25, (2):183-186.

-----.(2001) *Social Theories of the Press. Constituents of Communication Research 1840s to 1920s*. New York and Oxford: Rowman & Littlefield Publishers, inc.

Harvey, L. (1987) *Myths of the Chicago School of Sociology*. Aldershot, Brookfield: Avebury.

Jensen, K. B. (2008) 'Communication Theory and Philosophy' in

Wolfgang Donsbach (ed.). *The International Encyclopedia of Communication*. Blackwell Publishing. Blackwell Online. 15 June 2008: http://www.communicationencyclopedia.com/subcriber/uid=1125/tocnode?id=g9781405131995-chunk_g97814051319958_ss104-1>

Katz, E., J. D. Peters, Tamar Liebes and Avril Orloff (eds.) (2003) *Canonic Texts in Media Research*. Cambridge, Oxford and Malden: Polity Press.

Lang, Kurt (1989), 'Communications Research: Origins and Development', in Eric Barnouw and George Gerbner, *International Encyclopedia of Communictions*. NewYork and Oxford: Oxford University Press:369-374.

Martín A. Manuel (2003) *Teoría de la Comunicación: una Propuesta*, Madrid: Tecnos.

Matthews, F. H. (1977) *Quest for an American Sociology: Robert E. Park and the Chicago School*. Montreal: McGrill-Queen's University Press.

Mead, G. H. (1934) *Mind, Self and Society*. London and Chicago: The University of Chicago Press (edited and with translation of Charles W. Morris).

Muhlmann, G. and E. Plenel (eds.). (2008) *Le Journaliste et le Sociologue. Robert Ezra Park*. Paris: Seuil.

Muhlmann, G. (2008) 'Presse et Démocratie', in Géraldine M. and E. Plenel, *Le Journaliste et le Sociologue. Robert Ezra Park*. Paris: Seuil:19-31.

Nerone, J. (2006) 'The Public and the Party Period', in Jeremy Packer and Craig Robertson (eds.). *Thinking with James Carey. Essays on Communications, Transportation, History*. New York and Oxford: Peter Lang:157-176.

Park, D. and J. Pooley (eds.). (2008) *The History of Media and Communication Research. Contested Memories*. Oxford, New York and Viena: Peter Lang.

Park, R. E. (2002 [1940]) 'News as Form of Knowledge: a Chapter in the Sociology of Knowledge', *The American Journal of Sociology*, vol. 45: (5):669-686.

-----.(1972 [1904]) *The Crowd and the Public and Other Essays*, Chicago: University of Chicago Press.

-----.(1950) *Race and Culture: Collected Papers of R. E. Park*, vol.I, (eds.). Hughes, E. C., Johnson, C. S., Masuoka, J., Redfield, R. and Wirth, L. New York: Glencoe and Free Press.

-----.(1941a) 'News and the Power of the Press', *The American Journal of Sociology*, 47 (July):1-11.

-----.(1941b) 'Morale and the News', *The American Journal of Sociology*, 47 (November):360-377.

-----.(1927) 'Topic Summaries of Current Literature: The American Newspaper', *The American Journal of Sociology*, vol. 32⊗5) (March):806-813.

-----.(1925) 'Community Organization and the Romantic Temper', *The Journal of Social Forces 3* (May): 673-677.

-----.(1923) 'The Natural History of the Newspaper', *The American Journal of Sociology*, vol 29: 3 (November): 273-289.

-----.(1922) *The Immigrant Press and its Control*, New York and London: Harper &

Brothers.

-----.(1916) 'The City: Suggestions for the Investigation of Human Behaviour in the City Environment', *The American Journal of Sociology*, vol. XX: 5 (March 1915):577-612.

Park, R. E. and E. Burgess (1970 [1921]) *Introduction to the Science of Sociology*. Chicago and London: The University of Chicago Press.

Peters, J. D. and P. Simonson (2004) 'From Hope to Disillusionment. Mass Communication Theory Coalesces, 1919-1933', in *Mass Communication and American Social Thought. Key Texts, 1919-1968*. Lanham, Boulder, New York, Toronto and Oxford: Rowman & Littlefield Publishers, inc.:13-20.

Peters, J. D. (2000 [1999]) *Speaking into the Air. A History of the Idea of Communication*. Chicago and London: The University of Chicago Press.

-----.(1989) 'Democracy and American Communication Theory: Dewey, Lippmann, Lazarsfeld', *Communication* 11: 199-220.

Peters, John D. (1986) 'Institutional Sources of Intellectual Poverty in Communication Research', *Communication Research*, vol. 13:4, October:527-559.

Pietilä, V. (2008) 'How Does a Discipline Become Institutionalized?, *in* David Park and Jefferson Pooley, *The History of Media and Communication Research. Contested Memories*. Oxford, New York and Vienna: Peter Lang:205-223.

Plenel, E. (2008) 'Actualit´r de Park', *in* G. Muhlmann and E. Plenel, *Le Journaliste et le Sociologue. Robert Ezra Park*, Paris: Seuil : 7-18.XXX

Polanyi, Karl (1944) *The Great Transformation: the Political and Economic Origins of our Time*. Boston: Beacon Press.

Pooley, J. (2007) 'Daniel Czitrom, James W. Carey, and The Chicago School', *Critical Studies in Media Communication*, vol. 24: (5):469-472.

Proulx, S. (2001) 'Les Recherches Nord-Américaines sur la Communication: L'Institutionnalisation d'un Champ d'Études', *L'Année Sociologique*, 50 :2: 467-485.

Rogers, E. M. (1994) *A History of Communication Study. A Biographical Approach*. New York and Toronto: The Free Press.

Ross, E. A. (1910) 'The Suppression of Important News', *Atlantic Monthly*, March:303-311.

-----.(1917-1918) 'Social Decadence', *The American Journal of Sociology*, vol. 23: 4 (Jan):620-632.

-----.(1904) 'Moot Points in Sociology. VIII. The Factors of Social Change', *The American Journal of Sociology*, vol. 10: (1):189-207.

-----.(1903a) 'Moot Points in Sociology. II. Social Laws', *The American Journal of Sociology*, vol. 8:6 (May):105-123.

-----.(1903b) 'Moot Points in Sociology. III. The Unit of Investigation', *The American Journal of Sociology*, vol. 9:1 (Jul):188-207.

-----.(1903c) 'Moot Points in Sociology. VIII. The Factors of Social Change', *The American Journal of Sociology*, vol. 9: 2 (Sep):349-372.

Small, A. and G. Vincent (1894), *An Introduction to the Study of Society*. New

York: American Book.
Small, A. (1915) 'The Bonds of Nationality', *The American Journal of Sociology*, vol. 20:4 (Jan):629-683.
Sandstrom, Kent (2008) 'Symbolic Interaction' *in* Wolfgang Donsbach (edt.), *The International Encyclopedia of Communication*. Blackwell Publishing. Blackwell Online. 15 June 2008:
http://www.communicationencyclopedia.com/subcriber/tocnode?id=g978405131995_chunk_g978140513199524_ss131-1
Saperas, E. (1992) *Introducció a les Teories de la Comunicació*. Barcelona: Editorial Pórtic, SA.
Schiller, D. (1996) *Theorizing Communication. A History*, New York: Oxford University Press.
Silva, F. C. (2007) 'Re-examining Mead. G. H. Mead on the 'Material Reproduction of Society'', *Journal of Classical Sociology*, vol. 7 (3):291-313.
Simonson, Peter and John D. Peters (2008), 'Communication and Media Studies, History to 1968', *in* Wolfgang Donsbach (edt.), *The International Encyclopedia of Communication*. Blackwell Publishing. Blackwell Online. 15 June 2008:
http://www.communicationencyclopedia.com/subcriber/tocnode?id=g9781405131995_chunkg97814051319958_ss88-1>
Thomas, W. and F. Znaniecki (1984 [1918-1920]) *The Polish Peasant in Europe and America*. Urbana and Chicago: University of Illinois Press (edited and abridged by Eli Zaretsky).

Edited by CHRISTOPHER HART

HEROINES AND HEROES. SYMBOLISM, EMBODIMENT, NARRATIVES & IDENTITY. ISBN 9780955124433. First published in 2008. Available from: http://www.lulu.com/4005570

Essays

Englishness and Espionage: Edith Cavell as the Good Spy. *Rosie White,* Northumbria University, England.
Elementary, "Docteur Barnes". *Caterina Calafat,* Universitat de les Illes Balears.
Cavalier Ideals, Exile and Spectacle in The Rover and The Second Half of the Rover. *Vanessa Coloura,* University of California, Santa Barbara.
Dante's Ugolino in 18th-century France: Reynolds, Fuseli, Flaxman and the Students of J-L David. *Aida Audeh,* Hamline University, USA.
From English Partner to American Action Hero: The Heroic Identity and Trans-national Appeal of the Bond Girl. *Lisa Funnell,* Wilfrid Laurier University, Waterloo, Ontario.
Bond, Smiley, The Jackal: A Spectral English Hero for a Post-Heroic England. *Alan Kirby,* Bellerbys College, Oxford.
Softboiled Heroes: Investigating Englishness in the Classical Hollywood Detective Film. *Philippa Gates,* Wilfrid Laurier University Waterloo, Ontario.
The English Christian Hero: Nelson of Trafalgar. *Christopher Hart,* University of Chester, England.
The Hero Under Fire. *Terry Phillips,* Liverpool Hope University, England.
Images of English Purity. A Comparative Study of Elizabeth I and Diana, Princess of Wales. *José I. Prieto Arranz,* Universitat de les Illes Balears
The 'Wicked Ladies': The Historical Romantic Fiction of the 1940s. *Mary Joannou,* Anglia Ruskin University, England.
Englishness and the 'Victim' Hero in One for My Baby by Tony Parsons. *Joanne Woodman,* Canterbury Christ Church University, England.
"Murder most Foul": Brutus as an English hero in Voltaire's La Mort de César. *Helena Agarez Medeiros,* Katholieke Universiteit, Belgium.
'I have married England': Two visions of Englishness in Interwar popular Fiction. *Jessica Meyer,* Oxford Brookes University, England.
Rob Roy an Anti-English Hero. *Beatriz Oria Gómez,* University of Zaragoza, Spain.
From the Decadent to the Dandy: Conceptualising Nineteenth-Century English Male Heroism in Edward Bulwer Lytton's the Last Days of Pompeii and Edgar Allan Poe's "The Fall of the House of Usher". *Marta Miquel Baldellou,* Universitat de Lleida, Spain.
Dandyism and French Heroism in Oscar Wilde.*Ignacio. Ramos Gay,* Universidad de Castilla-La Mancha, Spain
Em-bodying England: John Lydgate, Henry V and Hector of Troy. *Kate Ash,* University of Manchester, England.
Heroic Leadership, Mountain adventure and the English: John Hunt and Chris Bonington Compared. *Paul Gilchrist,* University of Brighton, England.

Edited by CHRISTOPHER HART

COLLECTION OF ESSAYS IN HONOUR OF TALCOTT PARSONS
ISBN 9781905984138 First published in 2009.
Available on line from: http://www.lulu.com/8175670

Chapter 1	**Functionalism and the Theory of Action.** *Helmut Staubmann,* University of Innsbruck, Austria.	
Chapter 2	**The Theory of Action After Parsons.** *Jan Balon,* Charles University, Prague, Czech Republic.	
Chapter 3	**Definition of the Situation as a Generalized Symbolic Medium.** *Victor Lidz* Drexel University College of Medicine, USA.	1
Chapter 4	**Parsonianism,' General Frameworks, Evolution An Exercise in Reflexivity.** *Matteo Bortolini,* University of Padua, Italy.	
Chapter 5	**Adaptive Structure and the Problem of Order.** *R. E Hilbert,* University of Oklahoma, *and Charles Wright,* Oklahoma City University, USA.	
Chapter 6	**Collective Learning as Social Change: Integrating Complex Adaptive Systems and Structuration with Parsons's Theory of Action.** *David R. Schwandt,* The George Washington University, USA.	
Chapter 7	**The Autonomy of the Spirit of Society: Talcott Parsons on Max Weber's Conception of Religion and Society.** *Yuri Contreras-Véjar,* New School for Social Research, New York, USA.	
Chapter 8	**The Place of Law in Talcott Parsons's American Societal Community.** *A. Javier Treviño,* Department of Sociology Wheaton College, USA.	
Chapter 9	**Toward a Theory of Health Attainment: A Causal Model of Parsons' Sick Role.** *Jennifer Harris Kraly,* Case Western Reserve University, USA.	
Chapter 10	**Talcott Parsons' Sociology of the Nation-State.** *Daniel Chernilo,* Departamento de Ciencias Sociales Universidad Alberto Hurtado, Chille.	
Chapter 11	**Talcott Parsons's Weberian Analysis of National Socialism.** *Uta Gerhardt,* Heidelberg, Germany.	

www.ingramcontent.com/pod-product-compliance
Ingram Content Group UK Ltd.
Pitfield, Milton Keynes, MK11 3LW, UK
UKHW021318180426
11947UKWH00015B/1301